IMAGERY
Current Perspectives

IMAGERY
Current Perspectives

Edited by

Joseph E. Shorr
Institute for Psycho-Imagination Therapy
Los Angeles, California

Pennee Robin
Institute for Psycho-Imagination Therapy
Los Angeles, California

Jack A. Connella
Institute for Psycho-Imagination Therapy
Los Angeles, California

and

Milton Wolpin
University of Southern California
Los Angeles, California

Springer Science+Business Media, LLC

Library of Congress Cataloging in Publication Data

Imagery: current perspectives / edited by Joseph E. Shorr . . . [et al.].

p. cm.

Based on the Ninth Annual Conference of the American Association for the Study of Mental Imagery, held in conjunction with the Second World Conference on Mental Imagery, June 25-28, 1987, in Toronto, Canada, and the Tenth Annual Conference of the American Association for the Study of Mental Imagery, held June 17-19, 1988, in New Haven, Connecticut.

Includes bibliographical references.

ISBN 978-1-4899-0878-0

1. Imagery (Psychology)—Therapeutic use—Congresses. 2. Imagery (Psychology)—Congresses. I. Shorr, Joseph E. II. American Association for the Study of Mental Imagerey. Conference (9th: 1987: Toronto, Canada) III. American Association for the Study of mental Imagery. Conference (10th: 1988: New Haven, Conn.)

RC489.F35I44 1989 89-77532

616.89'14—dc20 CIP

Based on the Ninth Annual Conference of the American Association for the Study of Mental Imagery, held in conjunction with the Second World Conference on Mental Imagery, June 25-28, 1987, in Toronto, Canada, and the Tenth Annual Conference of the American Association for the Study of Mental Imagery, held June 17-19, 1988, in New Haven, Connecticut

ISBN 978-1-4899-0878-0 ISBN 978-1-4899-0876-6 (eBook)
DOI 10.1007/978-1-4899-0876-6

Softcover reprint of the hardcover 1st edition 1989

Originally published by Plenum Press, New York in 1989

PREFACE

The fifth volume of Imagery emanates from the matrix of presentations offered after the conventions of the American Association for Mental Imagery for the years 1987 and 1988. The first meeting was held in Toronto; the second at Yale University.

An overview of the presentations covered such a variety of subjects that we thought the subtitle would be most appropriately--Current Perspectives.

For the first time in five volumes, two contributions are related to anthropological imagery by Caughey and Brink. John Caughey, whose book, Imaginary Social Worlds pioneered the social psychology approach to the silent inner imagination, offers a fine chapter in anthropological imagery of his own experiences with Sufi mystics in Pakistan and Micronesian Islanders in the Western Pacific compared to middle-class Americans. Nicholas Brink follows with a chapter on "The Healing Powers of the Native American Medicine Wheel."

Theoretical studies with interesting experimental designs are presented by Huneycutt, "A Functional Analysis of Imagined Interaction Activity in Everyday Life" by Kunzendorf and Hoyle on "Auditory Percepts, Mental Images and Hypnotic Hallucinations: Similarities and Differences in Auditory Evoked Potentials"; and by Giambia and Grodsky on "Task--Unrelated Images and Thoughts While Reading."

The relationship between creativity and mental imgery is presented by H. Rosenberg and W. Trusheim entitled, "Creative Transformations: How Visual Artists, Musicians and Dancers Use Mental Imagery in Their Work," and Colalillo-Kates discusses "Dreamjourneys: Using Guided Imagery and Transformational Fantasy With Children."

The everpresent theoretical problem of the nature of consciousness and the self is presented by Boruss and Moore in a chapter called "Notions of Consciousness and Reality"; and by D. Rosenberg in a chapter subtitled "The Metaphor of Parts of Self: Finding Real Self and Emergent Identity."

"Measuring Manifest Dream Content" by Snell, Gunn, Schuck and Mosley is the next chapter relating images and dreams.

The chapters discussing the clinical use of imagery with patients begins with an introduction to the theoretical use of such therapy by J. Shorr called "The Existential Question and the Imaginary Situation as Therapy." This is followed by M. S. Cerney's "The Use of Imagery in Grief Therapy." Then Mark Ettin's chapter called "Points of View: Working with Spontaneous Images in Group Therapy." This is followed by David Tansey's article titled "Use of Three Boxes, a Psycho-Imagination Therapy Special Image, with a Schizophrenic Population."

"Sexual Jealousy: Evaluation and Assessment Using the Principles of Psycho-Imagination Therapy" by Pennee Robin and Jack Connella is the last article that completes the clinical work.

"Emotive Imagery and Pain Tolerance" by Linda Smith and Milton Wolpin examines the relationship between pain, imagery and health.

The fifth volume has perhaps a wider application of Mental Imagery than in any of the four previous volumes.

Finally, I wish to thank Pat Vann of Plenum Press for her cooperation and support in the development of all of the volumes called "Imagery."

Joseph E. Shorr

CONTENTS

AUDITORY PERCEPTS, MENTAL IMAGES, AND HYPNOTIC HALLUCINATIONS: SIMILARITIES AND DIFFERENCES IN AUDITORY EVOKED POTENTIALS

Robert G. Kunzendorf and Diane Hoyle

University of Lowell

ABSTRACT

In past research, percepts, images, and hallucinations have been shown to have similar sensory and physiological underpinnings, but different cognitive effects. In the present psychophysiological study of these sensory similarities and cognitive differences, auditory evoked potentials (AEPs) were obtained (a) while 12 select subjects mentally imaged the evoking tone as louder versus softer, and (b) while they hypnotically hallucinated the evoking tone as louder versus softer. The results of this study indicate that eidetically imaged loudness versus softness and hypnotically hallucinated loudness versus softness, like perceived loudness versus softness, affect the amplitude of early "sensory" components in the AEP. The results also indicate that imaged loudness and softness affect a later "image-monitoring" component in the left-hemisphere AEP, whereas hallucinated loudness and softness--like perceived loudness and softness--do not affect this later component.

This research presentation explores the manner in which images and hallucinations are similar to percepts, but different from each other. The first part of this presentation reviews past research indicating that vivid images and hallucinations are psychophysiologically similar to percepts. The second part reviews behavioral evidence that vivid images and hallucinations are different from each other. The final part presents new research confirming that vivid images and hallucinations are psychophysiologically different as well.

PSYCHOPHYSIOLOGICAL SIMILARITIES

Evidence that images, hallucinations, and percepts are psychophysiologically similar emerged in some of the earliest reports of psychological experimentation. For example, Darwin (1803) made the following report:

> Close your eyes, and cover them with your hat; think for a minute on a tune, which you are accustomed to, and endeavour to sing it with as little activity of mind as possible. Suddenly uncover and open your eyes, and in one second of time the iris will contract itself, but you will perceive the day more luminous for several seconds, owing to the accumulation

of sensorial power in the optic nerve.

Then again close and cover your eyes, and think intensely on a cube of ivory two inches diameter, attending first to the north and south sides of it, and then to the other four sides of it; then get a clear image in your mind's eye of all the sides of the same cube coloured red; and then of it coloured green; and then of it coloured blue; lastly, open your eyes as in the former experiment, and after the first second of time allowed for the contraction of the iris, you will not perceive any increase of the light of day, or dazzling; because now there is no accumulation of sensorial power in the optic nerve; that having been expended by its action in thinking over visible objects.

This experiment is not easy to be made at first, but by a few patient trials the fact appears very certain; and shews clearly that our ideas of imagination are repetitions of the motions of the nerve, which were originally occasioned by the stimulus of external bodies; because they equally expend the sensorial power in the organ of sense. (pp. 156-157)

In other early experimentation later replicated by Oswald (1957), Gruithuisen (1812) observed that vivid visual imagery produces negative after-images which, like the negative after-images of perception, maintain a fixed retinal location as the eye moves. Likewise in the auditory modality, Gruithuisen observed that vivid imagery produces peripheral after-effects:

Once in a dream I heard a cannon fired off beside me, whereupon I awoke, and my ears hurt (especially the right ear, on which side the cannon stood), and I perceived a ringing in my ears as would be the case in reality. (p. 237)[1]

Inasmuch as visual and auditory after-imagery originate in the sensory transmitter (Craig, 1940; Zwicker, 1964), any visual images that induce after-imagery must innervate the corticofugal pathways to the retina (Van Hasselt, 1972-73), and any auditory images that induce after-imagery must innervate the corticofugal pathways to the cochlea (Klinke & Galley, 1974).

Like early studies of image-induced after-images, recent electrophysiological studies also show that peripheral nerves are centrifugally innervated during vivid imaging. In a study of chemically induced hallucinations, Krill, Wieland, and Ostfeld (1960) observed significant changes in the electroretinograms (ERGs) of human subjects who experienced visual hallucinations and no change in the retinal activity of control subjects who received either nonhallucinogenic doses or nonhallucinogenic analogues of two drugs. In a study of verbally suggested hallucinations in a schizophrenic patient with electrode implants, Guerrero-Figueroa and Heath (1964) observed larger and then smaller evoked potentials in the optic tract, when the evoking light was hallucinated to be brighter and then dimmer.

In a study comparing the electroretinographic effects of percepts and of nonhallucinatory images, Kunzendorf (1984) obtained normal unimodal ERGs when eidetic imagers and control subjects perceived green flashes of light, and normal bimodal ERGs when eidetic imagers and control subjects perceived red flashes of light. Kunzendorf also obtained unimodal ERGs when the eidetic subjects imagined that red flashes were vivid green flashes, and bimodal ERGs when the eidetic subjects imagined that green flashes were vivid red flashes.

[1] Translation by Michael Chapman

In Pavlovian conditioning studies of visual responses in humans, Bogoslovksii and Semenovskaya (1959) and Freedman and Ronchi (1964) obtained increases in both the subjective brightness and the ERG amplitude of a dim light, when the light was accompanied by a conditioned stimulus that had previously been paired with a bright light. In an operant conditioning study of visual responses, Roger and Galand (1981) found that human subjects could voluntarily augment peripherally generated components of the visual evoked potential (VEP), and reported that most successful augmenters "associated the [evoking] flash with complex imagined sights such as bomb explosions" (p. 481).

Similarly, in an operant conditioning study of auditory responses, Finley and Johnson (1983) found that humans could voluntarily augment peripherally generated components of the auditory evoked potential (AEP). Finally, in hypnosis research on auditory responses, Deehan and Robertson (1980) reported that the AEP was abolished completely when negative hallucinations were hypnotically suggested.

BEHAVIORAL AND PSYCHOLOGICAL DIFFERENCES

The above evidence indicates that, as hallucinated sensations and imaged sensations and remembered sensations become quantitatively more vivid, they become physiologically more similar to the vivid sensations of perception. Such evidence, however, does not necessarily support Hume's (1739/1979) commonly accepted assertion that hallucinations and images and percepts are qualitatively indistinguishable. Although early behavioral experiments seemed to indicate that Hume's assertion was correct, recent behavioral research clearly shows otherwise.

The classic example of an experiment favoring Hume was conducted by Perky (1910). She instructed subjects to visualize their free associations on a background screen, and to report everything that they visually imaged. Unbeknownst to the subjects, Perky projected subliminal stimuli onto the screen. As a result, subjects incorrectly reported that they were visually imaging some of the subliminal stimuli. These erroneous reports seem to provide strong support for Hume's theory that perceptual experience usually is more vivid than imaginary experience, but otherwise is indistinguishable from mental imagery.

However, the reports of Perky's subjects provide equally strong support for Kunzendorf's (1987-88) theory of cognitive-state monitoring. According to monitoring theory, the brain normally registers or "monitors" both the peripheral innervation of perceptual sensations and the central innervation of mentally imaged sensations. Subjectively, such monitoring provides subjects with a sensationless awareness of whether their sensations are "centrally innervated" images or "peripherally innervated" percepts. But only under normal circumstances do subjects monitor the source of their sensations. When peripherally innervated sensations are subliminal, they are too brief or too weak to monitor. Thus, in Perky's study, the sensations of "unmonitored" subliminal percepts were immediately mistaken for imaged sensations, and in Kunzendorf's (1984-85) follow-up study, the sensations of "unmonitored" subliminal percepts were memorially confused not only with imaged sensations, but also with supraliminally perceived sensations.

Both for Kunzendorf's monitoring theory and for Hume's theory, the truly critical issue is whether supraliminal percepts and vivid images are confusable--an issue which Perky's experiment did not address, but which recent research has addressed. Hume's theory asserts that mental images of greater vividness are less distinguishable from normal percepts and, by such definition, are more hallucinatory in nature. In contrast, monitoring theory asserts that mental images of greater vividness, because they require central innervation of greater strength, are more easily "monitored" by the brain and more quickly discriminated from normal percepts. In addition, monitoring theory asserts that hallucinations--vivid hallucinations of physical bodies, as well as faint hallucinations of ghost-like entities--arise whem hypnosis or sleep or schizophrenia attenuates cognitive-state monitoring.

Consistent with monitoring theory and not with Humean theory, a recent experiment by Kunzendorf (1985-86) showed that supraliminal percepts are normally discriminated more quickly from vivid images (which are more easily "monitored") than from faint images. Moreover, this same experiment by Kunzendorf showed that during "unmonitored" states of deep hypnosis, supraliminal percepts are discriminated less quickly from vivid images than from faint images.

Other recent studies suggest that sleep and schizophrenia, like hypnosis in Kunzendorf's (1985-86) study, attenuate the monitoring of images and increase the incidence of hallucinations but do not necessarily increase the vividness of images. Johnson, Kahan, and Raye (1984) reported that wakeful subjects cannot memorially discriminate actual dreams, which they have previously imaged and reported, from descriptions of dreams, which they have previously perceived. Flor-Henri (in press) noted that many schizophrenics' hallucinations of voices are not vividly experienced "in the external world," but are faintly experienced "inside the head."

A schizophrenic hallucination, an hallucinatory dream, and an hypnotic hallucination are <u>hallucinatory</u> because they are not experienced as "self-generated" images. Moreover, an hallucination is qualitatively different from a vivid image, because imaged sensations are subjectively accompanied by the sensationless awareness <u>that they are "self-generated</u>." According to monitoring theory, this self-awareness is the subjective quality of a neural process that monitors the "central" source of imaged sensations.

PSYCHOPHYSIOLOGICAL DIFFERENCES

The remainder of this presentation describes new evidence regarding the neural substrates of the "source monitoring" process. Such evidence shows that, although percepts and images and hallucinations have similar effects on the peripheral nervous system (PNS), images have unique effects on the central nervous system (CNS): left-hemisphere effects that may be indicative of image-monitoring.

In light of recent research into left-hemisphere effects of hypnosis and schizophrenia, the current research into left-hemisphere effects of imaging is focused on cortical components of the auditory evoked potential (AEP). Gruzelier, Thomas, Brow, Conway, Golds, Jutai, Liddiard, McCormack, Perry, and Rhonder (1987) found that the <u>state of hypnosis</u> attenuates cortical AEP components from the left temporal lobe, but they did not test for any effects of hallucinatory imaging in the hypnotic state. Very similarly, Roemer, Shagass, Straumanis, and Amadeo (1979) found that <u>schizophrenic states</u> disrupt cortical AEP components from the left temporal lobe, but did not test for any effects of hallucinatory imaging in such states.

In the present AEP research, the effects of hypnotically hallucinating an evoking tone as louder or softer were compared to the effects of wakefully imaging the evoking tone as louder or softer. The search for

AEP differences between images and hallucinations is focused on left-hemisphere components with 300-500 msec latencies, and the search for AEP similarities between images and hallucinations (and percepts) is focused on two subcortical or "sensory" components. The first "sensory" component extends from stimulus onset to Wave V (the positively charged AEP trough occurring 6 msecs after stimulus onset); the innervation underlying this first component travels from the cochlea to the inferior colliculus (Allison, 1984; Picton, Hillyard, Krausz, & Galambos, 1974). The second "sensory" component extends from Na (the negatively charged AEP peak occurring 16-25 msecs after stimulus onset) to P1 (the AEP trough occurring 50-80 msecs after stimulus onset); the innervation underlying this second component ascends from the thalamus to the temporal-parietal cortex (Polich & Starr, 1983).

Method

Subjects. Twelve undergraduates from the University of Lowell were selected to participate in this study and were paid for their participation. These select subjects included three eidetic imagers high in hypnotizability, three eidetic imagers low in hypnotizability, three average auditory imagers high in hypnotizability, and three average auditory imagers low in hypnotizability. Thus, eidetic imagery and hypnotic susceptibility are independent factors in this experiment, even though they may be correlated variables in the population at large (Wilson & Barber, 1983).

On Weitzenhoffer and Hilgard's (1962) Stanford Hypnotic Susceptibility Scale, Form C, the six highly hypnotizable subjects had a mean score of 10.2 out of 12 (SD = 0.8). The six subjects of low hypnotizability had a mean score of 3.0 out of 12 (SD = 2.1).

On screening tests, the six eidetic imagers successfully imaged an 80 dB SPL tone sounding louder and then softer. (Although the proportion of college students experiencing auditory eidetic images has not been determined, Kunzendorf [in press] has found that less than 10% of the college population experiences visual eidetic images, which produce visual after-images obeying Emmert's Law.) On Kunzendorf's (1980) Vividness of Auditory Imagery Questionnaire (VAIQ), the six eidetic imagers had a mean score of 1.2 (SD = 0.2), where "1 = as vivid as normal hearing" and "5 = no image could be heard." In contrast, the six average imagers in this study had a mean VAIQ score of 3.2 (SD = 1.3).

Apparatus

In order to evoke brain potentials for computer averaging, a 120 Hz tone lasting 55 msecs was generated 80 times with an IBM Personal Computer, once every 1.5 secs. The tone was binaurally presented at 80 dB SPL though 8-ohm earphones with shielding added. Brain potentials, electroencephalograms (EEGs), were recorded from the left and right hemispheres by affixing miniature disc electrodes at T3 and T4 (International 10-20 System) and by referencing them ipsilaterally to ear-clip electrodes. For each hemisphere, recordings between 0.3 Hz and 3 kHz were amplified with a Grass Instruments 7P511 AC Amplifier. Upon every presentation of the evoking tone, the amplified EEGs from both hemispheres were sampled 300 times, once every 2 msecs, and were digitized with a Tecmar PC-Mate Lab Master. Any digitized EEGs with a floor or ceiling effect in either hemisphere were bilaterally rejected by computer. Following 80 unrejected presentations of the evoking tone, the digitized EEGs were averaged with an IBM Personal Computer. The computer-averaged evoked potentials, one for the left hemisphere and one for the right hemisphere, were plotted on two channels of a Grass Instruments 79 EEG/Polygraph.

Procedure

During the first phase of this experiment, while each of the individually tested subjects was in a state of wakefulness, three sets of bilateral AEPs were obtained. For one set of AEPs, the subject was instructed "just to listen to the 80 tones." For another set of AEPs, the subject was instructed "to image the 80 tones sounding much louder than they really are." For the third set of AEPs, the subject was instructed "to image the 80 tones sounding much softer than they really are, by imaging background music that blocks them out." The order of these three conditions of instruction varied across subjects.

During the second phase, after the subject was administered Weitzenhoffer and Hilgard's (1962) instructions for inducing hypnosis, three more sets of bilateral AEPs were obtained. For one set, the subject was instructed "to listen to the 80 tones." For another set, the subject was authoritatively instructed "to hear the 80 tones louder than ever before." For the remaining set, the subject was authoritatively instructed "to hear the 80 tones softer than ever before, as loud music begins to block them out."

Results

"Sensory Components" of the AEP. The current study was designed, in part, to examine the effects of auditory imaging and auditory hallucinating on two "sensory" components of the AEP. The earliest of these "sensory" components extends from stimulus onset (the cochlea) to Wave V (the inferior colliculus). The effects of auditory perceiving, auditory imaging, and auditory hallucinating on this peripherally innervated component of the AEP are shown in Figure 1 and Figure 2. For the unhypnotizable eidetic imager in Figure 1(A), this earliest component enlarges when the louder 90 dB tone is heard and recedes when the softer 70 dB is heard, in accord with previous findings (Picton, Hillyard, Krausz, & Galambos, 1974). For the same subject in Figure 1(B), and for the hypnotizable eidetic imager in Figure 2(A), this earliest component enlarges when the 80 dB tone is imaged to sound louder and recedes when the 80 dB tone is imaged to sound softer. Also, for the hypnotizable subject in Figure 2(B), this peripherally innervated component enlarges when the 80 dB tone is hallucinated to be louder and recedes when the 80 dB tone is hallucinated to be softer. However, these percept-like effects of wakeful and hypnotic imaging on this earliest component of the AEP occurred only for the eidetic imagers of Figure 1 and Figure 2--and only in the left hemisphere of the eidetic imager in Figure 2. The other subjects' imaging and hallucinating produced no measurable effect on this very early and very small component.

The other "sensory" component currently under examination extends from Na (the thalamus) to P1 (the temporal-parietal cortex). The effects of auditory perceiving, auditory imaging, and auditory hallucinating on this second "sensory" component are summarized in Table 1 and exemplified in Figures 1 and 2. For the unhypnotizable eidetic imager in Figure 1(A), this second component enlarges when the louder 90 dB tone is heard and recedes when the softer 70 dB tone is heard, in accord with previous findings (Picton, Hillyard, Frausz, & Galambos, 1974). Also, for the eidetic imager in Figure 1(B), for the hypnotizable eidetic imager in Figure 2(A), and for all six eidetic imagers in Table 1, this second component enlarges when the 80 dB tone is imaged to sound louder and recedes when the 80 dB tone is imaged to sound softer. Finally, for the hypnotizable subject in Figure 2(B), and for all six hypnotizable subjects in Table 1, the second "sensory" component enlarges when the 80 dB tone is hallucinated to be louder and recedes when the 80 dB tone is hallucinated to be softer. (In the hypnotic phase, the three unhypnotizable eidetic imagers no longer exhibited any sensory effects of imaging--because, as they indicated after

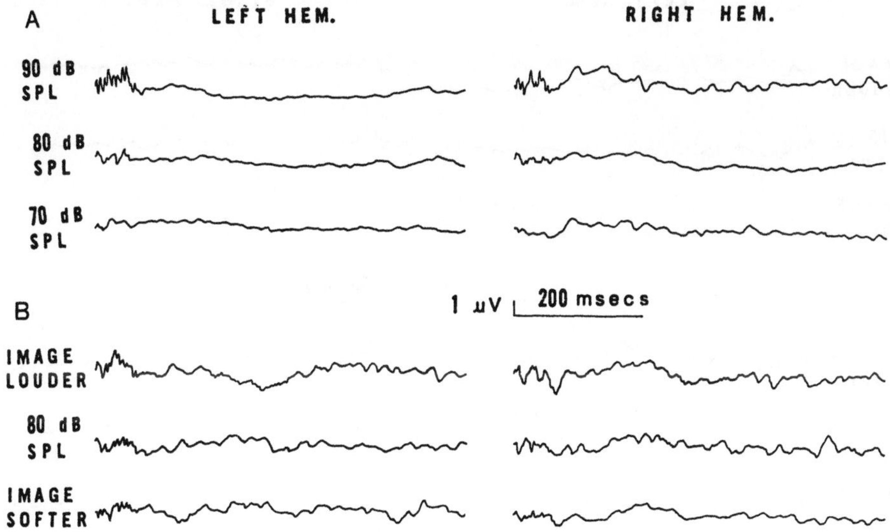

Figure 1. Tracings of a subject's evoked potentials (A) for louder and softer percepts of the evoking tone, (B) for louder and softer images of the evoking tone. (This subject is one of the unhypnotizable eidetic imagers.)

the experiment, they did not <u>voluntarily image</u> when they were given <u>authoritative</u> hypnotic suggestions to <u>hallucinate</u>.)

Consistent with these descriptive statistics, an analysis of variance for the <u>sensory components</u> in Table 1 revealed (a) a main effect of the three instructions, $F(2,16) = 17.22$, $p < .001$, (b) a three-way interaction among the instructions, the waking and hypnotic phases, and the levels of eidetic imagery, $F(2,16) = 5.36$, $p < .025$, and (c) a three-way interaction among the instructions, the waking and hypnotic phases, and the levels of hypnotic susceptibility, $F(2,16) = 3.85$, $p < .05$. For the main effect, a trend test revealed a linear increase in the second <u>sensory component</u> across instructions, $F(1,16) = 34.40$, $p < .001$. For the first interaction, a trend test indicated that, in the waking phase, this linear increase in the second component across instructions was greater for eidetic imagers than for average imagers, $F(1,10) = 24.52$, $p < .001$. For the second interaction, a trend test indicated that in the hypnotic phase, this linear increase in the second component across instructions was greater for subjects of high hypnotizability than for subjects of low hypnotizability, $F(1,10) = 9.87$, $p < .025$.

<u>The "Monitoring" Component in the Left Hemisphere</u>. Finally, the current study was designed to compare the effect of mental imaging and the effect of hypnotic hallucinating on late AEP components in the left hemisphere. The particular component worthy of further analysis extends from N3 (the most negatively charged peak between P3 and P4) to P4 (the most positively charged trough 450-500 msecs after stimulus onset).

The effects of auditory imaging and auditory hallucinating on N3-P4 in the left hemisphere are summarized in Table 3 and exemplified in Figures 1 and 2. For the perceiver in Figure 1(A), this left-hemisphere component is unaffected when the louder 90dB tone is heard and when the softer 70 dB tone is heard. In contrast, for all 12 subjects in Table 3, including the eidetic imagers in Figure 1(B) and Figure 2(A), this left-hemsphere component enlarges when the 80 dB tone is imaged to sound louder and when the 80 dB tone is imaged to sound softer. Finally, for the hypnotic

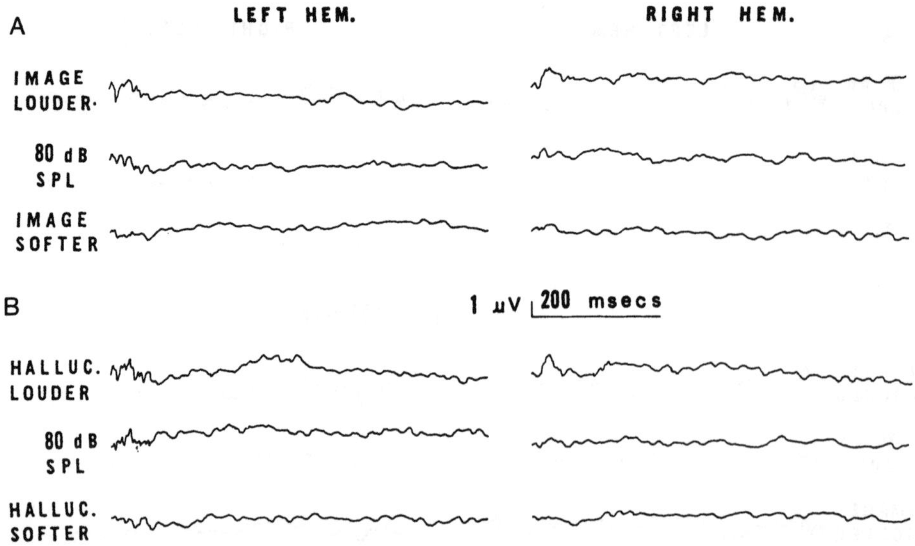

Figure 2. Tracings of a subject's evoked potentials (A) for louder and softer images of the evoking tone, (B) for louder and softer hallucinations of the evoking tone. (This subject is one of the hypnotizable eidetic imagers.)

hallucinator in Figure 2(B), and for all 12 subjects in Table 3, this left-hemisphere component is unaffected when the 80 dB tone is hallucinated to be louder and when the 80 dB tone is hallucinated to be softer. (Unhypnotizable subjects exhibited no N3-P4 effects during hypnosis, just as they exhibited no "sensory" effects during hypnosis--because they neither hallucinated nor imaged when given authoritative suggestions "to hear" a louder or softer tone).

An analysis of variance for the N3-P4 components in Table 3 confirmed the presence of an interaction among the three instructions, the waking versus hypnotic phases, and the two hemispheres, $F(2,16) = 4.63$, $p < .05$. Moreover, a trend test for this N3-P4 interaction indicated that in the left hemisphere, the quadratic trend across instructions was greater during the waking phase than during the hypnotic phase, $F(1,11) = 14.22$, $p < .005$.

CONCLUSION

The results of the present experiment indicate that eidetically imaged loudness versus softness and hypnotically hallucinated loudness versus softness, like perceived loudness versus softness, affect the amplitude of early "sensory" components in the AEP. The results also indicate that imaged loudness and softness affect a later "source monitoring" component in the left-hemisphere AEP, whereas hallucinated loudness and softness--like perceived loudness and softness--do not affect this later component.

The earliest "sensory" component under examination, Wave V at 0-6 msecs of the auditory evoked potential, enlarged when two eidetic imagers imaged the evoking tone as louder and receded when they imaged the evoking tone as softer. For one of these eidetic subjects, the hypnotizable one, Wave V also enlarged when the subject hallucinated the evoking tone as louder and receded when she hallucinated it as softer. Given that this earliest sensory component reflects innervation from the cochlea to the inferior colliculus (ALlison, 1984; Picton, Hillyard, & Krausz, 1974), the results of these two subjects suggest that vivid auditory images centrifugally

Table 1. Amplitude (in μV) of AEP "Sensory Component" from Na to P1

Hypn. susc.	Instru.		Waking Phase: Eidetic imagers LHem.	Eidetic imagers RHem.	Eidetic imagers L+R/2	Average imagers LHem.	Average imagers RHem.	Average imagers L+R/2
High	Image louder	M	1.37	1.27	1.32	1.61	1.33	1.47
		SD	.32	.64		.21	.23	
	Just listen	M	1.00	0.87	0.94	1.64	1.04	1.34
		SD	.44	.47		.07	.15	
	Image softer	M	0.77	0.77	0.77	1.58	1.18	1.38
		SD	.21	.29		.31	.03	
Low	Image louder	M	1.67	1.33	1.50	1.33	0.94	1.14
		SD	.31	.83		.42	.15	
	Just Listen	M	1.17	1.07	1.12	1.40	1.17	1.29
		SD	.06	.61		.72	.15	
	Image softer	M	0.73	0.74	0.74	1.17	1.07	1.12
		SD	.12	.38		.21	.38	
Hi&Lo	I.loud	M			1.41[a]			1.30
	Listen	M			1.03			1.31
	I.soft	M			0.75[b]			1.25.

Hypn. susc.	Instru.		Hypnotic Phase: Eidetic imagers LHem.	Eidetic imagers RHem.	Eidetic imagers L+R/2	Average imagers LHem.	Average imagers RHem.	Average imagers L+R/2	Eid&Ave (L+R/2)
High	Halluc. louder	M	1.53	1.44	1.49	1.43	1.25	1.34	1.41[c]
		SD	.46	.50		.30	.53		
	Just listen	M	1.20	0.90	1.05	1.21	0.90	1.06	1.05
		SD	.20	.36		.47	.56		
	Halluc. softer	M	0.93	0.87	0.90	0.93	0.90	0.92	0.91[d]
		SD	.12	.15		.26	.35		
Low	Halluc. louder	M	1.30	0.76	1.03	1.23	1.10	1.17	1.10
		SD	.36	.15		.15	.46		
	Just listen	M	1.30	1.07	1.19	1.13	1.10	1.12	1.15
		SD	.17	.31		.81	.17		
	Halluc. softer	M	1.30	0.67	0.99	1.13	0.97	1.05	1.02[e]
		SD	.10	.31		.61	.38		

[a] Significantly > Listen Mean of 1.03, $t(5) = 4.96$, $p < .01$.
[b] Significantly < Listen Mean of 1.03, $t(5) = 3.05$, $p < .05$.
[c] Significantly > Listen Mean of 1.05, $t(5) = 3.18$, $p < .05$.
[d] Marginally < Listen Mean of 1.05, $t(5) = 2.10$, $p < .10$.
[e] Insignificantly < Listen Mean of 1.15, $t(5) = 0.96$.

Table 2. Amplitude (in μV) of AEP "Monitoring Component from N3 to P4

Hypn. susc.	Instr.		Waking Phase					
			Eidetic imagers		Average imagers		Eid. & ave.	
			LHem.	RHem.	LHem.	RHem.	LHem.	RHem.
High								
	Image louder	M	1.03	0.57	0.70	0.50		
		SD	.32	.12	.26	.27		
	Just listen	M	0.60	0.74	0.21	0.41		
		SD	.26	.29	.20	.34		
	Image softer	M	0.87	0.63	0.65	0.51		
		SD	.12	.21	.33	.25		
Low								
	Image louder	M	1.10	0.77	0.87	0.87		
		SD	.17	.40	.46	.31		
	Just listen	M	0.77	0.83	0.43	0.57		
		SD	.48	.35	.41	.31		
	Image softer	M	0.93	0.67	0.83	0.87		
		SD	.23	.12	.25	.12		
Hi&Lo								
	I.loud	M					0.93a	0.68
	Listen	M					0.50	0.64
	I.soft	M					0.82b	0.67

Hypn. susc.	Instr.		Hypnotic Phase					
			Eidetic imagers		Average imagers		Eid. & ave.	
			LHem.	RHem.	LHem.	RHem.	LHem.	RHem.
High								
	Halluc. louder	M	0.61	0.90	0.68	0.63		
		SD	.19	.30	.30	.21		
	Just listen	M	0.60	0.87	0.51	0.46		
		SD	.35	.15	.15	.16		
	Halluc. softer	M	0.74	0.70	0.61	0.49		
		SD	.15	.10	.39	.28		
Low								
	Halluc. louder	M	0.73	0.47	0.80	1.00		
		SD	.46	.32	.69	.53		
	Just listen	M	0.73	0.60	0.67	0.97		
		SD	.31	.20	.23	.47		
	Halluc. softer	M	0.50	0.50	0.74	0.73		
		SD	.26	.10	.38	.42		
Hi&Lo								
	H.loud	M					0.71c	0.75
	Listen	M					0.63	0.73
	H.soft	M					0.65	0.61

[a]Significantly > Listen Mean of 0.50, $t(11) = 5.68$, $p < .01$

[b]Significantly < Listen Mean of 0.50, $t(11) = 3.51$, p .01

[c]Insignificantly > Listen Mean of 0.63, $t(11) = 0.82$

innervate the cochlea and the brain stem, just as vivid visual images centrifugally innervate the retina and the optic nerve (Kunzendorf, 1983; Guerrero-Figueroa & Heath, 1964). If any weaker centrifugal effects of auditory imaging were present in the other eidetic and hypnotic subjects, those effects were probably too small to measure with the current amount of averaging and the current rate of sampling, inasmuch as brain stem AEPs are often averaged from 1000 EEGs sampled at 2000 Hz.

The Na-P1 "sensory" component--which, at 20-65 msecs, exhibits more measurability with less averaging--enlarged when all six eidetic imagers imaged the evoking tone as louder and receded when they imaged the evoking tone as softer. The Na-P1 component also enlarged when all six hypnotizable subjects hallucinated the evoking tone as louder and receded when they hallucinated it as softer. Like Wave V, this component is a "sensory" component, because its amlitude is not a function of attention but is a function of loudness (Polich & Starr, 1983)--real and imaged loudness!

Whereas eidetic imaging and hypnotic hallucinating had similar effects on "sensory" components of the AEp, they had different effects on a later left-hemisphere component, N3-P4. In the left hemisphere, N3-P4 enlarged when the evoking tone was imaged to be louder or softer, consistent with Kunzendorf's contention that the hallucinating brain does not monitor the source of sensations, N3-P4 did not enlarge when the evoking tone was hypnotically hallucinated to be louder or softer. In conclusion, then, it is suggested that N3-P4 may reflect the left hemisphere's monitoring of "centrally innervated" or "self-generated" sensations.

REFERENCES

Allison, T. (1984). Recording and interpreting event-related potentials. In E. Donchin (Ed.), Cognitive psychophysiology: Event-related potentials and the study of cognition (pp. 1-36). Hillsdale, N.J.: Lawrence Erlbaum.

Bogoslovskii, A., & Semenovskaya, E. (1959). Conditioned reflex changes in the human electroretinogram. Buletin of Experimental Biology and Medicine (translated from Russian), 47, 265-269.

Craig, K.J.W. (1940). Origin of visual after-images. Nature, 145, 512.

Darwin, E. (1803). Zoonomia (Vol. 1). Boston: D. Carlisle.

Deehan, C., & Robertson, A. W. (1980). Changes in auditory evoked potentials induced by hypnotic suggestion. In M. Pajntar, E. Roskar, & M. Lavric (Eds.), Hypnosis in psychotherapy and psychosomatic medicine (pp. 93-95). Ljubljana: University Press.

Finley, W. W., & Johnson, G. (1983). Operant control of auditory brainstem potentials in man. International Journal of Neuroscience, 21, 161-170.

Flor-Henri, P. (in press). Schizophrenic hallucinations in the context of psychophysiological studies of schizophrenia. In R. G. Kunzendorf & A. A. Sheikh (Eds.), The psychophysiology of mental imagery: Theory, research, and application. Farmingdale, N.Y.: Baywood.

Freedman, S. J., & Ronchi, L. (1964). Adaptation and training effects in ERG: IV. Overview of eight years. Atti della Fondazione Giorgo Ronchi, 19, 542-565.

Gruithuisen, F.V.P. (1812). Beyträge zur Physiognosie und Eautognosie, für Freunde der Naturforschung auf dem Erfahrungswege. München: I.J. Lentner.

Gruzelier, J., Thomas, M., Brow, T., Conway, A., Golds, J., Jutai, J., Liddiard, D., McCormack, K., Perry, A., & Rhonder, J. (1987). Involvement of the left hemisphere in hypnotic induction: Electrodermal, haptic, electrocortical, and divided visual field evidence. In S. Taneli, C. Perris, & D. Kemali (Eds.), Advances in biological

psychiatry: Vol. 16, Neurophysiological correlates of relaxation and psychopathology (pp. 6-17). Basel: S. Karger.
Guerrero-Figueroa, R., & Heath, R. G. (1964). Evoked responses and changes during attentive factors in man. Archives of Neurology, 10, 74-84.
Hume, D. (1979). A treatise of human nature (excerpt from 1739 edition). In R. I. Watson (Ed.), Basic writings in the history of psychology (pp. 51-62). New York: Oxford University Press.
Johnson, M. K., Kahan, T. L., & Raye, C. L. (1984). Dreams and reality monitoring. Journal of Experimental Psychology: General, 113, 329-344.
Klinke, R., & Galley, N. (1974). Efferent innervation of vestibular and auditory receptors. Physiological Reviews, 54, 316-357.
Krill, A. E., Wieland, A. M., & Ostfeld, A. M. (1960). The effect of two hallucinogenic agents on human retinal function. Archives of Opthalmology, 64, 724-733.
Kunzendorf, R. G. (1980). Imagery and consciousness: A scientific analysis of the mind-body problem (Doctoral dissertation, University of Virginia, 1979). Dissertation Abstracts International, 40, 3448B-3449B.
Kunzendorf, R. G. (1984). Centrifugal effects of eidetic imaging on flash electroretinograms and autonomic responses. Journal of Mental Imagery, 8, 67-76.
Kunzendorf, R. G. (1984-1985). Subconscious percepts as "unmonitored" percepts: An empirical study. Imagination, Cognition, and Personality, 4, 367-375.
Kunzendorf, R. G. (1985-1986). Hypnotic hallucinations as "unmonitored" images: An empirical study. Imagination, Cognition, and Personality, 5, 255-270.
Kunzendorf, R. G. (1987-88). Self-consciousness as the monitoring of cognitive states: A theoretical perspective. Imagination, Cognition, and Personality, 7, 3-22.
Kunzendorf, R. G. (in press). Afterimages of eidetic images: A developmental study. Journal of Mental Imagery.
Oswald, I. (1957). After-images from retina and brain, Quarterly Journal of Experimental Psychology, 9, 88-100.
Perky, C. W. (1910). An experimental study of imagination. American Journal of Psychology, 21, 422-452.
Picton, T. W., Hillyard, S. A., Krausz, H. I., & Galambos, R. (1974). Human auditory evoked potentials: I. Evaluation of components. Electroencephalography and Clinical Neurophysiology, 36, 179-190.
Polich, J. M., & Starr, A. (1983). Middle-, late-, and long-latency auditory evoked potentials. In E. J. Moore (Ed.), Bases of auditory brainstem evoked responses (pp. 345-361). New York: Grune & Stratton.
Roemer, R. A., Shagass, C., Straumanis, J. J., & Amadeo, M. (1979). Somatosensory and auditory evoked potential studies of functional differences between the cerebral hemispheres in psychosis. Biological Psychiatry, 14, 357-373.
Roger, M., & Galand, G. (1981). Operant conditioning of visual evoked potentials in man. Psychophysiology, 18, 477-482.
Van Hasselt, P. (1972-1973). The centrifugal control of retinal function: A review. Ophthalmological Research, 4, 298-320.
Weitzenhoffer, A. M., & Hilgard, E. R. (1962). Stanford Hypnotic Susceptibility Scale, Form C. Palo Alto, CA: Consulting Psychologists Press.
Wilson, S. C., & Barber, T. X. (1983). The fantasy-prone personality: Implications for understanding imagery, hypnosis, and parapsychological phenomena. In A.A. Sheikh (Ed.), Imagery: Current theory, research, and application (pp. 340-387). New York: J. Wiley & Sons.
Zwicker, E. (1964). "Negative afterimage" in hearing. Journal of the Acoustical Society of America, 36, 2413-2415.

A FUNCTIONAL ANALYSIS OF IMAGINED INTERACTION ACTIVITY IN EVERYDAY LIFE

James M. Honeycutt

Department of Speech Communication
Louisiana State University
Baton Rouge, LA

ABSTRACT

A program of research examining imagined interactions in everyday life is described. Imagined interactions are a type of cognition in which individuals imagine themselves having dialogue with others. They reflect a type of imagery in which communicators experience various message strategies with others. A multidimensional instrument reflecting imagined interaction characteristics has resulted in eight dimensions of imagined interaction features. Imagined interactions may serve a variety of functions including rehearsal, increasing self-understanding, and catharsis in the form of tension relief from anxiety-producing situations. Therapeutic benefits also accrue from imagined interactions.

It is a pleasure to be here speaking at Yale today on imagined interactions in everyday life. Within the field of human communication, the study of mental imagery has been discussed under the labels of intrapersonal communication and social cognition. I believe the study of mental imagery is increasingly vital and important given the advent of new work technologies which may provide individuals more free time to be introspective, daydream, or fantasize. Ultimately, the question arises if this increased free time is spent on functional or dysfunctional thoughts, some of which may include imagined interactions. Caughey (1984) surmises that when an individual's attention is not taken up by demanding tasks, the self's attention shifts inward to a world of inner imagery and silent language. He argues and I agree that this is a pervasive phenomenon largely ignored by social science. I believe the study of covert dialogue or what my colleagues and I have termed "imagined interactions" can enlighten us in this area.

During the last 10 years, there has been an interest within my field on information processing and how this affects communication behavior and outcomes such as interpersonal attraction. For example, in some studies in the area of initial interaction, an individual arbitrarily designated in an experimental role as a "perceiver" may be induced to believe that he/she will be meeting a stranger who will be of some personality disposition (e.g., friendly/unfriendly, similar/dissimilar other). The interaction may be sequentially analyzed in some fashion and postinteraction ratings of the other's social status and likeability may be gathered (e.g., Street & Murphy, 1987; Capella, 1984; Berger, 1979; Ickes et al., 1982).

In situations such as these, we may expect the perceiver to "rehearse" what he or she will do during the anticipated encounter. Thus, the perceiver is placing him or herself in some role and developing a cognitive representation of planned interaction. The perceiver is having what we refer to as "imagined interactions" (Edwards, Honeycutt, & Zagacki, 1988; Honeycutt, Zagacki, & Edwards, in press; Zagacki, Edwards, & Honeycutt, forthcoming).

Imagined interactions are a type of daydreaming that tend to occur with significant others (e.g., romantic partners, friends, relatives) as opposed to total strangers we never expect to meet. Thus far, we have deliberately restricted our study of imagined interactions to real-life others as opposed to fictional characters. We have examined the characteristics of these in everyday life. It is my hope to learn more about the form and functions of imagined interactions in daily situations. In our conception, imagined interactions are not simply internal thoughts or fantasies. Rather, an imagined interaction takes place when the self is involved in internal dialogue with a real-life significant other. More is said on this later when I will discuss a working definition of imagined interactions. Imagined interactions (IIs) may serve a variety of general and specific functions. Furthermore, the process of having an II serves to develop cognitive representations of the self. In this regard, an individual having an II is afforded the luxury of visualizing him or herself in a variety of roles, situations, and hypothetical scenes. For example, an individual may imagine an interview with a company recruiter. If the individual anticipates negative reactions to some things he/she imagines saying, then the individual may "rewrite" the II in such a way as to anticipate favorable outcomes (Edwards et al., 1988).

Today, I will partition my address into four major areas. First, I will detail how the interest in studying IIs began and how our research program at LSU started to emerge. I will review some of our survey findings such as the relationship between loneliness and general features of IIs. Second, I will discuss the theoretical foundations behind the II concept. Finally, I will speculate on the therapeutic benefits of IIs and present some sample journal accounts of II functions.

CREATION OF THE II RESEARCH PROGRAM

Excluding books, I assume that all of us read any combination of journal articles, conference papers, essays, or book chapters on a regular basis. Occasionally we may come across an article that really excites us and creates an "a-ha" experience. This kind of experience happened to me in April of 1986. One of my research interests is in marital and family communication. I came across an intriguing, psychotherapy article on "imagined interactions and the family" by Rosenblatt and Meyer in the April issue of Family Relations. These therapists discussed the notion of imagined interactions occurring between the client and family of origin (parents) and between client and therapist. They discussed imagined interactions in terms of thinking through how to solve a problem or thinking through an interaction with another who is physically or emotionally unavailable. They argue that IIs have many characteristics of real conversations and that they may be fragmentary, extended, rambling, repetitive, or coherent. IIs may occur frequently during the course of an individual's day. Most involve actors in conversation with significant others, such as family members, close friends, intimates, or work partners.

Rosenblatt and Meyer (1986) discuss four general functions of IIs. First, they can serve a rehearsal function for interaction that is anticipated and one is anxious about it. Second, they can help individuals talk through problems with another who is physically unavailable. Third, IIs may help the self obtain a greater sense of one's feelings. Fourth, IIs may help one to recreate past events in order to determine if an alternative course of action could have led to different outcomes. This is related to Greene's (1984) activation of procedural records for behavioral situations. As individuals engage in IIs, procedural records may be activated which can prescribe behaviors to be enacted for particular circumstances.

Our research program started after two of my colleagues, Renee Edwards and Kenneth S. Zagacki were also excited about the II construct and how it could be examined and extended within the human communication discipline in terms of cognitive planning for anticipated interaction episodes. In order to create a cohesive research team, we have systematically rotated author ordering with each of us contributing relatively the same amount of input into projects. From a theoretical stance, we saw the concept as one way to operationalize the study of intrapersonal communication; the study of internal communication as they affect communication in interpersonal relationships. From a practical viewpoint, we believed that if we could begin to identify the topics of IIs in everyday interaction, and how this related to such personality constructs as loneliness, then we may be in a position to counsel lonely individuals how to have IIs that help them prepare for actual conversational encounters. We also believed that the content of IIs may provide us with insight on problems affecting individuals with interpersonal relationships.

Survey of Imagined Interaction (SII)

Singer (1978) has described how studies of daydreaming and the stream of conscious can be conducted with surveys and has called for more research in this area. Based on what Rosenblatt and Meyer (1986) had speculated concerning the existence of IIs in clients, Renee Edwards and I started to develop a survey instrument called the SII (Survey of Imagined Interaction) designed to measure if individuals have a variety of IIs, topical content, who they are with, how discrepant or similar they are to real interactions, how vague or detailed they are, and the purpose for having them.

The SII begins by describing IIs as "those 'mental interactions' we have with others who are not physically present," and goes on to describe some potential characteristics of IIs (Edwards, Honeycutt, and Zagacki, 1988; Zagacki, Edwards, and Honeycutt, forthcoming). The survey is divided into two sections. Section 1 includes statements about IIs using 7 point Likert-type items ranging from 1) very strong disagreement, to 7) very strong agreement. Section 1 reflects general features about IIs such as whether the self or other talks more in the II, how pleasant their II's tend to be, discrepancy of the II with real interaction, the scene of the II, and if their II's are primarily verbal, visual, or a mixture.

Section 2 is concerned with the characteristics of a specific II in which respondents are asked to write out sample lines of dialogue. Table 1 contains two sample protocols and some of the descriptive data pertinent to each protocol. The first protocol concerns child management. A husband reports an II with his wife in which he questions the example she is setting for their son. He reports having "mostly positive" feelings about the II. The second protocol involves a wife imagining a conversation with her husband in which he accuses her of being too sensitive while she feels concern. The wife reports feeling good about the II because it allowed her to rehearse what she would later say to her husband. Aside from indicating the topics of the II and how the self felt about the II, respondents also indicate when and where they experienced it. they also are asked if they re-experienced the II as they wrote it down and the ease of reporting the alternating lines of dialogue. After giving the sample II protocol, there are a number of items reflecting the functions of the II as well as some items adapted from Hecht's (1978) Communication Satisfaction Inventory. We are interested in measuring satisfaction with the reported II and relating it to various factors in the SII. For example, one may report negative emotions about the II content, but feel satisfied with the II since it allows one to voice his or her views.

A principle components analysis of Section 1 has revealed an eight factor solution with good reliabilities (Zagacki et al., forthcoming). The first factor reflects "discrepancy" between having an II and reports of real conversations. The second factor concerns "pleasantness" or how pleasant an individual's IIs tend to be across a variety of topics, situations, and interaction partners. The third factor reflects "activity" or how often individuals report having IIs. Factor 4 reflects "dominance" or how much one believes he/she talked in the II compared to the other interactor. The fifth factor reflects "specificity" in terms of how detailed and developed an individual's IIs are. The sixth factor signifies "retroactive IIs" in which an II occurs after an important encounter. Factor 7 was

Table 1

Sample SII Protocols

Gender: Male
Age: 41
Relationship to self: wife
How long ago it took place: yesterday
Scene of the II: home
Topic(s) discussed: proper method of child training
Self-reported emotions about the II: mostly positive

Me: Don't keep yelling at the child. Either punish him or give him a whippin'. You should listen to yourself. All that yelling makes you sound exactly like some of our less intelligent neighbors. This only encourages Jeremy to do the same thing in return.

Wife: He's my child and if I think he should be yelled at, then I'll do it.

Me: That's typical female intelligence. If you're stupid, tell everybody. Then double up and raise your children to be just as stupid as you are.

Gender: Female
Age: 21
Relationship to self: husband
How long ago it took place: 10 minutes
Scene of the II: home
Topic(s) discussed: my expectations and his attitude toward me
Self-reported emotions about the II: felt better because I had an idea about what I was going to say.

Me: You know, you really hurt my feelings by your comments a few minutes ago.

Husband: Why? That's stupid! They had nothing to do with you. You shouldn't be so sensitive.

Me: They had everything to do with me. When you snap at me like that, when I'm just being concerned, it hurts my feelings. It makes me feel like you have something to hide. I mean, I just asked you a simple question and you get all sarcastic. I don't understand why you have to react that way.

labeled "variety" and represents the diversity of topics and individuals that individuals report characterize their IIs. Finally, the eighth factor reflects "proactive IIs" which occur before an important encounter or meeting. A stepwise regression of communication satisfaction on these factors has revealed that the pleasant ($\beta = .40$) and nonretroactive ($\beta = -.14$) features are significant predictors, overall $F(2, 242) = 25.95$, $p = .000$, $r^2 = .18$.

A factor analysis of the function items in Section 2 yielded a three-factor solution. Factor 1 reflects "increased understanding" of oneself such as clarifying feelings and thoughts. The second factor reflects "rehearsal" for an anticipated encounter. The third factor represents "catharsis." In this situation, the II functions to reduce uncertainty and relieve tension about the other's behaviors.

The psychometric properties of the SII are reviewed elsewhere (Zagacki et al., forthcoming). The SII is a multidimensional instrument. Thus, it is possible for researchers to use some or all of the subscales depending on the samples of individuals under study. It is easy to administer and hence, can be used to assess imagined interactions in everyday life. Currently, I am surveying elderly populations using some of the subscales. I have created other versions of the SII for use in marital and dating relationships as well as for assessing the content of an II before a real encounter occurred.

Relation Between Loneliness and SII Factors

Elsewhere, we have reported that individuals who are higher in loneliness report having IIs that are more discrepant from real interaction (Edwards et al., 1988). Using the revised UCLA loneliness scale (Russell, Peplau, & Cutrona, 1980), our early work revealed that loneliness scores were negatively associated with having IIs and with having IIs making the self feel more confident. In addition, lonely individuals experienced less communication satisfaction and more negative emotions with their IIs than did non-lonely individuals. Thus, lonely individuals appeared to experience more dysfunctional IIs. More recently, we have found negative correlations between loneliness and the catharsis function, having a greater number and variety of IIs, and having IIs that are detailed and specific (Zagacki et al., forthcoming). It also appears that loneliness is best predicted by having IIs that are discrepant ($\beta = .27$) and vague ($\beta = -.21$ for the "specificity" factor, overall $F(2, 242) = 17.55$, $p = .000$, $r^2 = .12$).

We have speculated that lonely individuals may have fewer IIs because they have fewer actual interactions to review or rehearse. thus, this low number of interactions may leave lonely individuals with no real resources for constructing (or reviewing) later IIs (Honeycutt et al., in press).

THEORETICAL FOUNDATIONS OF THE IMAGINED INTERACTION CONSTRUCT

We have formally defined IIs as process of cognition whereby actors imagine themselves in interaction with others (Edwards et al., 1988). Imagined interactions involve the actor in contrived dialogue with anticipated others. As such, they reflect a specific mode of "imagery" in which communicators experience cognitive representations of conversations. In addition, IIs may occur in different modes--verbal, visual, or both (Zagacki, et al., forthcoming). In forming an image of the scene of the II, they may image the other, and/or they may image the self, with functions and outcomes varying with the mode of imagery.

The notion of "imagined interactions" is more inclusive than imagined dialogue or conversation. The term "interaction" connotes more than verbal dialogue as nonverbal images come to the mind of the imaginer. For example, some of my students indicate how they can detail the visual scene of an imagined interaction (e.g., a professor's office before protesting an exam grade) in addition to anticipated dialogue. For a few, the visual images seem stronger than the verbal dialogue.

Since imagined interactions can contain visual data, they may indicate a mode of thinking distinct from the traditional propositional mode (Zagacki et al., forthcoming). Cognitive decision-making (Honeycutt et al., in press) refers to the process whereby actors examine cognitive schemata, lists, networks of propositional information, or other cognitive structures for appropriate communicative behaviors. In this view, actors have available information encoded in propositions; they simply draw on these propositions in order to determine what behaviors best suit any given communicative exigencies. Imagined interactions, however, are in principle different from propositional thinking insofar as they may involve actors in imagined dialogue with anticipated others.

Imagined interactions are attempts to simulate real-life conversations with others and in particular, significant others as revealed in our data. thus, imagined interactions may allow actors to access information from or similar to that contained in cognitive structures, such as cognitive scripts (Schank & Abelson, 1977; Kellermann, 1984), and/or procedural records (Greene, 1984; see also Edwards et al., 1988). Relatedly, imagined interactions may allow actors to solve communication problems ordinarily worked out in more propositionally located operations. But imagined interactions afford actors the opportunity to envision the act of discoursing with others, anticipating their responses, and even assuming others' roles.

Imagined interactions should not be confused with internal self-talk. Howell (1986) discusses "internal monologue" as talking with oneself. According to Howell, individuals want to concentrate fully on a topic but their minds wander. If the individual happens to be in an emotional state, irrelevant thoughts multiply. Attention is divided between these thoughts and what the individual should be doing in the encounter. "The more intense and constant the internal monologue, the lower a person's ability to pick up cues from the environment and respond sensibly to them" (Howell, 1986, p. 114).

In contrast, IIs are internal dialogue. Instead of merely responding to our conjured thoughts, we may respond to imagined remarks by the other. While IIs tend to occur before and after actual encounters (Edwards et al., 1988), they may occur during an encounter. Here, I would like to open up the debate. Actually, I believe that most IIs occur before or after real encounters as opposed to occurring within an actual conversation. Yet, it is possible that in some situations, the II may occur milliseconds before an actual utterance as a way of anticipating how the other will respond. Of course, cognitive psychologists will readily inform us as to the problem of limited cognitive capacity and information overload. To argue that IIs occur within an ongoing conversation posits an incredible information processing capacity for human beings who have enough difficulty attending to their own thoughts, let alone anticipating another's responses (Hewes, 1986). Still, the scenario of a job interview comes to mind. In this situation, the interviewee may imagine and "predict" what the next probing question will be because he/she has figured out the line or sequence of questions. According to speech act theory (Jackson & Jacobs, 1980), it appears that a line of questions already posed allows prediction of follow-up questions and remarks. Figure 1 reveals the symbolic location of IIs within a dyad. Both interactors may pro and retroactively imagine what

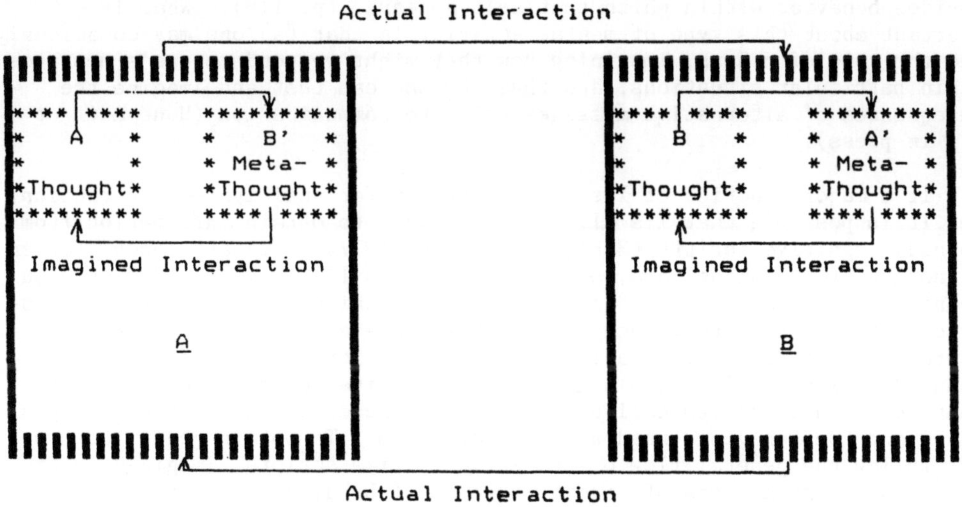

Figure 1. Symbolic location of imagined interactions. A has internal cognitions, thoughts, and beliefs which affect imagined interactions with B. This is signified by the asterisk boxes (*) and the lined arrows going to and from the internal representations of self. Imagined interactions may occur before as well as after a real interaction has taken place. Imagined interactions may affect actual dialogue and responses.

the self and other says. Box A represents internal thoughts directed toward oneself from the perspective of interactor "A." Box B' represents Laing's (1969) metaperspective. A is imagining the perceptions of B or what A thinks B is thinking.

The study of imagined interactions is exciting because it can inform us on conjured plans for communicative encounters and reveal representations of self. An individual having an II is in a position in which he or she can take into account another's perspective. This metaperspective may reveal empathy or projection depending on the fit of the II with real interaction. In addition, the luxury of conversational control (e.g., self talks first, self talks more than other) allows one to project him or herself in a variety of situations and roles.

Symbolic interactionism and script theory have provided the theoretical foundation for the II construct. Mead (1934) described the internalized conversation of gestures and showed that individuals can have present a variety of scenarios for envisioning the alternative possible overt completions of any given act in which individuals are involved. The individual can "test out implicitly the various possible completions of an already initiated act in advance of actual completion of the act," and thus choose "the one which it is most desirable to perform explicitly or carry into overt effect" (Mead, 1934; p. 117). This process pertains, in part, to what Mead called the individual's internal conversation with him/herself. These internal dialogues could involve taking the role of others to see ourselves as others see us. According to Manis and Meltzer (1978), this type of pre-communicative mental activity is a peculiar type of activity that goes on in the experience of the person. The person responds to him or herself. Mead adds that this activity is essential to the constitution of the self-concept: "That the person should be responding to himself is necessary to the self, and it is this sort of social conduct which provides behavior within which that self appears" (p. 118). What is important about this type of mental activity is that (a) one may consciously take the role of others, imagining how they might respond to one's messages within particular situations, and thus (b) one can test and imagine the consequences of alternative messages prior to communication (Honeycutt et al., in press).

If a major function of IIs are rehearsing for anticipated interaction, then it is possible that IIs allows individuals to obtain information from learned, cognitive scripts (Schank & Abelson, 1977). We have speculated on the notion of "planning" and how this relates to II activity. Research on planning usually assumes that actors access planning behaviors from paticular cognitive structures, such as cognitive schemata and scripts or procedural records (Zagacki et al., forthcoming). Script theorists (e.g., Schank & Abelson, 1977) have argued that cognitive scripts are related to planning in that scripts call up cognitive representations of specific goal states and the behaviors needed to achieve them. To obtain goals, actors must follow the general flow of the script. Like scripts, imagined interactions are abstractions of ongoing streams of behavior to which central tendencies are extracted and sorted. However, they may not accurately represent real conversations, and may be both functional and dysfunctional.

For example, Caughey (1984) argues that inner conversations can maintain reality by rehearsing for expected conversations and by reconstructing past conversations. By inner talk, we bind ourselves within a culturally constructed framework. Caughey points out how ethnographic studies of inner conversations help us to retain a sense of values and keep our purposes ahead of us. One area of research in this area which we are pursuing is how IIs function to help foreign students at American universities retain their cultural identity as well as rehearsing for English encounters. For students learning English as a second language, we wonder if their IIs occur in their native language, English, or a mixture?

Regarding dysfunctional uses of inner conversation, Caughey (1984) speculates that erroneously rehearsing for anticipated encounters may lead to the construction of a faulty script for behavioral enactment. There is the problem of "letting one's images of how one would like things to be distort one's expectation of how they are actually likely to be" (Caughey, 1984; p. 142). I would add that individuals may overestimate their ability to persuade others in their IIs to adopt their positions given the luxury of conversational control in which they can go back and continually "rewrite" the script. We have found that the self reports talking more in the II than the partner. This may be therapeutic in increasing self-awareness.

THERAPEUTIC BENEFITS OF IIS

When we begin to analyze the functions of IIs, there is an implicit belief that there are therapeutic benefits at some level, whether it be increased self-awareness, tension-relief, or feeling pleasant thoughts about the II. Support for this assumption is available in a study by Schultz (1978) investigating the use of imagery to alleviate depression. He studied four imagery conditions across 60 depressed male psychiatric patients. One condition labeled the "aggressive imagery procedure" had depressed males recalling someone saying something which angered the self. In the "socially gratifying imagery" condition, the individual was instructed to recall someone saying something which was very pleasing. The "positive imagery" condition had the patient recall a place he used to visit in order to relax. Finally, the "free imagery" condition had patients reporting all images, thoughts, fantasies, and ideas which occurred to him without trying to direct his thoughts.

Ratings of depressive feelings taken 10 minutes after the imagery induction revealed that the first two conditions produced lower levels of depression than the less socially oriented conditions. I would argue that the aggressive and socially gratifying inductions forced the patient to have retroactive IIs that were negative and pleasant, respectively. Schultz also reports that in comparing the socially gratifying and positive imagery conditions, depression was lowered after the socially gratifying induction.

It is my hope to be able to train individuals to have IIs that make them feel better. Recall the findings on the dysfunctional use of IIs for the lonely. We need more research on the therapeutic uses of IIs. Further evidence of the general and therapeutic functions of IIs is presented below in the form of journal accounts I have had some of my students collect. Having been exposed to the II concept, students often report having them even though they had not previously thought about the experience as an instance of imagined interaction. Journal accounts of IIs tend to be more impressionistic and reveal more about emotions than pure survey data.

SAMPLE JOURNAL ACCOUNTS

Following is an account of an II where rehearsal helped in enhancing confidence though the real interaction did not fulfill expectations. In a sense, the individual was rehearsing the wrong script. However, she believed that the act of rehearsing was helpful.

> Recently, I had to confront my father about moving out of the dorm and into an apartment. I was quite nervous about the whole confrontation, so before I discussed the issue with him, I kind of rehearsed what I was going to say to him and I tried to anticipate his reaction.
>
> Our spring break is when I had to talk to my father, so for about two weeks beforehand, I was rehearsing. It seemed like every time I would think about it, I would change my approach a little bit. But my father's reaction, in my mind, was always the same. He would tell me that he did not want me to move into an apartment. In my imagination, I would tell him of all the benefits an apartment would have. I would have more privacy, there would not be as much noise so it would be easier to study, it is less expensive than the dorm, and a meal plan, and on and on.
>
> The time finally arose when I had to confront him. Again, I imagined what I was going to say to him and then I went ahead and opened the discussion. To my surprise, I did not even use my plan of action. I did not even list the benefits of the apartment vs the dorm. Nevertheless, we discussed it and my father agreed to my moving out which also contradicted my imagined interaction. I thought that this was kind of strange because usually my imagined interactions were similar in at least some ways to the actual conversation, but this one was completely opposite. At first I thought that all of that "practicing" was just a waste of time, since I did not use what I had practiced, but I think I was a little more confident about the discussion since I had gone over in my head the points of view that I wanted to get across. Maybe this helped since he agreed to let me move out. In this case, I am glad that they were different from the outcome. If they had gone the way I imagined, I would still be living in the dorm next semester.

The next account also reveals the discrepancy between an II and a real interaction. However, the individual goes on to indicate that some IIs are congruent with real episodes.

> Last summer I met a girl in Florida and we wrote each other for quite some time. We both kept saying we wanted to see each other, but our plans never materialized. Finally, in September she was going to fly to New Orleans to see me. From the moment she told me she was coming to visit, I began imagining what it would be like when we saw each other. I figured we would embrace passionately at the airport and have a million things to say to each other. I figured we would go out Friday night to the French Quarter and go to bars. She had never been to a bar before. At the time the drinking age was 18 in New Orleans and 21 in Alabama (her home state). Saturday I planned for us to go to the Riverwalk all day and then go out again that night. Sunday morning I was supposed to bring her to Biloxi where she had a ride home to Alabama.
>
> Well, welcome to reality. When she got off the plane, we kind of half-hugged each other and really didn't know what to say to each other. Most of our conversation was small talk. After we got to my house and showered, we went to the French Quarter. We probably didn't stay there any longer than an hour before we decided that we were exhausted and ready to get some sleep. Surprisingly, Saturday was pretty much like I had planned. We spent the whole day at the Riverwalk and really enjoyed ourselves. However, Saturday night was a different story. We began the night as I had planned by going to bars. Then the real excitement began. At about one o'clock in the morning she told me she had to make a phone call. After she got off the phone, I was informed that she had to leave for Biloxi right then. Instead of spending a nice evening out with her, I spent most of the night going to Mississippi. This was definitely a good example of an imagined interaction being quite different than the actual experience.
>
> Fortunately, all of my imagined interactions were not this disappointed. Because my present girlfriend is living in New Orleans this semester, I often have imagined interactions about the two of us. For instance, I often imagine us embracing and kissing when we see each other on Fridays. These imagined interactions are often fulfilled and then some. I also imagine things we are going to say to each other and these dialogues are also fulfilled. We often both tell each other how much we thought about each other and how much we missed each other.

Personally, I have found that the more familiar I am with a situation or the closer I am to a person, the more accurate my imagined interactions will be.

The next journal sample contains an account of a woman imagining seeing a lover who has been away. This seems to serve a rehearsal and psychological contact function.

> Andy and I both have had numerous imagined interactions concerning our relationship. An imagined interaction is a process that helps people in the construction of social reality. A person may develop visual or verbal scripts in their head to help them deal with certain situations. Imagined interactions serve specific functions: rehearsal for actual upcoming communication situations, evaluation after an important encounter, obtaining a greater sense of our own feelings, and improving

our own self knowledge. Perhaps the best example of imagined interactions being used in Andy's and my relationship occurred during our separation last summer.

It was a very difficult time for both of us because we missed each other so much. The thing that helped each of us deal with the pain was the use of imagined interactions. I was amazed to discover that we both had imagined interactions over the same thing--the moment that we would be reunited at the end of the summer. Whenever I was feeling lonely or especially missing Andy, I would think about the moment we would be able to see each other again. I would imagine the inevitable embrace, kiss, and words of love that we would give to each other. I would rehearse over and over again in my head the things that I would tell Andy at that moment. Things like "I love you more than anything else in the world." At the actual moment, we did hug, kiss, and give romantic proclamations of love to one another, but then there was an awkward moment of silence for two reasons. First, we had each gone over in our head that moment so many times that we neglected to think about what would come next. Second, we were still in shock that we had finally been reunited. Now, we both laugh when we think of that moment because we realize how rehearsed the whole thing was on both of our parts. Nevertheless, imagining conversations with each other and being together again helped us survive the separation. Through the process we learned a lot about what we felt about each other also.

The role of perceptions in our relationship exposes probably our biggest weakness. We have had arguments over the time we've known each other simply because one or the other of us misunderstood what the other was trying to convey in a given statement. For example, once I became upset because Andy said, "I need some time alone" to me. I perceived the statement as meaning "I want to break from this relationship for awhile." I discovered after a teary, accusatory argument that what Andy really meant was that he needed to study because he had some tests.

In contrast to the previous account in an intact relationship, the next account represents what we have called the "post-termination stage" of relationships (Edwards et al., 1988). This occurs when a romantic or dating relationship has ended but an individual may think about the ex-partner and reconstructs previous encounters or imagines future encounters. IIs in this stage can create a type of "psychological contact" with the ex-partner.

I had a relationship in high school with a girl who was serious as far as high school relationships go. We dated for almost a year and then broke up. Even though I was the one who terminated the relationship, I was also the one who was the most lonely afterwards. I can remember keeping up with the girl through our mutual friends. I wanted to know who she was dating, what they were going, and whether or not she still liked me. I would have imagined interaction with this girl where I would tell her the things that bothered me about her. She would change the behaviors that I did not like and then we would get back together.

For whatever reasons, I was not able to come straight out and talk to her about the problems I was having with her. Instead I just terminated the relationship. I often still imagined being with this girl years afterwards and would go over in my mind things we had said and what could have been said different. Sort of a cross between fantasizing and imagined interaction. A couple of years after high school and probably four years since we had dated, we met in a college town and had a few dates. Within a very short time, maybe two weeks, our relationship was right back to where it was before I terminated it with her in high school. Again she showed behavior that was close to that which I had not been able to accept in high school and again I terminated the relationship. This time, however, we both sort of broke contact and did not make an effort to reach one another. Although I still think about this person on occasion, it is only because she was a big part of my past and I tend to reflect on my past experiences and relationships at times.

CURRENT RESEARCH

Presently, we are investigating the functions of IIs in elderly populations. The SII factors are being correlated with measures of hopelessness. This is being done in order to determine if the content of IIs can inform therapists on the depressive thoughts of the elderly. Increasingly, hopelessness and suicidal tendencies in the elderly have been of concern to gerontological researchers (Osgood, 1985). I believe that IIs may compensate for the lack of real interaction in some cases. This in turn may be related to feelings of hopelessness and depression.

We are analyzing emotional affect and its association with the imagined interaction features and functions. We are relating imagined interaction activity to conversational sensitivity (Daly, Vangelisti, & Daughton, 1987). This is of theoretical interest because it has been posited that individuals who are stimulated and sensitive to the nuances of conversation develop these skills through varied communication experiences. There may be a role of imagined interaction activity in producing sensitivity. By producing procedural records in imagining an upcoming conversation, individuals may activate nodes that allow a person to be sensitive in the interaction. Thus, there should be a correspondence between the proactive dimension and conversational sensitivity. These are just a small sample of the research being conducted in our center.

Our research is taking a functional approach to the analysis of IIs. This approach has allowed us to create a typology of functions. We are interested in determining if the specific functions we have identified so far are generalizable across a variety of situations, tasks, and/or relationships.

REFERENCES

Berger, C. R. (1979). Beyond initial interaction: Uncertainty, understanding, and the development of interpersonal relationships. In H. Giles and R. St. Clair (Eds.), Language and social psychology. Oxford: Basil Blackwell.

Capella, J. N. (1984). The relevance of the microstructure of interaction to relationship change. Journal of Social and Personal Relationships, 1, 239-264.

Caughey, J. L. (1984). Imaginary social worlds. Lincoln, NE: University of Nebraska Press.

Daly, J. A., Vangelisti, A., and Daughton, S. M. (1987). The nature and correlates of conversational sensitivity. Human Communication Research, 14, 167-202.

Edwards, R., Honeycutt, J. M., and Zagacki, K. S. (1988). Imagined interaction as an element of social cognition. Western Journal of Speech Communication, 52, 23-45.

Greene, J. O. (1984). A cognitive approach to human communication: An action-assembly theory. Communication Monographs, 51, 289-306.

Hecht, M. L. (1978). The conceptualization and measurement of interpersonal communication satisfaction. Human Communication Research, 4, 253-264.

Hewes, D. E. (1986). A socio-egocentric model of group decision-making. In R. Y. Hirokawa and M. S. Poole (Eds.), Communication and group decision-making. Beverly Hills, CA: Sage.

Honeycutt, J. M., Zagacki, K. S., and Edwards, R. (in press). Intrapersonal communication, social cognition and imagined interactions. In C. Roberts and K. Watson (Eds.), Readings in intrapersonal communication. Spectra.

Howell, W. S. (1986). Coping with internal monologue. In J. Stewart (Eds.), Bridges not walls: A book about interpersonal communication. New York: Random House.

Ickes, W., Patterson, M. L., Rajecki, D. W., and Tanford, S. (1982). Behavioral and cognitive consequences of reciprocal vs compensatory responses to preinteraction expectancies. Social Cognition, 1, 160-190.

Jackson, S., and Jacobs, S. (1980). Structure of conversational argument: Pragmatic bases for the enthymeme. Quarterly Journal of Speech, 66, 251-265.

Kellermann, K. (1984). Scripts: What are they? How can you tell? And why should you care? Paper presented at the annual Speech Communication Association Convention. Chicago (November).

Laing, R. D. (1969). Self and others. London: Tavistock.

Manis, J. G., & Meltzer, B. N. (1978). Symbolic interaction: A reader in social psychology. Boston: Allyn and Bacon.

Mead, G. H. (1934). Mind, self and society. Chicago: University of Chicago Press.

Osgood, N. (1985). Suicide in the elderly: A practitioner's guide to diagnosis and mental health intervention. Rockville, MD: Aspen.

Rosenblatt, P. C., & Meyer, C. (1986). Imagined interactions and the family. Family Relations, 35, 319-324.

Russell, D. W., Peplau, L. A., & Cutrona, C. E. (1980). The revised UCLA loneliness scale: Concurrent and discriminant validity evidence. Journal of Personality and Social Psychology, 39, 472-480.

Schank, R., & Abelson, R. (1977). Scripts, plans, goals and understanding: An inquiry into human knowledge structures. Hillsdale, NJ: Lawrence Erlbaum.

Schultz, K. D. (1978). Imagery and the control of depression. In J. L. Singer & K. S. Pope (Eds.), The power of human imagination. NY: Plenum.

Singer, J. L. (1978). Experimental studies of daydreaming and the stream of thought. In K. S. Pope & J. L. Singer (Eds.), The stream of consciousness. New York: Plenum.

Street, R. L., Jr., & Murphy, T. L. (1987). Interpersonal orientation and speech behavior. Communication Monographs, 54, 42-62.

Zagacki, K. S., Edwards, R., & Honeycutt, J. M. (forthcoming). Imagined interactions, social cognition and intrapersonal communication: Elaboration of a theoretical construct. Top two papers to be presented before the Intreapersonal Communication Commission of the Speech Communication Association as the annual conference, New Orleans, November 1988.

TASK-UNRELATED IMAGES AND THOUGHTS WHILE READING

Leonard M. Giambra and Alicia Grodsky

Gerontology Research Center
National Institute on Aging
Baltimore, MD 21223

ABSTRACT

The study of task-unrelated images and thoughts (TUITS) has typically been conducted during non-semantic tasks such as sustained attention or vigilance tasks. This study investigated TUIT frequency during a semantic task, reading. Reading material may differ in both difficulty and interest to the reader. While interest attracts the reader's attention, difficulty requires the conscious control of attention. Both interest and difficulty were predicted to be inversely related to TUIT frequency. In this study, 59 men and women, 18-39 years old, recorded their TUIT frequency while reading four separate nonfiction passages (low interest-low difficulty, low interest-high difficulty, high interest-low difficulty, and high interest-high difficulty). Analyses of variance found that greater interest resulted in significantly ($p < .05$) fewer TUITs. Difficulty did not significantly ($p > .05$) affect TUIT frequency. Thus, interesting text attracts more attention to it and reduces attention to internal stimuli, i.e., TUITs. More difficult text did not produce fewer TUITs than less difficult texts.

Daydreaming, or mindwandering, results when an individual has thoughts and images unrelated to an ongoing task. Thus, daydreams may be operationally defined as task-unrelated images and thoughts (TUITS). Laboratory studies of TUITs have used tasks where vigilance or sustained attention is required to detect and respond to simple stimuli (see, for example, Giambra (in press) and Abrobus (1968)). These simple stimuli require relatively shallow processing. A reasonable and important extension of the laboratory work on task-unrelated images and thoughts would be to a central task requiring deep information processing, specifically, semantic processing. Reading is such a task. Not only will the study of TUITs during reading provide important information about TUITs during a semantically rich and engaging task, but it will also provide information about TUITs with an ecologically valid and ubiquitous task.

Unlike a vigilance task, reading is not transparent with regard to its salient components and requirements; for example, the person's interest in the task and the difficulty of the task. In a vigilance task it is relatively easy to know the subject's likely level of interest, usually very low; it is more difficult to know a subject's interest in some reading material. Similar considerations apply in determining the difficulty of a vigilance or a reading task. Furthermore, there is likely to be a much wider range of interest and difficulty in any text material than in any vigilance task. The surest method for determining both interest and difficulty of text material is to have the individual read the material and rate its interest and difficulty. This experiment was an investigation of the influence of the subject's interest in text and its difficulty on the likelihood of task-unrelated images and thoughts while reading that text.

How might interest and difficulty be interpreted in information processing terms so as to allow for a prediction of the influence of interest and difficulty on task-unrelated imagery and thought likelihood? Webster's New World Dictionary (1972) defines the verb "interest" as "to excite the attention or curiosity of." Thus, we might characterize text that is interesting as text that will attract the attention of the reader. The attraction of attention is to be construed as essentially automatic in the sense that no conscious effort of will is exercised by the person. The attention of the individual is drawn to the text since it is inherently interesting to him or her. Interest, of course, is continuous--from completely uninteresting or completely interested. The greater the interest the greater the attraction of the individual's attention to the reading text. It is reasonable to expect that the occurrence of task-unrelated images and thoughts and the degree of one's interest are related. Specifically, the greater the attraction of attention to a text, the less likely it would be that task-unrelated images and thoughts would occur. This should include both spontaneous (unbidden) and deliberate TUITs.

Webster's New World Dictionary (1972) defines the adjective "difficult" as "hard to do, make, manage, understand, etc.; involving trouble or requiring extra effort, skill or thought." When we approach a difficult task we set our mind to it in a deliberate, conscious manner. Thus, a difficult text demands that we direct and maintain our full attention to it in a conscious, controlled manner. It would follow that when our attention is fully engaged by a difficult passage that task-unrelated images and thoughts would be minimized. Thus, we would predict an inverse relationship between difficulty and TUIT likelihood.

METHOD

Subjects

Thirty women and 29 men from 18-39 years of age participated. All were from the Baltimore-Washington area and had at least some college education.

Procedure and Stimuli

Each subject read four nonfictional passages. The pool of text consisted of 23 passages in four topic areas (astronomy, biology, political science, and psychology). All passages were printed on paper, on one side per page. Four passages from this pool were selected for each subject. Two passages were selected so as to be of high interest and two passages were selected to be of low interest. Within each pair of low and high interest passages, one was selected to be easily comprehended and one was selected to be difficult to comprehend. The potential interest level for all passages for a subject was determined by the subject's ratings of interest for brief descriptions of the passage contents. Passage difficulty ratings were determined by having college educated raters read and judge each of the 23 passages. Each subject presentation order of the four interest-difficulty combinations was determined by a Latin Square of size four.

Three two-hour sessions were used. Each session involved 2-8 subjects. During the first session, subjects were trained to become aware of and report their spontaneous and deliberate task-unrelated images and thoughts (TUITs). They indicated on each passage the point at which either kind of TUIT ended. Three practice passages were used to train the subjects to record their TUITs while reading. During each of the second and third sessions, subjects read two passages with a rest break of five to ten minutes between passages. Each passage was read for 12 minutes and both spontaneous and deliberate TUITs were indicated on the passages. A 10 item multiple-choice test on the passage content was taken immediately after the 12 minute reading period. Subjects then rated each passage on interest and difficulty.

The interest rating scale was as follows:

(0) I was NOT interested in this material at all and did not enjoy reading it.

(1) I was only slightly interested in this material and would NOT like to read further on this topic. It is among the most uninteresting material I've read in the past year.

(2) I was interested in this material, but it is not one of my favorite topics.

(3) This material was so interesting that I truly enjoyed reading it.

(4) This is the most interesting material I've read in the past year and I would like to read even more on this topic.

The difficulty rating scale was as follows:

(0) This material was easy to read and to understand.

(1) This material was not hard to read and I did not have much trouble understanding what I was reading.

(2) This material was difficult, but I was able to understand what I was reading.

(3) This was not the most difficult material I've ever read, but it was still so difficult that I had to work to try to understand it.

(4) This is the most difficult material I've read in the past year or so, and I had to work as hard as I possibly could to try to understand it.

RESULTS

There was considerable variation between the a priori assignments of interest and difficulty to the four passages and the actual assignments based upon the post-reading ratings. This variation made the use of the a priori assignments of limited usefulness. Therefore, the subsequent analyses were based only on the post-reading ratings of passage interest and difficulty.

Each subject read and rated four passages on interest. From these passages two were selected; one had the highest (either a 2, 3, or 4), and one had the lowest (either a 0 or 1) interest ratings. Subjects who did not meet this criterion or who had an interest rating difference of less than two for the two selected passages were excluded from the analyses of variance (ANOVAs). A Sex X Interest (Low, High) ANOVA, with repeated measures on interest, was performed for each of the three TUIT measures. The main effect of Interest was significant for Total TUITs, $\underline{F}(1,42) = 4{,}59$, $\underline{p} < .05$. As hypothesized the mean frequency of Total TUITs was greater for the low interest than for the high interest passages (see Table 1). The interest effect for Spontaneous TUITs approached significance, $\underline{F}(1,42) = 2.72$, $\underline{p} < .11$; again, low interest resulted in more TUITs than high interest (see Table 1). The Interest X Sex interaction was significant, $\underline{p} < .01$, for Deliberate TUITs, $\underline{F}(1,42) = 5.51$. For men, the deliberate TUIT frequency was greater at low interest than at high interest; for

Table 1

Mean Frequency of Task-Unrelated Images and Thoughts for Low and High Interest Passages

Type:	Total		Spontaneous		Deliberate	
Interest:	Low	High	Low	High	Low	High
Female	6.6	6.1	4.9	4.1	1.6	2.0
Male	7.7	5.5	5.1	4.1	2.6	1.4

women, the inverse was true (see Table 1) of the six low-high interest comparisons this was the only one where high interest produced more TUITs than low interest. Each subject also rated the four passages on difficulty. From these passages, the highest (either a 2, 3, or 4) and lowest (either a 0 or 1) rated passages were selected. Subjects who did not have passages did not have a difficulty rating difference of two or more. A Sex X Difficulty (Low, High ANOVA, with repeated measures on Difficulty, was performed on the three TUIT measures. No effects with probability levels of .05 or less were obtained. Although not significant, the means for the high and low difficulty passages are provided in Table 2.

DISCUSSION

Interest was found to influence the frequency of task-unrelated imagery and thought; low interest produced more frequent TUITs than high interest. For men the relationship was consistent across all TUIT measures; for women the relationship was not evident for deliberate TUITs. Thus, it would appear that an interesting text acts as if it is attracting--and holding for longer periods--the attention of the reader. How the attraction is operated or engaged or modified is open to speculation. Perhaps, interest reflects motivation, which increases text saliency, and which lowers the saliency of internally generated stimuli. Alternatively, interest may be inversely related to task-unrelated imagery and thought likelihood because greater interest in external stimuli acts to increase the inhibition of internal stimuli. Other hypotheses about the effect of interest do not presume that higher interest results from a greater attraction of attention. It may be that it is simply a matter of capacity. That is, greater interest uses more resources, as a result of more extensive text processing, leaving less capacity available to support the occurrence of TUITs.

Table 2

Mean Frequency of Task-Unrelated Images and Thoughts for Low and High Difficult Passages

Type:	Total		Spontaneous		Deliberate	
Difficulty:	Low	High	Low	High	Low	High
Female	6.2	6.9	4.1	4.8	2.1	2.1
Male	8.0	8.4	5.8	5.3	2.2	3.0

The difficulty of the text material was found to have no significant effect upon TUIT frequency. This was most surprising since, on an intuitive basis, difficulty appears to be more powerfully related to the attentional aspects of text material than interest. However, since difficulty requires conscious, deliberate efforts to focus attention, the inverse relationship is more sensitive to failures of concentration. Failures could come about through fatigue or other physiological factors, but the most likely source of failures to concentrate is psychological. A failure to concentrate results from a conscious decision to stop concentrating. Such a decision could be the result of overwhelming difficulty, of a low level of motivation, etc. Thus, when there is a failure to concentrate at higher levels of difficulty, we could see an increase of TUITs, especially deliberate TUITs. This outcome can result in no apparent relationship between difficulty and TUIT likelihood. At low difficulty levels, because the cognitive demand is low, more TUITs may occur because of available capacity. At high levels, TUITs may occur because the extreme effort required leads to a withdrawal from the task. This hypothesis can only be examined in a subsequent study.

REFERENCES

Antrobus, J. S. (1968). Information theory and stimulus-independent thought. British Journal of Psychology, 59, 423-430.

Giambra, L. M. (1989). Task-unrelated-thought frequency as a function of age: A laboratory study. Psychology and Aging, 4.

Guralnik, D. B. (Ed.)(1972). Webster's new world dictionary of the American language. New York: World.

SOCIAL DIMENSIONS OF MENTAL IMAGERY:

AN ANTHROPOLOGICAL APPROACH

John L. Caughey

University of Maryland
College Park

In this chapter I want to consider several potential contributions which cultural anthropology might make to the study of mental imagery associated with daydreams, fantasies, memories and anticipations. I say "potential contributions" because, as yet, anthropology has devoted little attention to this pervasive and significant aspect of human experience. To be sure, there has been some work on culture and dreaming, and on altered states of consciousness, such as trance (Kennedy and Langness, 1981). Otherwise, it seems hardly to have occurred to most anthropologists that it might be worthwhile investigating the role of mental imagery in the cultures they have studied. However, standard anthropological approaches can be readily adapted to the study of imagery in a way which could contribute significantly to our understanding of the subject. I would like to illustrate some of these possibilities by describing my own fieldwork with three exotic groups: with Sufi Mystics in Pakistan, with Trukese Islanders in the Western Pacific, and with middle class Americans in Washington and Baltimore.

The first and most important contribution anthropoogy might make is its cross-cultural, comparative perspective. Whatever aspect of human experience we are trying to explore, it aids our understanding to see how the phenomenon works in other cultural settings (Wallace, 1968). By studying carefully how mental imagery is conceptualized and experienced in other societies, we might greatly advance our general understanding of the subject. Secondly, the contrasting patterns of other cultures highlight distinctive features of our own system which familiarity may make it difficult to identify (Caughey, 1986). Further, the contrast may help us to better identify the cultural lenses with which we think about mental imagery. To some significant degree, our own understanding of the subject is influenced by our own cultural conditioning. Finally, cross cultural perspectives may be useful because people in some non-western cultures have developed sophisticated and powerful techniques for working with mental imagery from which we may have much to learn. But let me illustrate with examples from my own fieldwork.

ANTHROPOLOGICAL APPROACHES TO CULTURE STUDY

When I was a graduate student in Anthropology in the 1960's, I already knew that I wanted to study American culture. But I was advised by my professors to do fieldwork elsewhere first. This advice was based on the logic of the points raised above, particularly the idea that one can see one's own culture better after cross-cultural experience. Also, as I was beginning to learn, claims to a full-fledged anthropological identity are partially validated through recounting tales of adventurous encounters with magic in Timbuctoo, or with malaria in the New Guinea highlands. All this plus the opportunity to spend a year on an island in the Western Pacific was fully persuasive. So some 20 years ago I set off to study Faanakkar, a small island in the Truk group of the Caroline Islands of Micronesia. It proved to be a most interesting place, a beautiful island with green mountains, a blue lagoon, and a drastically different traditional culture much of which was still going strong; they had a matrilineal kinship system, exotic magical practices, a radically different cosmology, and so forth.

I did not go to Faanakkar to study mental imagery; like most anthropologists, then and now, I had little appreciation for the importance of the subject. An interest in imagery, however, was forced upon me in the course using standard anthropological methods to pursue traditional anthropological topics. Moreover, it is just these topics and methods which I think can be usefully adapted to the study of mental imagery.

In the first place I was interested in the study of Faanakkar "culture" and how this culture affected various aspects of the people's lives. In one standard use of the term in contemporary anthropology culture refers not to objects and behaviors, but to the world view or system of meaning by which people understand their experience and generate forms of action (Goodenough, 1981; Shweder and Levine, 1984; Holland and Quinn, 1987). In this sense, culture is seen as a learned socially constructed cognitive system with which people think, perceive, and behave. Given this approach, I was interested in trying to discover how the people of Faanakkar thought about, perceived, and experienced life from their point of view. I was interested, for example, in their cosmology, including their sense that the flat (not round) world has a solid cover like a great inverted bowl. This belief affected experience. In looking up at a blue sky they see not an insubstantial colored haze, but a solid blue dome (Caughey, 1977). As I will suggest, this sense of culture--as a relative, socially constructed meaning system--has important implications for understanding mental imagery.

I was also expected to study "social organization," how were social relationships culturally organized and experienced on Faanakkar? I was interested in the different identities, roles, and forms of interaction. How, for example, did men relate to their various iney ("mothers," not only one's biological mother, but one's mother's sisters and maternal cousins were understood as one's "mothers")? What patterns, characterized the relations of magical curers and clients? This concern reflected the taken for granted anthropological assumption that "social relationships constitute the single most important feature of life in every society" (Spradley and McCurdy, 1972:112). Much of life has to do with how one's personal relations are organized and experienced. One's desires, goals, emotional states, frustrations, sense of self, etc., are all tangled up in the experience of social relationships. However, this is not only an individual psychological issue, it is also a cultural phenomenon since the way people experience social relations is heavily influenced by how these relationships are culturally constituted within particular culturally organized groups. It is also taken for granted in anthropology that "social relations" refers to real interactions between actual people (kinsmen, friends, etc.) operating in each other's presence. This, I was to find, is an unfortunate, erroneous, restricted perspective which overlooks the powerful importance of experiencing social relations through mental imagery.

In order to pursue the ethnographic study of culture and social organization, I was expected to make use of the standard anthropological method of "participant observation." This approach rests on the assumption that an adequate understanding of the insider's experience requires one to move out of a detached, objective, outsider stance. One interviews people in depth to be sure, but also as far as is feasible one also seeks to experience their world, to become an observing participant in their activities. The more radical proponents of this approach even suggest that one must become the phenomenon one is studying (Mehan and Wood, 1975; Caughey, 1986). Through such engagement, one gains a privileged observational position, and one often develops closer rapport with informants who may subsequently "open up" more in interviewing phases of the study. But mainly one seeks to attain an insider's feel for the subjective experience of the phenomenon one is studying. So it was that in my attempts to understand the cultural organization of Faanakkar social relationships through participant observation that I was led directly into the study of mental imagery.

SPIRIT INTERACTIONS ON FAANAKKAR

One regular and fairly elaborate social activity on Faanakkar was the fishing party, a set of men who swim out together into the lagoon to spear fish. I wanted not only to ask people about such expeditions--I wanted to go along, to participate, and observe. Despite some initial reluctance, this was permitted, so metal spear in hand, I began often to accompany these expeditions. Fishing parties it turned out were characterized by ritualistic rules because they were explicitly conceptualized as war parties. At first I assumed that this was due to the danger of sharks who, attracted by the smell of fish blood, rapidly appeared in the water around us. While there was healthy respect for this danger, the main concern was focused on supernatural creates known as sea demons. I had already begun to learn that the Trukese believed in the existence of a large set of ghosts and god-like spirits, that they knew the names of these creatures, that there was considerable interest in and lore about their doings in the sky world--love affairs, feasts, feuds, etc. I vaguely characterized their beliefs and conversations as "mythology" and "religion" and wrongly assumed that they had little to do with the experience of social relationships. I fitted what I was learning about sea demons into the same framework. I learned that there were believed to be nine such creatures in the lagoon, that they fought with each other, that they could change into different shapes--sometimes vague and insubstantial, sometimes ugly, sometimes assuming the form of a beautiful woman. I assumed these to be interesting but basically irrelevant, false, superstitious beliefs with little or no experiential significance. Local concerns about there beings focused on the fact that through their malevolence they could cause an illness in people called saat, which led to physical weakness, fevers, anxieties, and sometimes insanity and death. It was believed that somehow the sea demon could enter a person and gradually "devour" the soul. Again I simply took this as a quaint "folk explanation" for some illness. Then I began to learn that illness was preceded or accompanied by seemingly outlandish reports of having somehow encountered these beings, of having seen and socially interacted with them. This struck me--given my secular western ethnocentrism--as impossible. Yet I heard serious accounts of personal experiences like this from people I trusted and knew well. How could they claim to have seen, spoken with, and even made love to non-existent sea demons?

Then I had the following experience. It had rained during our afternoon fishing trip and I felt tired and chilled when we returned to shore. Soon after I began to feel ill with chills and fevers. Over the next several days I became progressively worse. I lost all appetite for food and I became so weak I could hardly walk. The chills and fevers became acute. During the fevers I experienced strange irrational feelings and anxieties. I wanted to pick up the phone, call the doctor, take an ambulance to the hospital, but there were no phones, doctors, ambulances or hospitals. I lay on my sleeping mat on the floor of the shack and wondered if I was going to die. From the beginning my adopted kinsmen assumed that I was afflicted with saat. They checked with the local diviner who worked his magic and found that, yes, I was possessed by not one but two sea demons--Iku and Sowneeooc--who were inside my chest eating my soul. My kinsmen urged me to take the local treatment in order to try to drive out the demons. "Unless you do so," they warned, "you will likely get worse, go crazy, and die." While I was not cheered by this assessment, I was reluctant to take the cure--I knew it involved magical spells and consumption of local "medicine." I was skeptical--I thought it might make me worse. Then I met one of the sea demons. In the midst of a severe bout of fever and chills, I suddenly experienced an involuntary fantasy or visionary state. I saw before me a red sea and a red haze and felt strongly that there was a presence out there, a soothing siren-like presence, enticing me into the red haze. I felt drawn towards the redness, but I also felt frightened and reluctant to let myself go. I jerked myself back and "woke up," as it were, on my sleeping mat, sweating heavily. When I told my kinsmen, they said, "Oh, yes, that's typical of saat. It's lucky you didn't go with the sea demon, you would never have come back." To this I replied, "Give me the sea demon treatment." So they collected a set of herbs from the mountain and prepared hot stones and bowls of medicine. To the accompaniment of spells, they steamed me with some of the medicine, rubbed more on my body, and gave me the rest to drink. The next day I was better and the day after it was as if I had never been sick.

This experience of forced participant observation changed my situation in a variety of different ways. In the first place, people opened up to me more about this realm. "See," they said, "now you know spirits are real" and they talked with me freely about their own experiences. Secondly, the experience made me less smugly ethnocentric about the "non-existence" of supernatural beings, though, in the end, I remained skeptical. But more importantly for the purpose of this essay, the experience demonstrated to me how it was that people interacted with sea demons. It wasn't that they saw the sea demons in front of them through regular external perception--it was that they saw and often vividly interacted with sea demons--and other ghosts and spirits--through dreams, fantasies, and visionary experiences. These experiences were social. The person entered a psychological state such as a daydream, assumed a self, encountered an image of another being and interacted with it. It was, that is, through processes of mental imagery that they vividly and powerfully experienced subjective social interactions with sea demons. After this, I came to see that Trukese social organization could not be properly or adequately understood through the usual anthropological lens. Social interactions on Faanakkar involved not just objective real interactions among a set of real people, it also included pervasive, regular experiences of social interactions through imagery--through dreams, fantasy, trance, etc., which were culturally legitimated as real and significant. These experiences were considered just as subjectively meaningful as what we would call "real" interactions. People carried out a complex set of friendship relations, kinship relations, love relations, and antagonistic enemy relations with spirits through experiences of inner imagery. Furthermore, these experiences were not just subjectively powerful--they had important social and psychological consequences. In the first place, they importantly affected real interactions--people often made important choices about actual social interactions because of information or advice they received during interactions with spirits. Secondly, it seemed that important psychological dimensions were involved. For example, imaginary relations with spirits seemed to provide healing "compensations" for difficulties in real love affairs, kinship relations, and the like (Caughey, 1977).

MEDIA FIGURES AS GODS IN AMERICAN SOCIETY

After returning to the United States, I began studying middle class American social organization. Again I was interested in how culture affects our experience of standard relationships--friendship, marital relations, love affairs, etc. In trying to analyze the results of interviews and observations, I often made use of the cross cultural perspective including my own study--I would think about friendship on Faanakkar, Truk, and what the expectations, rewards, and strains were. The similarities or contrasts with our society highlighted patterns in American friendship. At one point, in the fall of 1971, I was thinking, "Of course the Trukese have all these imaginary interactions with gods and spirits they've never actually met and we don't," and then I thought, "But wait a minute," I had talked recently with a young woman who had expressed to me the importance, in her social world, of then popular TV talkshow host Dick Cavett. "Dick," she made it clear, was of extreme significance to her in a "social" way--she had never actually met the man, but her heart was his. She was in love with a god-like figure she had never actually met.

This realization eventually led me into an extensive ethnographic investigation of the social significance of American media figures, and their parallels to non-western gods (Caughey, 1984). I interviewed several hundred informants and I also carefully watched my own experience of the media through "self-ethnography" (Caughey, 1982). Like the Trukese, I concluded, we know about a set of god-like figures beyond the circle of our actual acquaintances. In fact, we know about hundreds of unmet media figures: musicians, sports figures, politicians, talkshow hosts, movie actors, authors, fictional characters, and the like. Like the Trukese, we not only know who these people are, we take great interest in lore about their social activities--their successes and failures, their salary disputes, divorces, diets, etc. Furthermore, Americans not only know <u>about</u> such beings, we feel strongly about them, we hate some, admire others, and "like" or even "love" still others. And not only this, Americans regularly <u>interact</u> with them. First we interact, in a sense, through various forms of the media, as when we identify with a character in a movie or respond to a face talking at us out of the television. We also interact with those beings through mental imagery. Quite often Americans <u>dream</u> about media figures--here the sleeping individual dreams--and hence <u>experiences</u>--a conversation or other meeting with an image of the celebrity. Even more commonly, the individual experiences interactions with the unmet figure through fantasy. For example, each of the most common relations young people develop with media figures has an important fantasy dimension. In admiration relations--where the fan casts the media figure in the role of mentor and role model--people regularly imagine meeting the idol and becoming close friends with them. Thus the individual subjectively experiences a vivid social interaction with the media figure. Like Trukese society, American social organization cannot be adequately understood by limiting ourselves to a consideration of actual social relations. Americans know about numerous media figures and they also experience regular imaginary social interactions with images of them. Like the Trukese with their spirits these relations are often subjectively meaningful and they are often socially and psychologically significant. These relationships are important to self-conceptualization and where the media figure is cast as role model, the person may use the imaginary social relationship as a basis for real world behavior. Similarly media love relationships seem often to provide a compensatory working through of problems in actual love relationships (Caughey, 1984; 1988).

IMAGINARY INTERACTIONS WITH IMAGES OF KNOWN OTHERS

As I probed this area further, I also began to see another familiar experience in a new light. It is, I realized, not just media figures that we imaginatively interact with through mental imagery; our imaginary worlds--dreams, memories, anticipations and fantasies--are all intensely social. Sometimes, to be sure, we may dream of being alone--of walking, for example, through a deserted landscape. Far more commonly (97% of the time in my dream sample) the individual dreams of encountering other beings and of playing out interactions with images of these beings (Caughey, 1984: 89). The same principle seems to apply to memories, anticipations, and fantasies. Sometimes the imagined others are media figures and occasionally they are totally made up creatures of our imagination. More commonly the imagined others are mental images of beings we actually know. The great majority of our experiences of mental imagery consist of interactions with exquisitely vivid imaginary replicas of known others--kinsmen, lovers, friends, co-workers, and the like. Put another way, our study of American social relationships remain one dimensional until we recognize and explore the fact that every significant actual relationship has important imaginary dimensions. I do not just experience "real" interactions with my friend. I interact with my images of her--I dream about her, I vividly reexperience past social interactions with her through memory, I project upcoming interactions through anticipation, and I play with our relationship through fantasy interactions. These imaginary relationships have been neglected but they are a pervasive and significant aspect of American social experience. Except when the individual is engaged in a demanding task or an engrossing actual interaction, his or her attention is likely to be caught up in imaginary interactions. The person's attention slips away into inner worlds of mental imagery--to memories, fantasies, inner conversations, anticipations and the like. Given the time Americans spend in imaginary interactions through media consumption, dreams, and working imagination, we probably spend more time in imaginary interactions than we do in actual social relations (Caughey, 1984).

Secondly, these interactions are often subjectively vivid. Thinking about an upcoming encounter is often a powerful experience with much of the compelling emotional tone of actual interactions. I do not just "think about" the future--I experience it--I am, as it were, teleported into an imagined version of the future where I experience visually and linguistically an encounter with the imagined other. Finally, these relations are socially and psychologically significant. For example, we prepare scripts and make important decisions about how to actually behave through imaginary rehearsals of upcoming encounters. Through memory and fantasy interactions we work through and repair the damage from past and current actual interactions (Caughey, 1984).

SOCIAL STRAIN IN AMERICA--REAL AND IMAGINARY

As I investigated this area further, I became more and more struck by the problematic aspects of American social organization--the difficulties we experience in work relations, marriages, divorces, parenting, and friendship. These problems are all pervasively and complexly reflected in our imaginary social worlds--as I further found during an excursion into the study of "mental illness" through field work on an urban psychiatric ward. The severely disturbed or "psychotic American" does not usually lead a solitary existence. The individual typically imagines him or herself to be entangled in elaborate self-other relations--as with delusionary representations of media figures, actual acquaintances, or purely imagined creatures (Caughey, 1984). The person is immersed, that is, in what Cameron (1954) referred to as the "paranoid pseudo community." I was impressed again by the vivid emotionally powerful significance of these imagined beings and their relation to the person's actual situation. Unfortunately, at least on the ward I studied, the psychiatrists were not much interested in the structure and functioning of their imagined interactions--they viewed them as symptoms of illness and wanted not to explore but to eliminate them. Looking elsewhere, about this time, I had the opportunity to study again in a non-western culture, this time in northern Pakistan.

SPIRIT INTERACTIONS OF SUFIS IN PAKISTAN

In Pakistan I located a situation in which curers were intensely interested in working therapeutically with mental imagery. On a cliff in the Margalla Hills of Pakistan a mystic and his followers operated a pilgrimage center. Their cultural framework was based on Sufism, a form of Eastern philosophy combining Islamic and Hindu psychology and mysticism. Along with other activities, including treating people with physical ailments, they worked psychologically with two general kinds of clients. The first were people with various kinds of difficulties which we would characterize as "psychological problems." As on Truk, anxieties and depression were typically conceptualized as having supernatural causes associated with evil spirits, witches, and sorcery. People might be afflicted by an evil spirit, who was acting independently or who had been directed at them by a sorcerer. In such cases, the mystic would attempt to use his own power to subdue or drive out the evil spirit or supernaturally empower the client to accomplish this. Mental imagery was a key dimension. Dreams, trance, and meditative states were the arenas in which these battles were fought. The afflicted individual and the mystic sometimes acted out these psychic dramas, as when the individual was possessed by an evil spirit--acted agitated--and was physically subdued and sometimes whipped. The second type of clients were "seekers" who wanted to attain higher levels of functioning. Here the person was instructed on how to follow an inner "path" (tarigat) of psycho-spiritual development involving the cultivation of qualities such as patience, peace, and mastery. In some cases, the seeker would withdraw temporarily from ordinary life to pursue the path; in other cases, the person was given practices which would allow him/her to practice in "the world"; that is, in the midst of ordinary life. Along with other exercises, much use was made of mental imagery.

The following account illustrates some of the cultural concepts involved. A disciple on the path was given an exercise in which he was expected to maintain quiet steady meditation against intrusive images. He was to sit in a pool of water at the edge of a swift running river in the mountains. First he drew a magic circle around the place where he would sit; next he assumed a meditative state and sought to hold it for several hours. It was expected that distracting spirits would attempt to loosen his concentration as, for example, when ugly demons with drums and musical instruments would come to the edge of the circle and make loud, distracting noises. When the image of a beautiful woman appeared, the disciple lost his concentration and let the woman into the circle of his consciousness; at this same moment he was suddenly swept away down the river. The mystic, his teacher, though miles away, immediately knew, through intuitive perception, what had happened. He assumed a trance state and using his own power, overcame the spirit. At this moment the disciple was saved and pulled from the water by travelers on the shore.

Such stories of spirit battles provide legitimating conceptual support for less dramatic but also interesting forms of mental imagery work. For example, in one technique, the "mirror of consciousness," the individual seeks to monitor the flow of ordinary consciousness. He or she seeks to clear away and purify imagery involving negative worldly values and also watches for "indications," images which might be interpreted as communications from the teacher. In another technique, the individual deliberately calls to mind a mental picture of his/her teacher's face. Once this is accomplished, it is believed that the teacher can send his own spirit to merge with that image. Thus, the image provides a vehicle for disciple-teacher interaction in which the teacher can give advice, warnings, or encouragement to the disciple. Here we see how a practice in mental imagery conceptualized as significant allows for a powerful imagined interaction. It gives the individual a sense of help and power in trying to handle his/her difficulties. Overall, it seemed that clients benefited significantly from deliberate use of imagined social dramas in which they acted out battles with negative beings or in which they drew on supportive interactions with images of their teacher.

IMAGINARY INTERACTIONS IN AMERICAN THERAPY

Back in the United States, I began to look for a situation in which people were deliberately using mental imagery techniques to work with self-other relations. I hoped to find an American situation analogous to the shrine I had studied in Pakistan. This proved easier than expected. In considering various possibilities, I became aware of two patterns I had previously only been dimly aware of. Like the culture in general, American psychology has given relatively little significance to mental imagery, but there are a variety of western psychologies and therapies now working intensely with mental imagery (Shorr, 1983). Secondly, principles of Eastern psychology and philosophy have become surprisingly prevalent in the United States (Ellwood, 1979). Sometimes techniques from Sufism, Vedantta, Zen, Tibetan, Buddhism, and the like, are being adopted in American therapies in combination with western techniques. This cultural borrowing and synthesis reflects recognition that Eastern systems--more oriented to the experiential use of imagery--have important lessons for western therapies. Eventually I chose to do research at a place I will call "The Place." Here two American psychologists work with middle class clients, mostly Washington professionals, who are disturbed or discontent and/or who are seeking higher levels of functioning.

The cultural framework these psychologists operate with involves a combination of Eastern and Western psychology. Both psychologists have extensive training in Gestalt therapy, thus much use is made of mental imagery techniques involving focus on self-other relations with considerable emphasis on "psycho drama" style acting out of social relations. At the same time both psychologists have extensively studied Eastern psychology, particularly a brand of Indian mysticism, as developed in an organization headed by an Indian teacher and his successor, which involves practices such as chanting, meditation, visualization, and other Eastern techniques.

The psychologists at the center run a variety of programs; they train other therapists interested in their "experiential" approach, they do individual therapy, and they do group therapy. In all, these programs blend Eastern and Western techniques. Through participant observation I plan to study all of their programs. Currently I am attending their training program for therapists. For six months (February-July, 1988) I involved myself as a participant in one of their group therapy programs.

This proved a fascinating vehicle for the study of the imaginary dimensions of American social organization. What we identified as clients' problem areas were all self-other difficulties involving individual versions of widely shared problems in the cultural structioning of American social relationships. The five group members were afflicted with emotionally difficult social relations with spouses, boy or girl friends, co-workers, parents, and friends, and often these were conceptualized as interconnected. Each of the members was expected to discuss the ongoing state of these relationships with the therapist and the group, but such talk was mostly seen as a prelude to experiential "work" on these relations and this work involved deliberate use of imagined interactions. Clients were also expected to work on these relations outside the session. This work too was largely "imaginary."

Sessions took place in a small room with American furnishings combined with Eastern touches including a picture of the Guru on the wall, statues of the dancing Indian goddess Kali, and of Ganesh "the remover of obstacles." Sessions invariably began with a period of meditation, the leader asking clients to breathe rhythmically, to "go inside," and perhaps to mentally visualize some quiet scene or to contemplate some issues--such as one's coming death. Emphasis was placed on seeking attunement with one's higher or "true self."

After discussion of the past week's events, clients were encouraged to play out versions of ongoing social dramas. Sometimes a significant figure would be imagined as sitting in a chair, and the person would be asked to speak with them. At times members of the group were chosen by the client to play the role of some currently significant figure. Here is an example. After discussing his current situation, one of the men, Steve, who was having continued difficulties with his ex-wife, was invited to pick one of the women in the group to play her role, while one of the men acted as his "alter-ego," encouraging him to act more aggressively in order to break free from the passive situation he felt stuck in. The scene ended with Steve pinned back against the bookcase, his ex-wife threatening him, "I'm going to get you for this," as she squeezed her fingers around his neck. Characteristically, Steve was unable to respond; he stood, passive, while his wife strangled him, making no effort to break free, despite encouragement from his "alter ego," from me, and from other members of the group. As one woman suggested, he seemed paralyzed, "almost as if he is being crucified." We and he agreed, so the therapist then told Steve to put out his arms, to simulate crucifixion, and there he hung and there the work ended. The leader seemed deliberately to leave Steve hanging there, as it were, his problem unresolved. Then as people sat down she set up the steps which would follow, a further play with mental imagery and imagined interactions. "This [next] week," she told Steve, "I want you to look for imagery during your regular meditations; see what comes up and try to go with it." Then she told two stories. One was about an Indian guru who had to take a sword and "symbolically kill" a female goddess who was blocking his spiritual and psychological progress. The other was an account of a similar experience of her own. She had been plagued by nightmare visions of a hostile, aggressive and disdainful male figure who had haunted her dreams and who had begun to appear in her meditations. Under the guidance of her Indian teacher, she had done psychic battles with this figure, including some dramatic acting out, and eventually overcame him. Thus, without directly saying so, she had cued Steve and other members of the group to look for and to expect pertinent imagery, she had set out a general "script" for dealing with it, and she had offered authoritative legitimation for the culturally unsupported idea of taking it seriously and "going with it."

The next week Steve gave a dramatic report of the unexpectly "wild" imagery he had experienced, all of which involved imagined social interactions. The day after group he had "seen" an image of a knife in his meditation and felt and imagined the possibility of cutting his wife with it. However, he had recoiled from this feeling as too literally aggressive. That night he had a vivid dream in which he managed to escape from his ex-wife's sexual advances. The next morning, after recalling and replaying this dream, he had a dream-like memory of the recent group therapy scene.

> It was like I was here again being crucified with her fingers around my neck, feeling helpless. Then in frustration, I imagined breaking the hold with my hands and shoving her away . . . . Then the image stopped, I thought "how curious" and then I drifted to other matters. I started to think what I needed to do at the office that day, and then I thought, "wait a minute, this is maybe an important experience." So I deliberately put myself back into the scene, and it kind of took hold of me. I pushed her away hard, saying, "I hate you, stop killing me," and her face seemed to change before me, different, ugly witch-like faces passed and somehow settled into an image like the wicked witch in the "Wizard of Oz," so then, spontaneously, I imagined myself throwing a bucket of water on her. She dissolved in a hideous, satisfying manner.

He added brief descriptions of several other images. One of which he "went with." Coming into his kitchen, half asleep in the morning, he had been struck by the sight of a table knife, gleaming silver on his plastic breakfast table. He went with his feeling, he picked it up, then stabbed the air with it, and then slashed it sword-like around himself, as if cutting "ties or threads" which were binding him to his ex-wife, "it was like playing cops and robbers as a child; I knew I was playing, but it was vivid, I really got into it." This report was greeted with surprise and appreciation by the group with the leader repeatedly emphasizing how "good" it was and also countering Steve's apologies about all this seeming "kind of crazy." No, she kept saying, this is "good," "powerful," "great!" These imaginary experiences accepted by the group as significant were then used as script for group drama. It worked powerfully, not only for Steve, but for others, and various new dramas were created as spinoffs from it. The following week others reported vivid imagery, including a woman who had dreams of wicked witches, which, in turn, fed into the following week's drama in which another of the men powerfully enacted the symbolic killing of his mother and several other figures in the group, including the therapist.

CONCLUSION

Anthropological approaches offer a useful supplement to the psychological study of imagery. Comparative, ethnographic research in American and nonwestern settings provides an important opportunity to explore how mental imagery works in various culturally structured social settings. Research in nonwestern settings, such as those I studied in Truk and Pakistan, show us how mental imagery is conceptualized and experienced in other cultural systems. As described here, for example, where experiences of mental imagery are defined as "real" interactions with spirit beings, these images may play a significant role in personal and societal functioning. Understandings of such nonwestern systems can also be valuable in highlighting aspects of American imagery. For example, the Trukese cases illuminate an analogous feature of contemporary American experience. Like the Trukese with their spirits, contemporary Americans not only know about numerous god-like media figures, they form a variety of imaginary social relationships with images of these beings that may play important roles in personal and societal functioning.

Ethnographic research in therapeutic settings like "The Place" can also be illuminating. Because these groups encourage people to pay attention to and to report on imagery in a non-experimental context, they offer a special window on the nature of imagery experiences and how they are related to contemporary middle class society. The research I have done so far suggests that while imagery experience is partly connected to peculiarities of individual psychological make-up, it is also strongly influenced by widespread culturally constituted strains in the cultural organization of American social relationships. In addition, we can watch, in settings like "The Place," how nonwestern techniques are being adapted and transformed into an American therapeutic context as people work with imagery and how these techniques mesh or clash with American patterns. We can also begin to consider the extent to which such new therapies may be effective in dealing with chronic American social psychological syndromes.

To effectively do such research, I suggest, requires a commitment to participant observation. In order to understand and explore how these inner experiences work, and in order to gain adequate rapport with informants, it is necessary to go beyond a detached outside interviewer posture and enter into this kind of world. Anthropology provides important models for participant observation which can be readily adopted to such imagery research.

Finally, research so far suggests that work on mental imagery has a crucial social dimension. What one finds at "The Place" indicates that to a very significant extent the phenomenological experiences of dreams, memories, anticipations, and fantasies involve the subjective experience of social relations with images of other people. This pervasive experience constitutes a kind of murky nether world which mirrors the realm of actual social experience. It represents a significant reflection of the stresses and strains in the actual American social system. Within this realm, it would also appear, lie important possibilities for therapeutically dealing with culturally constituted psychological distress associated with particular American relationships through the deliberate playing out of imaginary social dramas. But whatever the ultimate therapeutic value of such techniques, it seems unquestionable that research on such areas could shed important light on the social nature of mental imagery. Also, looked at another way, those of us interested in mental imagery can use such evidence to argue that an adequate understanding of American social relationships demands attention to mental imagery.

REFERENCES

Cameron, N. (1959). The paranoid pseudo community revisited. American Journal of Sociology, 65, 56.

Caughey, J. L. (1977). Faanakkar: Cultural Values in a Micronesian Society. Philadelphia: University of Pennsylvania Publications in Anthropology, 2.

Caughey, J. L. (1982). Ethnography, introspection, and Reflexive culture studies. Prospects, 9.

Caughey, J. L. (1984). Imaginary Social Worlds: A Cultural Approach. Lincoln: University of Nebraska Press.

Caughey, J. L. (1986). On the anthropology of America. In H. Varenne (Ed.) Symbolizing America. Lincoln: University of Nebraska Press.

Caughey, J. L. (1988). Fictional identities and the construction of self in adolescence. Adolescent Psychiatry. Forthcoming.

Ellwood, R.S. (1979). Alternative Altars: Unconventional and Eastern Spirituality in America. Chicago: University of Chicago Press.

Goodenough, W. H. (1981). Culture, Language, and Society. Menlo Park, CA: Benjamin/Cummings.

Holland, D. and Quinn, N. (1987). Cultural Models in Language and Thought. Cambridge: Cambridge University Press.

Kennedy, J. G. and Langness, L. L. (1981). Introduction. Special issue on dreams. Ethos, 9.

Mehan, H. and Wood, H. (1975). The Reality of Ethnomethodology. New York: Wiley.

Shorr, J. (1983). Psychotherapy Through Imagery. New York: Thieme-Stratton.

Shweder, R. A. and LeVine, R. (1984). Culture Theory. Cambridge: Cambridge University Press.

Spradley, J. and McCurdy, D. Anthropology: The Cultural Perspective. New York: Wiley.

Wallace, A. F. C. (1968). Anthropological contributions to the study of personality. In E. Norbeck, D. Price-Williams, S. W. McCord (Eds.), The Study of Personality. New York: Holt, Rinehart and Winston.

THE HEALING POWERS OF THE NATIVE AMERICAN MEDICINE WHEEL

Nicholas E. Brink

Private Practice
Lewisburg, PA

Atop Wyoming's Big Horn Mountains is an elaborate configuration of stones. These stones lie in a pattern resembling a large 28-spoke wheel, 80 feet across. It is estimated that perhaps five million similar stone circles or medicine wheels, from 5 to 30 feet in diameter, existed across North America. Artifacts found at the Majorville wheel in Alberta, Canada, indicate the age of this medicine wheel is from 4000 to 5000 years old, built at the time of the construction of the Egyptian pyramids. Eddy (1977) described these, and other medicine wheels, many from 100 to 200 feet across. His evidence suggests that these wheels were used as calendars and instruments of astronomy. Anthropologists might attach a religious significance to such artifacts as the medicine wheel and the medicine bundle, believing these places and objects were used in the worship of the sun, stars, or moon.

Native American literature and "teaching tales" suggest that neither the astronomical nor religious significance seem adequate in describing the significance of the medicine wheel. The medicine wheel functions more centrally in life and provides a framework for growth and direction in one's life. The medicine wheel has implications for psychology and psychotherapy.

THE MEDICINE WHEEL

The medicine wheel is a concept and life process among the Native American, providing the individual with emotional and healing strength and direction to life. In a concrete form, the wheel is symbolized by the four directions, most concretely, as rocks on the ground designating the four directions, but also found in other symbols, shields, medicine bundles and ceremonies. Each direction is represented by an animal, a color and personal characteristics. The medicine wheel is personal to each individual and its meaning is fluid and different from individual to individual. For example, the medicine wheel of Hyemeyohsts Storm (1972) describes East as the color gold, as represented by the Eagle and with the traits of being farsighted, concrete, rational, and action oriented. South is the Mouse, green, and the childlike, trusting, innocent, sexual and physical side of the individual. West is the Black Bear and is the individual's deeper, darker, introspective, and emotional side. North, the White Buffalo, is wisdom, understanding, strength and spirituality.

Understanding the characteristics of animals is a very important and beautiful aspect of the medicine wheel, an aspect that is not well understood or used by this writer because of his limited involvement with animals. This paper presents the more personal use of the medicine wheel to this writer as a psychologist.

The Medicine Wheel, in the abstract sense, is life and a truth greater than life, yet it is different for every individual. It is recognized as real, yet evasive, and difficult to define. When a child is born, the child's parents search or wait for a vision that characterizes the child. This vision is described in terms of one of the four directions, and provides a name for the child. A major task in life is the search of the four directions to become a complete person. The process of the search is most important and lifelong, and a specific goal of the search is not assumed or expected. As the four directions are searched, the personal meaning to the individual continually changes.

THE VISION QUEST

For the Native American the search of the four directions is seen as a continual vision quest. This concept was popularized in literature in the book, Lame Deer, Seeker of Visions, by John Fire Lame Deer and Richard Erdoes (1972). The book begins by describing the vision experience when being "alone on the hilltop." Such a quest is initiated intentionally with no expectations as to what will be seen or found. The unknown is faced with anticipation for discovery and change. What is seen or experienced on such a quest is considered relevant and valuable in one's life. The visions experienced can be referenced to or by the medicine wheel. The visions gained when being totally alone, as when "alone on a hilltop," are considered North or spiritual visions, visions of understanding and wisdom.

Don Juan, the teacher of Carlos Castaneda (1974), speaks of the tonal and the nagual. The "tonal is the organizer of the world . . . . The tonal is everything we know." As an individual moves through life, knowledge narrows our expectations and reality. The nagual is the unknown, that which is beyond the tonal, and by facing it, our world can expand. Andrews (1987) teaches the value of finding and facing the unknown. Visions on a hilltop are one means of such expansion. The nagual is "where power hovers." The many vision experiences of Castaneda are Don Juan's means to lead Castaneda to grow and use the nagual. Great fear is experienced in such expansion. Dealing with traumatic images is a source for growth and change (Brink, 1979).

The teaching tales of the Native American frequently have their source in these visions. Brink (1983) presented three distinctions between the Native American tale and the Euro-American Judeo-Christian fables and fairy tales.

CHARACTERISTICS OF THE MEDICINE WHEEL

The medicine wheel concept and process provides important therapeutic or healthy directions. First, the Medicine Wheel provides for continued growth and change throughout life. Second, the Medicine Wheel is a mirror, reflecting who we are, pulling from within us what is most important. Third, as we use the four directions as a mirror, as we begin to think we have an answer, that answer dissolves to become something else. This evasiveness of the Medicine Wheel may be its greatest power, even though this evasiveness may seem to be a weakness to the White Culture. Fourth, the Medicine Wheel has implications for all of life, whether for the individual, for work, play or sleep. The following is an elaboration of these four characteristics.

<u>The Medicine Wheel Promotes Change</u>

Our European heritage generally assumes the unchangeable nature of adults. Many models of psychology suggest that children grow and change, but adults are resistant to change. One theme frequently expressed in our Christian heritage is that man is born in sin and continually battles evil without the hope of real change in this condition. From many different directions, we are told we cannot change.

In contrast, the Native American is born with the spirit of the community being that change is expected, that life is the continued search of four directions with the goal being continued growth towards completeness. Though the parents provide a child with a description by naming the child as a result of visions at the time of birth, that name is changeable or added to through further visions.

<u>The Medicine Wheel as a Mirror</u>

The reference of the medicine wheel as a mirror has been made in Native American literature (Storm, 1972; Andrews, 1984). The wheel reflects the individual's characteristics in his or her search of the four directions. The medicine wheel incorporates the dynamic nature of a mirror (as explained in the next section) as different from a photograph. Many of the models of psychology provide reductionistic descriptions of the individual which do not accurately acknowledge the moment-to-moment changes in life. For example, a model may suggest that people may be either introverts or extroverts, ignoring the many occasions in an introvert's life when he or she is an extrovert. Seeing oneself using some psychological models or tests of personality is like trying to shave while looking at a photograph whereas the medicine wheel is like using a mirror.

<u>The Power of the Evasiveness in Meaning</u>

In reading the <u>Book of the Hopi</u> by Frank Waters (1972), this writer initially found the Hopi's use of symbols very annoying. Each symbol has a multitude of meanings. From a rational orientation, symbols with more than one meaning are confusing and meaningless. In our rational culture, the color green should not represent death or envy as well as life and growth. Over the years, I have learned to appreciate the diversity in the meaning of Native American symbols.

Each direction of the medicine wheel is described in a number of ways. For example, for the medicine wheel of Hyemeyohsts Storm, East is the eagle and embodies the characteristics of the eagle, e.g., farsighted. East is the sunrise, the beginning and the color gold. East represents the rational, doing or action oriented aspect of life. In the diversity of this description there is an intuitive unity. Yet, these descriptors provide flexibility for change from moment to moment when other aspects of the eagle are noted. Storm's South is the mouse and the color is green. South reflects the individual's sexual, physical or childlike side, including the traits of trust, playfulness and innocence. Again, there is an intuitive unity in this diversity and the descriptors add greater flexibility to mirroring the individual. When the West and North are added, the dynamic picture in the mirror becomes complete.

The diverse meaning of Native American symbols makes the medicine wheel a dynamic mirror. In attempting to see oneself in this mirror, the image is always changing and elusive. The individual's search leads to finding a personal meaning. For example, the rational and emotional distinction is recognized as a reality, but in facing West, one's emotional side, and searching for an understanding in the emotional, the emotional side dissolves into rational understanding. A phrase used by Roni Tower in her address at the 1987 AASMI Conference, that is, "Man plans and God laughs," illustrates the evasiveness of the North-South or spiritual-understanding and physical-innocence dimension. Are the plans of man or the laughter of God the North or the South? A similar phrase revealing the same elusive nature of the North South dimension is "everything is important but nothing is important."

This laughter of God is also reflected in the Heyoehkah of the Sioux or the Koyemsi (Mudhead) Kachina of the Hopi. These members of the tribe are the Jungian trickster archtype. The Heyoehkah does everything backwards, wearing clothing backwards and performing many of the spiritual rituals backwards. Such backwardness and humor prevent the community from taking any idea too seriously and, thus, promotes flexibility.

At one moment one sees oneself clearly in that mirror, but the next moment life moves on and the mirror shows a different reflection. The multitude of meanings found in dreams, imagery work and vision quests can be overwhelming, but a clearer expression of real life rather than looking at a photograph.

The Reflection of Life

The medicine wheel reflects an entire life, instantaneous moments in life or any interval in between. The wheel reflects therapy from beginning to end, a single session, or a moment in a session. The pursuit of the medicine wheel begins in the East and moves clockwise. East is dawn, birth, the beginning of a search, or an individual's decision to begin therapy.

Moving South, the physical, trusting, innocent side of life is the stage of life of childhood, of learning to walk and take charge of one's life. South is gaining trust in oneself, trust in the healing powers that come from within, and trust in one's therapist. South gives one the strength to face the West.

West, the dark emotional side of the individual, is the struggle of life, of being responsible to marriage, children, and one's profession. West is getting down to work in therapy, exploring the emotional pains of life, and facing the unknown. Facing these unknowns lead to greater understanding and spiritual growth, the North.

North is the spiritual experience that comes from deep emotional understanding, the peak experience in therapy, or the flash of insight. It is wisdom gained from life's experience. North provides the understanding and wisdom to make the appropriate decision in life, the East, of using the wisdom and understanding to continue in life and begin the circle anew. Each moment in life is reflected on the medicine wheel.

USING THE MEDICINE WHEEL

The Nature of the Journey

Lame Deer's trip to be alone on a hilltop was noted as a spiritual or North vision (Deer & Erdoes, 1972). The characteristics of each direction suggest the nature of the vision quest.

The journey begins in the East with the decision to seek spiritual understanding. The therapeutic equivalent is the client deciding to initiate therapy.

The journey takes the individual first to the South. The South experience provides the trust and innocence or openness necessary to continue on the journey. For both Lynn Andrews and Michael Harner (1980), this journey took them to a waterfall, and the vision was seen in the daylight in the mist of the waterfall. For Carlos Castaneda (1974), he was instructed to see the world through squinted eyes to intentionally blur his vision. Many of the experiences of childhood provide the source for the South vision. What child has not spun to get dizzy, or seen visions in the clouds? One favorite South experiences from my childhood, which continues in my office, is to see things in knots of the knotty pine paneling. The Rorschach cards provide a similar experience. The experience occurs through opening oneself to experiencing the environment in a new manner. The experience requires the individual to perceive in a trusting and innocent manner. The equivalent in therapy is the development of rapport.

With this light, trusting and playful childlike attitude, strength is gained to face the deep, emotional and frequently painful experiences of the West. The West experience is to go down deep in the dark to attain a vision. Lynn Andrews went deep into a cave. Michael Harner suggests any image of a hole, tunnel or cave. The therapeutic images of going down in an elevator or of going into a cave have generally been considered a means of listening to one's subconscious, of touching deep emotional feelings. Desoille (1966) uses the imagery of descending into a body of water. Dreamwork in therapy is another rich source for such East visions. Such East visions provide the emotional energy to continue on with the journey to the North.

The North vision, the spiritual vision of wisdom and understanding, is attained through being totally alone. Lynn Andrews was left by her mentor alone in a cabin during the winter in a remote portion of Manitoba for an extended period of time. Lame Deer went to the top of a mountain. In this state of total aloneness and with the emotional energy of the West, and the trusting and innocence of the South, a vision of understanding and wisdom is attained. In therapy, situations of being alone are frequently explored and challenging ones are often prescribed. During the therapy session, experiencing going down in an elevator frequently results in finding emptiness or a void. Exploring that emptiness or void can lead the client to find that which fills the void. When the client identifies an empty or void experience, the "affect bridge" of John Watkins (1971) is frequently used to initiate such an imagery journey. John Watkins has the client identify and describe an affect and then instructs the client to carry that feeling while going on such a journey.

The spiritual experience of a North provides the individual with an "act of power," or a decision of what needs to be done upon returning to the East, the place of "doing." The "act of power" then provides the beginning of the continued journey.

The Medicine Bundle and Medicine Shield

Medicine bundles or medicine shields are created to provide the individual with concrete ways of remembering and reviving the visions. The medicine bundle is a leather pouch filled with objects such as stones, feathers, herbs, etc., that provide special meaning or connection to the visions. A medicine shield is a hide stretched over a frame and decorated in ways to recall or revive the experiences of vision quests. Such objects can be very useful in therapy. Clients are instructed to find something to represent a spiritual learning experience, carry that object or place it in some conspicuous place as a constant reminder that awakens feelings of the experience. These objects evoke the vision experience similar to Roberto Assagioli's use of evocative words (Assagioli, 1973). Assagioli's Law III is "ideas and images tend to awaken emotions and feelings that correspond to them." Thus, whether an evocative word or an object in a medicine bundle, the feelings and emotions of the vision are awakened.

Among the Native Americans, such visions are very individual and personal. These visions can also become a central part of the community and a rich source of ritual, as when reenacted by the community, upon direction of Medicine Man. During the fall of the American Indian, between the time of Custer and Wounded Knee, the Indians were looking for strength. One major source of energy was the "Sun Dance," which spread across the plains. This dance began with a vision of one medicine man. Black Elk also had a powerful vision that was frequently reenacted by his tribe to bring this tribe strength (Neihardt, 1932). Such reenactment, as with the medicine bundle and medicine shield, is a means of retaining the power of the experience of the vision.

Facing One's Tormentor

Visions, generally of the West and North, are initially experienced as very frightening. In the books written by Lynn Andrews and Carlos Castaneda, such frightening experiences were so severe that they would elicit such severe physical reactions as vomiting. One repeated theme in the Native American literature is that power is gained through facing such frightening experiences. In therapy, these experiences identify a "tormentor" and facing the tormentor results in loss of its power and, thus, gaining great strength over it. Typically, individuals enter therapy running from problems, and one goal is to reverse that attempt to escape and to face the tormentor. Visions, again, provide a rich source of situations where the client has the opportunity to face a tormentor (Brink, 1979). Frequently the medicine person creates such experiences to force the client to face the tormentor. Jay Haley's (1984) "Ordeal Therapy" is one source of how such experiences can be used in therapy.

APPLICATIONS IN THERAPY

The Four Directions

Again, the direction of the search for the Native American is to begin in the East and move clockwise. This direction of search is the same for psychotherapy.

A 25 year old woman came for therapy because of unhappiness in her relationships with men. She complained of feeling distant in these relationships. The decision to seek therapy was an action of the East.

During the first session, imagery was used to attain relaxation. She was asked to turn her mind inward, becoming aware of her body sensations, sensations of tension and sensations of relaxation. Then she was led in imagery on a walk along a mountain path. These exercises were South experiences, physical and trusting experiences, first to increase her awareness of her body, and then a playful trusting exercise of examining what she saw along a mountain path.

During the second session she visualized going down in an elevator and seeing as the doors opened. She was ready to face this emotional and dark experience of the West. Behind one door she faced a void of darkness. The following session she chose to return to that darkness where she saw a faint source of light. She approached the light and found a chute through which she jumped into the light. She found herself flying along a coast line. This experience was very exhilarating. Though she did not know specifically to where she was flying, she sensed that she had a direction. She left the darkness of the West and was on her way to the understanding of the North, with the unspoken sense of a spiritual experience. Conscious understanding was attained when she saw a restaurant on a point jutting out into the water and she saw a car driving in. She landed to meet her mother, father, and music teacher. She wanted to tell them she could fly but she knew she could not. Her father would say "that's nice," discounting the significance of flying to her. Her mother would say "that's impossible," and her music teacher would try to take credit for her ability to fly. This realization returned her to the East with an understanding of her need to find someone who would be understanding.

Facing One's Tormentor

By facing one's tormentor, personal power is gained. Fear of the unknown is one major tormentor in life. Any change is facing, to some degree, the unknown. By facing one's tormentor, one is saying that one is ready to experience the unknown of change.

An obvious tormentor to a person attempting to quit smoking is the craving for a cigarette. Facing this feeling, the individual might discover that his or her mouth is dry or cottony, experience chest tightness, or cold and clammy hands or feet. For each individual this experience is different. As such feelings are faced and experienced fully, the feelings change, diminish or move to a different place within the body. When the individual experiences the evasiveness of such feelings, discovers that the feelings are not as intense or frightening as expected, or that the mind easily wanders away from the feelings, power is gained over these feelings. As other aspects of the addiction are revealed, these aspects, too, are faced in a similar manner. Similarly, facing the physical sensations of Premenstrual Syndrome provides power to reduce the common behavioral responses to these symptoms.

Facing such feelings is working primarily on the East-West axis. Power is found over the emotions of the West, when examined using rationality of the East. Power is also found over rationality of the East when getting in touch with the emotionality of the West. An example is of the client troubled by psychosomatic symptoms of panic and anxiety. Typically, the client with psychosomatic symptoms is an East oriented person not "in touch" with feelings. Whereas Watkins (1971) proposes the affect bridge, Araoz (1985) speaks of the somatic bridge. Araoz instructs the client to carry the somatic experience on an imagery journey as Watkins asks the client to carry the feelings. In using the imagery of the medicine wheel, the road signs on the East-West bridge are different at either end. At the East end, going West, the bridge is called somatic, and at the West end, going East, it is called affect. For the client with psychosomatic symptoms, he or she is to carry the symptom on the imagery journey to find the affect. By using imagery to uncover the thinking pattern and fear causing the anxiety, power over the anxiety is gained (Brink, 1987).

One of the most severe tormentors in our times is cancer. There have been numerous examples of how facing the tormentor of cancer has caused tremendous change within the individual. One example of the spontaneous imagery of a patient with benign fibroid tumors but with special relevance to the medicine wheel was presented by Eugenia Pickett (1988). In a personal communication with Eugenia Pickett, she assured this writer that neither she nor the client had any direct knowledge of the medicine wheel. Yet this client produced the following spontaneous image:

> I enter the land of deep sleep from the West, and am dancing in a counter-clockwise direction over the charred earth. In a scooping motion flower springs from the earth and marks the South. I spin around, moving to the East, and as I do, snow falls over the entire area. Then I move to the North, spread my arms to the heavens and wait . . . a long time. The moon rises and everything is crystalline, purifying the space, preparing it so it can grow green again in the spring. There are bits and pieces of charred wood showing through the snow and it looks like a large grave for many people. In the East I can see the beginning of a new day-glow of morning illuminating the flower of the South. The sky glows red, and there is something I must do before the sun rises. I rake through the snow and ashes, looking for something among the buttons and snaps and broken bits of things. And I find what I am looking for--a moon crystal. It is a crystal from the past, still here, and I put it in my pocket as the sun comes up on a clear blue-white day. The sun melts the snow. Water seeps into the earth, and tender little shoots appear.

She then continues the imagery ending with "I feel like I have everything I need and that I am all right, and that some kind of cleansing process has begun."

This incredible insight into the symbols of the four directions, yet proceeding, first, in the reverse of the usual direction of movement of the medicine wheel, as might be done by a Heyoehkah, to reverse the evil growth or to let go of something in one's life that was felt most important, in order to produce change, is a major goal in therapy to shrink tumors.

Marital Therapy

A major use of the East-West axis is in marital therapy. Lynn Andrews (1985) reports her conversation with Zoila, a Mayan Indian medicine woman. This Indian notes that white women generally live in the West, i.e., primarily exhibit their emotional side, and the white male lives in the East or is primarily rational. This incompleteness provides a clash in marriage that the only direction such a couple can find in common is their physical-sexual side, the South. She notes that the white culture lacks spirituality of the North.

Expanding this description of our white culture, the difference between the white male and female describes the sexual conflict found frequently in marital therapy. A frequent complaint by the wife is that the husband's approach to sex is "wham bam thank you ma'am." In such cases, the husband, if he allows himself to express his feelings, recognizes his impatience with the warmth and closeness sought by his wife. When the husband can take time to examine the emotional side, he can learn to appreciate the warmth.

Finding balance on this East-West bridge can provide solutions to such other marital problems as dealing with anger, guilt, fear and perfectionism. Adding the balance of the North-South bridge introduces the important ingredient of humor to overcome the problems caused by these emotions.

SUMMARY

Psychology has spoken of the four dimensions of the individual: the rational, the physical, the emotional, and the spiritual. The medicine wheel expands these four dimensions into a dynamic and meaningful model of mirroring human life and a model that promotes continual growth and change. East represents the rational, problem-solving, and action-oriented dimension, while West is the emotional, creative and spontaneous dimension. South, or the physical, sexual, trusting, and childlike dimension, is opposite the spiritual, knowing, and understanding dimension of the North. Life is to a life-long search of these four directions.

The power over life begins with beginning the search, an action of the East. Gaining trust of one's self is gained in the South. With this trust, one is able to face the more fearful experience of the darker, emotional, empty feelings of the West. This facing the West provides the strength to, alone, discover the spiritual dimension. Out of this discovery of the North, one finds an act of power performed in the East and, thus, continues on the journey of the medicine wheel.

Therapeutic experiences of the South include activities to help the individual gain faith and trust in oneself. Playful, supportive and ego strengthening exercises, frequently using imagery, are included in those activities. The activities to assist the individual to face the deep emotions of the West include the use of mental imagery of descending or going down into the earth or water and of facing one's tormentor. Experiences of the North occur when one is totally alone. Using mental imagery or a situation of total aloneness to face the void or emptiness in life is a North experience. Out of such "alone" experiences come decisions of power that greatly affect one's life.

REFERENCES

Andrews, L. V. Medicine Woman. New York: Harper & Row, 1981.
Andrews, L. V. Flight of the Seventh Moon. New York: Harper & Row, 1984.
Andrews, L. V. Jaguar Woman. New York: Harper & Row, 1985.
Andrews, L. V. Star Woman. New York: Warner Books, 1986.
Andrews, L. V. Crystalk Woman. New York: Warner Books, 1987.
Araoz, D. L. The New Hypnosis. New York: Brunner/Mazel, 1985.
Assogioli, R. The Act of Will. London: Wildwood House, 1973.
Brink, N. E. Dealing with traumatic images. Bulletin of the American Association of the Study of Mental Imagery, 1979, 2(2).
Brink, N. E. Imagery and family therapy. In Imagery, Vol. 3, ed. J. E. Shorr, G. Sobel-Whittington, P. Robin, and J. A. Connella. New York: Plenum, 1983.
Brink, N. E. Three stages of hypno-family therapy for psychosomatic problems. Imagination, Cognition and Personality, 1987, 6(3).
Brown, J. E. The Sacred Pipe, Black Elk's Account of The Seven Rites of the Oglala Sioux. New York: Penguin Books, 1953.
Castaneda, C. The Teachings of Don Juan, a Yaqui Way of Knowledge. Los Angeles: University of California Press, 1968.
Castaneda, C. A Separate Reality, Further Conversations with Don Juan. New York: Pocket Books, 1971.
Castaneda, C. Journey to Ixtlan, the Lessons of Don Juan. New York: Pocket Books, 1972.
Castaneda, C. Tales of Power. New York: Pocket Books, 1974.
Castaneda, C. The Second Ring of Power. New York: Pocket Books, 1977.

Castaneda, C. The Eagle's Gift. New York: Pocket Books, 1981.

Castaneda, C. The Fire from Within. New York: Simon & Schuster, 1984.

Castaneda, C. The Power of Silence, Further Lessons of Don Juan. New York: Simon & Schuster, 1987.

Deer, J. L., Erdoes, R. Lame Deer Seeker of Visions. New York: Pocket Books, 1972.

Desoille, R. The Directed Daydream. New York: Psychosynthesis Research Foundation, 1966.

Eddy, J. A. Probing the mystery of the medicine wheel. National Geographic, 1977, 151(1), 140-146.

Harner, M. The Way of the Shaman, a Guide to Power and Healing. New York: Bantam Books, 1982.

Haley, J. Ordeal Therapy. San Francisco: Jossey-Bass, 1984.

Neihardt, J. G. Black Elk Speaks. New York: Pocket Books, 1932.

Pickett, E. Fibroid tumors and response to guided imagery and music: Two case studies. Imagination, Cognition and Personality, 1988, 7(2), 165-176.

Storm, H. Seven Arrows. New York: Harper & Row, 1972.

Storm, H. Song of Heyoehkan. New York: Harper & Row, 1981.

Waters, F. Book of the Hopi. New York: Penguin Books, 1963.

Watkins, J. G. The affect bridge: A hypnoanalytic technique. International Journal of Clinical Hypnosis, 1971, 19, 21-27.

CREATIVE TRANSFORMATIONS: HOW VISUAL ARTISTS, MUSICIANS, AND DANCERS USE MENTAL IMAGERY IN THEIR WORK

Helane S. Rosenberg

Associate Professor
Rutgers University
New Brunswick, New Jersey

William Trusheim

Director of Fine and Performing Arts
Pequannock Township Schools
Pompton Plains, New Jersey

"Imagination whirls me around." So stated GD, a choreographer who was interviewed as part of the following package of research studies that focuses on how artists use mental imagery in making or performing art. And like GD, what all the various visual, musical, and dance artists, interviewed in the three studies reported here have in common is that imagination whirls them around. Imagination is a major force in the creative processes of all of these artists.

Yet, to paraphrase Shakespeare's Polonius, there is "method to their madness." Or, more appropriately, methods to these madnesses. The many imagery-related strategies, as unusual as they may seem to the non-artist (but not, of course, to the scholar of mental imagery) as essential are these strategies to the creation and performance of works of art. What's so compelling about the studies that follow is the degree to which these various artists have finely tuned their imagery processes, just as they have developed the technical/craft aspects of their chosen art forms. In fact, the links and the interactions between internal processes and external actions are inexorably forged and wonderfully synergistic.

BACKGROUND

The body of research that focuses on how various types of art-makers use mental imagery in their creative work is small, but rich. Even the early investigations are important to the studies reported here. Both Patrick (1937) and Roe in 1946 (1975) studied the creative processes of painters and painting. Each utilized the interview method to tap the rich resource of the working artist and provided conclusions that suggest that imagery experiences are important aspects of the artistic process. Eindhoven and Vinacke (1952) conducted a similar study of painters. The researchers found great individual differences in the process of these artists, in terms of imagery as well as other elements. They did provide case studies, however, which further describe how visual artists utilize imagery in their creative process.

Not until the 1980's did researchers seek to further delineate how visual artists, as well as artists working in other mediums, use imagery in their work. Nass (1984) interviewed composers to gain insight into the musical composition process. Although not the focus of study, Nass reported that composers do depend on imagery and that imagery modalities used by these composers ranged from auditory to kinesthetic to visual. Lindauer (1983) narrowed the focus to imagery and interviewed a number of working artists in a variety of artistic mediums. Subjects were questioned about the frequency, mode, clarity, vividness, control, locus, and variability of their imagery. Lindauer reported that imagery use by artists was a foregone conclusion for several of the subjects. All of Lindauer's subjects reported a high degree of vividness and clarity in their imagery. This study showed that information about artist's imagery can be easily obtained through the interview process and concludes with the assertion that "we [psychologists] have much to learn about imagery from the arts, more than those in the arts can learn about imagery from psychology" (p. 499).

The recent work of Rosenberg (1983, 1987a, 1987b) at Rutgers University suggested that both creative and performing artists, professionals and young students alike, rely on various mental imagery strategies to stimulate art-making and performance. Of major importance to the studies reported here artists is the iii System, a framework that describes the cyclic, oscillation, and connection aspects of how artists use imagination in their work (1983). The interview study (1987b), conducted with 13 visual artists, provided some initial conclusions in terms of the classification of mental imagery-related processes within all stages of the artistic process. Rosenberg found that artists depend on their mental imagery in three essential phases of art-making: collecting and storing images, art-making itself, and response to the completed paintings (pp. 83-91). This 1987 study also provided the studies reported here with a model interview guide and an efficient method of qualitative analysis.

OVERVIEW

The following three interview-based studies (each strongly linked to the iii System and to each other) describe and detail various aspects of the imagery-related processes of 26 musicians, 20 visual artists, and 6 dancer/choreographers. The first study focuses on visual artists and further delineates their use of imagery within their art-making process. Of particular importance are the descriptions concerning negotiation with images and the oscillation between internal and external. The second study focuses on musicians specifically brass performers. It describes these musicians' concepts of tone (interesting because of its unique focus to a large extent on auditory imagery), musical interpretation, and mental rehearsal and warm-up. The third study deals with dancers. It provides interesting case study information about how choreographers incorporate their visual and kinesthetic images into their dance pieces.

METHODS

Each of the three studies that follow employ similar methodology in terms of subjects, development and implementation of interview guide, interview process, and data analysis.

Subjects

The subjects for the three studies were professionals in each of their selected art fields; all the subjects made their living creating or performing in their respective fields, although most of the subjects did also teach in their art fields in order to supplement their income. All of the 20 visual artists had presented their work in group or individual shows at major professional galleries in the New York or Philadelphia area; most of these visual artists had received major grants or fellowships such as the Guggenheim or Rockefeller. All 26 musicians were eminent orchestral brass players; each played in one of the following major symphony orchestras: Baltimore Symphony Orchestra, Boston Symphony Orchestra, Chicago Symphony Orchestra, New York Philharmonic, and Philadelphia Orchestra. Several of these subjects enjoyed "world-class" status and many were regarded by their peers as the best in the world at what they do. The dancer/choreographers were equally meritorious; they were recipients of fellowships and awards, including a Tony, and had their works performed on Broadway and by major dance companies in New York City.

The Interview Guides

The interview guides for the three related studies were developed, piloted, and revised as necessary. Each guide consisted of a set of topics, subtopics, and possible probes which were common to all three series of interviews, as well as topics unique to each art form. The interview guide consisted of a series of open-ended questions designed to draw on the artist's past experiences and current practices for answers. The general goals of the interviews were to ascertain the scope, depth, and importance of imagery in the art-making stages of each respondent.

The Interview Processes

All interviews were conducted face-to-face and were tape recorded and subsequently transcribed. The interviews lasted from 50 minutes to an hour and thirty minutes. A major concern during the interviews was the question of researcher bias. The problem of bias can never be totally eliminated from a research design of this type. Nevertheless, throughout the interview every effort was made to control bias. To minimize bias, the interviewers took a passive stance, allowing the respondents to draw on personal past experiences freely. Leading questions were avoided and various probes were employed to clarify possible confusions. (For example, the term "image" could mean to the visual artist the painting itself, not the mental picture.) Student interviewers received at least one semester's training in interview strategies and techniques. More importantly, each interviewer taught or practiced the same or a related art form as the interviewee.

ANALYSIS

All the transcriptions for each of the three series of interviews were transcribed and scanned independently by at least two judges. Imagery-related statements were coded and subsequently categorized. Since each interview was unique, based on different lines of questioning according to the nature of each discussion, statements from all parts of the interview were scanned to determine their subject matter. This was not always a straightforward process because some respondents spoke about a particular topic in a question about a different topic. Once the exact subject matter of each statement was determined, they were separated and placed in the appropriate category.

Among the 52 transcripts (26 musicians, 20 artists, and 6 dancers), the number of imagery-related response statements per interview ranged from 17 to 93. For the 20 visual artists, 694 statements were designated as imagery-related. These statements were subsequently organized into eight groupings: biographical information, training and mentors, sources and preliminaries for art-making, craft elements/external standards, early stages of art-making, negotiating with the work already in progress, the art-making process itself, and selling a work of art. For the 26 musicians, the 849 imagery-related statements were grouped into these eight topics: background and training, mentor-student relationship, warm-up, tone production, musical expression and interpretation, conductors' imagery, mental rehearsal, and reduction of performance anxiety. In the three interviews with the dancer/choreographers reported here (selected from the pilot sample of six interviews) a similar density of imagery-related statements seems to be emerging, although final count and complete categorization have yet to be determined.

RESULTS AND DISCUSSION

Following are the discussions and results of the study, presented art form by art form. It is important, however, to state some general conclusions, ones that help frame the specific conclusions and also to clarify both the unique and shared characteristics of the art-making processes to be discussed.

The art forms that we are discussing are primarily non-verbal ones. This factor is certainly a plus, in that we did not have to concern ourselves with the possible artful verbalizing about personal imagery that is the domain of the wordsmith.

Despite the non-verbal character of the art forms, almost every artist interviewed was highly verbal and eager to participate in the study and to communicate during the interview. This suggests that artists do not deserve to be labeled inarticulate, solitary, or out-of-touch. They make good subjects. We believe, however, and have been told by many of those interviewed, that the fact that the interviewers were themselves practicing artists in the various art forms enabled the initial contact to be extremely positive and sparked the flow of the interview process.

Finally, it is important to compare and contrast the groups of art-makers in terms of their respective art forms. Again, all are primarily non-verbal. In terms of the classification of creative or interpretive, two of the three groups are creative (making something from nothing--those being the visual artists and the choreographers) and one group is interpretive (that being the brass players). In terms of the individual versus ensemble classification, one group is individual (that being the visual artists) and the other two are ensemble artists--the choreographer and the musical performer.

VISUAL ARTISTS

The following discussion focuses on some aspects of five of the eight groupings: sources for art-making, early stages of art-making, negotiating with the work already in progress, the actual painting process (particularly the oscillation between internal and external), and selling a work of art. For this study, 20 artists (15 women and 5 men) were interviewed.

The Power of Stimulating Imagery: Sources for Art-Making

The visual artists in this sample paint widely diverse kinds of paintings in terms of both subjects (landscapes, still life, portraits, action scenes, people, and animals) and style (from almost photo realism to intensely expressionistic). Some of the artists describe how they have been inspired to paint by seeing an everyday object in their environment, such as a lone daffodil, for example. Others seem to be inspired more directly through their internal storehouse of objects and people. Yet all the artists interviewed are clearly aware that the original sources for material or subjects to be painted comes from the outside world. These artists seem to spend much of their time observing the world for the purpose of making art.

Many of the artists also describe specific techniques for collecting this material to be stored as images. One artist captures the world by pretending to be a camera herself: "I go out in the woods and pick a little area, whenever the sun is a certain way or a tree or something . . . . I just go shhh around like that [as if a camera panning the area] with a magnifying glass or choose a certain area" (CB). Interestingly, many of the artists also suggest that the decision about what to record as images rests as much with the objects as with themselves. Artists describe how they have been taken hostage or captivated or even captured to paint: "I see something that captures me" (EA). One artist acknowledges that he has to look at the appropriate places to begin with, but after that, he gives up control to the flowers in his landscapes: "The objects come out to me. I look at the right places and when I find them, they're startling. You want to paint that one" (JR). Others actually photograph the stimulating object or sketch constantly as a way not to forget.

Once the objects, people, or locations are stored as images, the artists similarly empower these images, giving them the ability to order the artist to begin working. The artists allow the images to return. During the interviews, many artists describe how these internal images re-emerge, ready to be subjects for paintings. One particular artist was not always delighted; he seemed compelled in a way that was out of his control. Yet he accepted the images' return: "My images come to me, whether I'm looking for them or not" (DJ). A second artist seemed happier with her re-emerging images: "Sometimes the thing just sort of comes to you in a flash and that just tickles me pink" (TS). A third artist describes her absolute trust in allowing herself to be stimulated to paint: "When I have images like this, I never believe they lead me astray. They're never wrong. They're true to me" (TS).

<u>Imagery's Role in the Early Painting Process</u>

The artists interviewed discussed many important issues that help place the early stages of the painting process within an imagery-related context. Preparation for art-making, holding and manipulating the stimulating image, and influence of the art materials. This discussion focuses on one issue of particular interest: the nature of the developing relationship between the painter and the stimulating image.

Once the object or image has captured the attention of the painter, an intensely personal relationship begins. In many cases, the artists questioned imbue their subjects or images with personal characteristics: "These guys become some of your little friends, your little companions. So you start getting a personal attachment. So the reason for this subject was that it was a friend" (JR). These artists know that the subjects don't have lives outside their paintings, yet within them they do have vivid existences: "I don't know what they eat for breakfast. But I know where they came from and I know how they change from picture to picture. I feel very friendly towards them" (AZ). This artist goes on to describe her long-term relationship with the woman who appears again and again in her work: "She means a lot to me because she's gone through a lot of transformations" (AZ). A relationship with images that begins this powerfully certainly suggests that an equally powerful relationship will exist with any painting that transforms the images onto the canvas; in fact, the paintings do reflect the strong attachment that these painters have with their subjects.

Negotiations with the Work in Progress: Conversations

The artists interviewed have developed a variety of imagery-related strategies as they begin the painting process in earnest. The most popular technique is to engage in various sorts of conversations with the internal images, the artistic materials, or even with the painting as a whole. One artist describes how he came to add one more daffodil to his work: There was a lot of personal character to that bulb. It told me that I had to paint it. I heard it that morning" (JR). Another artist explained what he did when he was "stuck." He spent some time looking at his paints and brushes and then knew how to proceed: "A lot of time the materials say what they're going to be sometimes to me. They tell me how to use them" (JC). A third artist describes a give-and-take procedure: "The materials really react to me and speak to me" (DS). In all three cases the artists quoted had little difficulty giving up control to images and paint brushes who they describe as being certainly focal, probably verbal.

Many artists go so far as to engage in conversations with more than images and art materials; some even with the developing work. These conversations, related during the interviews, are certainly among the most interesting imagery-related aspects of the painting process of these visual artists. One artist describes the give-and-take that occurs: "I always listen to the work. I will sit and talk with it a long time" (JH). Another artist relates specific information about the negotiations. For her, not only did the painting ask for assistance, but she voiced her affirmative response: "This is what I'm gonna be," it says, "Can you help me become that?" And I say, "Okay. How can I help you?" (LN). Another artist, in describing her conversations, performs a vaudeville-like routine, physically and vocally enacting both roles--the artist and the painting: "Paintings are a dialogue between the artist and the picture. You have to listen to what the painting wants you to do. It's a dialogue between the two of you. It says, 'I want a little bit more blue over here.' And you say, 'No, you were supposed to be white.'" (EG). In listening to the tape, the vocal tone and pitch of painter and painting are extraordinarily distinct from one another.

Fifteen of the 20 artists describe engaging in negotiations with their work, endowing their materials with distinct personalities, and empowering their subjects or images with artistic rights. It is important to note that at no time did these artists suggest, even when directly questioned about it, that they were speaking metaphorically in regard to images, subjects, materials, or paintings voicing opinions or offering perspectives. At least within the time that they make art, these artists fully believe that their images have wills and needs equal to or greater than those of the artist.

Oscillating Between Internal and External: Critical to Success

Much of the literature in mental imagery focuses to a large extent on the specifics of internal processes. Certainly these artists interviewed have well developed internal strategies. What seems apparent from interviewing them is the prescence of equally well-developed external procedures closely connected to the internal. These artists describe a variety of concurrent processes: painting the painting inside their heads and painting a similar or matching painting on the canvas. For these artists interviewed, either painting can lead the other. In fact, most of these artists reported that during their careers they have been stimulated to work internally for one painting and externally for another. Fourteen of the artists interviewed did seem to favor the procedure in which the external work is in charge; the materials or the early sketches of the work suggests how the painting will progress. These artists seem more than happy to give up control to the external. Eight of the artists interviewed describe procedures in which the internal painting leads the work; of these only four explained that they use the internal painting exclusively as leader in their art-making.

The classic model of an externally stimulated visual artist is one who sets up an easel out of doors and paints what he or she sees. The externally stimulated artists in this sample describe many more complex procedures. One such artist begins by passively allowing a colored marker to start the process. The following quote suggests that this artist's work is most certainly stimulated externally, almost as if the artist herself need not be present, except to be a critic of sorts: "Then I take a thin-line marker and I put it down almost like I'm hypnotized. I watch it cross over the colors very slowly and then I start to see the line suggesting something. I let it suggest something to start" (JB).

A second artist seems to be more excited by, but not much more present in, the externally stimulated work: "The canvas keeps me motivated. It's still kinda magic to me, when I see things form a canvas. When you have all these little lumps of color and a blank canvas. And just seeing the canvas change in how it's forming just keeps me going" (JR).

A third artist provides a detailed account of how she compares one external stage (the painting) with an earlier externalized stage (the sketch):

> I'll take a sketch. I'll enlarge. I'll put color. Sometimes I'll cut them out. Paste them. Paste them in different ways. It happens on the canvas, never in my mind, it's always external. Like the twenty sketches that kept happening. Then suddenly there's a canvas piece and then I go back to sketches. It's a back and forth. (EA)

The oscillation continues throughout art-making, always with a continued focus on the external. One artist describes how she experiments and changes a painting, not in her mind's eye, but on the canvas: "I can do a landscape and there's a red horse in this river. And days later, the red horse has been pulled out and there's a very light blue one instead" (BE).

Other artists describe how this oscillation is led by the internal painting. They seem to experiment first in their mind's eyes. They use the vocabulary of artists describing their externally stimulated practice, but to explain what is happening internally. Because most non-artists cannot comprehend how visual artists are able to draw and paint what they see in their mind's eyes, the procedures described by the internally stimulated artists seem almost magical: how wonderful to be able to capture on paper what's inside one's brain! Yet these artists are faced with many difficulties, resulting in part from the way in which they use imagery in their creative process.

One difficulty faced by these artists is discovering that the internal painting may seem fine, but the external one doesn't have the proper effect: "I can do it in my head. That doesn't mean it's going to work out like that in actuality. It might look exactly like it but might not work" (EA).

Because these artists are professionals, they are aware of what they must do to rectify the error. They must change the painting or change the image of the painting. This artist was unhappy with how the painting looked: "I do imagine the way the lime green would do to the painting and sometimes you imagine wrong because you don't know until you really see it" (BE). She went on to describe how she modified the stimulating image so that she could continue.

The visual artist also faces difficulty when neither the internal nor the external can remain constant. One artist describes how the images must change so that he can proceed: "Quite often, though, the images change as I'm working. I'll start with one and then it will become something else" (JH).

Another comes to grip with a bad internal/external fit by introducing a third party in the interaction: the artist himself. He began by matching the external to the internal, but when as the painting diverged, he described how he entered the work in progress and gave it permission to change: "It's completed in my mind before I start painting. Then when I go to the painting, I start reacting to what's happening on canvas and then it becomes a different painting" (JR).

Perhaps the internally stimulated artist's worst fear is to finish the painting internally and Walter Mitty-like failing to bring the fantasy to fruition. One painter describes being absorbed by the image and losing sight of the painting: "Inevitably when I'm three-quarters the way through a painting--no matter if it's an exciting painting or not, I'm bored. It takes me every ounce of energy to finish. Because it's already finished in my head" (EG). Because she is a professional, this artist completed her work. The need to have a number of completed pieces for her next New York show gave the oscillation a push in the direction of action.

Letting an Image Go: Selling a Work of Art

At some point in the interviews, almost all of the artists interviewed describe strong attachments to both the image that stimulates the work and to the work in progress. The sample seems divided, however, in the degree of attachment to the completed works. Also, the completed works seem to serve various purposes for the artists interviewed. Those artists who seem particularly attached to (and consequently unable to sell) their completed works describe these works, even though they are completed, as unfinished: "You know, I don't think my work is ever finished either" (JC). They seem to need to have the work in front of them in the studio in order to stimulate the next work or to use as an external match for the internal process. This external frame of reference stimulates both internal and external process as described by this artist:

> There's something about this [a painting] that I want to explore. And if it's not around, then I can't explore it in the same way. To me it just helps to have this stuff around . . . . I want to use it as material for other pieces. I consider this a finished piece, but I also use it again as raw material. (AZ)

This artist feels that one of her pieces sold to someone far away can no longer "do me any good." Neither the slide nor the memory of it can stimulate the work; she misses the piece and thinks about what it "sees" from the vantage point of the wall in the new owner's house. Clearly, the artist strongly identifies with her work.

A few of the artists, particularly those who seem less emotionally involved with their stimulating images, seem equally uninvolved with their creations. One artist in the sample often works to the specifications of architects and explains: "I think it's important to get rid of things" (CB). Most of the artists, however, describe a relationship with their work that is less intense than the first artist described or as cold as the second. These artists describe a process they go through which allows them to disconnect from their work and move on. One artist explains that initially: "I am not ready to relinquish the work, so I keep them around" (DS). But soon he feels distant from the process and the product and begins a new piece: "I know it's time to begin something new when I feel no attachment or connection to what's in my studio" (DS).

Another artist who has recently had great success in selling her work describes how difficult (but ultimately necessary) it was for her to "let go": "I just let these four pieces out of my studio" (EG).

Although art-making is an intensely personal process, and certainly evolves from a powerful image or object, the ultimate success of the professional artist rests first with the ability to permit this personal and powerful image to stimulate the work and then to distance self from the work that puts this image on the canvas for all to see. Those artists who describe themselves as successful (as well as psychologically strong) have tried valiantly to let their works speak for themselves by selling them to others.

MUSICIANS

Most skilled musical professionals recognize the significance of the mental ingredients in artistic performance and use them consciously in some way or another to enhance their playing. The findings presented here are based on the doctoral research of one of the co-authors (Trusheim, 1987), which involved eminent orchestral brass players (26 men) in five major American symphony orchestras mentioned above. The actual interview process focused on eight broad areas of potential imagery used by brass players. For the purpose of this article, five topics will be discussed. Each of these topics represents an important component in the process of musical performance for all players; a discussion of these areas proves most revealing in the identification of generalized imagery strategies and specific cases of imagery use in performance.

The Warm-up

The "Warm-up" is an important facet of performance because, in the words of a well-known trumpeter from the Chicago Symphony, it presents the movement when "you reacquaint yourself with the instrument each and every day." There are two predominant approaches to the warm-up--the standardized (or routinized) approach and the non-standardized approach. In the standardized approach, the player uses a set routine of exercises and etudes to prepare for actual playing. The non-standardized approach allows the material used for warm-up to very greatly according to the player's own assessment and perception of particular playing needs for that day. The most significant issue from an imagery standpoint, however, is that in both approaches, musicians depend on having a clear mental representation of a particular aspect of the sound or feel of playing which they strive to match as they approach the instrument for the first time on any given day:

> Warm-up is coupling ourselves to the instrument at the start of the day. My philosophy is to always return to the norms

> . . . and search out my finest quality of tone based on conceptual thought . . . . I try to sound my best at the very first note . . . . In my brain, I have worked for very high standards of musical concepts and sounds and I start with the norms and maneuver them into the extremes. (AJ)

These mental representations are present for the majority of players in the form of auditory or kinesthetic images which have been painstakingly developed through years of practice and performance. While different players concentrate on different points of focus--sound, feel, relaxation of the air column (for wind players), and frame of mind--a vivid mental image provides the necessary reference and becomes an important ingredient in the warm-up process.

Many players begin by calling up an auditory image of a specific sound that they wish to produce and then strive to match that as they play. Others use a kinesthetic image that guides them in achieving the proper "feel." Generally, those that concentrate on the feel of playing are looking for a relaxed and open air column. Still others look to develop a frame of mind which replicates the ambience of actually being onstage in a performance situation:

> Warm-up, I think for me, is more mental now--or psychological, you might say--than physical . . . I can come in to a concert a half hour before and my mind is on other things. . . I nurse myself into the frame of mind of playing a concert. You almost psyche yourself up, and by the end of my warm-up, I'm playing a little more bravura and with confidence--like what you've got to present when you go out on stage. (DT)

All of these approaches depend on imagery strategies and experiences to some degree.

Tone Production or "Concept" of Sound

The musical performance literature abounds in the use of the term "concept" of playing. "Concept" for musicians could perhaps best be described as an "ideal" sound or approach to playing a particular instrument. This "concept" is stored as a mental representation which may be multi-sensory for some players. Mental imagery plays a major role in the development of this concept--or ideal approach--and its subsequent use in actual performance.

The earliest stage in this process involves the development of a clear auditory image of an idealized sound or timbre. This occurs through the accumulation of a wide variety of listening and performance experiences and is an ongoing process throughout a player's career. With each and every experience, the stored image of the idealized sound is refined in one way or another based on the developing aesthetic discrimination of the player. A typical comment on this issue was offered by one of the tuba players in the study:

> The problem is that as soon as you get to the point where you can produce your ideal, . . . you'll go to a concert and you'll hear somebody do something, a little aspect of something . . . and you'll go back [to the practice room] and you can't do it. The ideal just went up! (WD)

This attitude was echoed by many of the players interviewed for this study indicating that the development of an ideal is surely a dynamic process which is "always open for renovation" (RG).

The next stage occurs as this stored image of proper instrumental timbre is recalled as an auditory image and used as a guide to performance. The vast majority of players report matter-of-factly on having the ability to create a vivid auditory image of the sound that they wish to produce on the instrument. This finding is not entirely unexpected since musicians are accustomed to dealing in sound throughout their musical lives and the development of a vivid aural image follows logically from all of their training, conditioning, and rehearsal and performance experiences. But simply forming the image is not the crucial point here. The majority of these players have also managed to incorporate the manipulation of this image into important aspects of their individualized approach to performance.

The most vital ingredient in actual sound production is the cultivation of the ability to hear accurately and vividly, in the mind's ear, the sound to be produced in actual playing. This vivid mental image is then used as a guide during actual performance. One of the horn players in the study states: "I like to use the slogan 'The music plays me.' The music that I have inside of my head is what plays the horn and that's what guides the product that comes out" (RG).

Time spent in imaging the sound directly influences the production of this sound as one plays the instrument. By way of example, one player suggests that "if you want to play the note louder, then hear it louder and then the mental side will tell the physical side what to do" (AJ).

Several other interesting responses show some alternative uses of imagery in the development of "concept" or good tone production. A number of players find that the mental representation of ideal sound has a visual, kinesthetic, or spatial aspect for them. Some view sound in terms of the visual image of a triangle:

> I think of sound as being sort of triangular or pyramid-shaped and the broadest part of that pyramid or triangle is the resonating point of the instrument. For me, the concept of that triangle or pyramid--depending on wheter you're looking at it two-dimensionally--establishes getting the sound to be broad and focused on as much fundamental or overtones in the sound. (CS)

One player recalls an experience he had as a young musician when he practiced in an open field and used various techniques to project his sound across the open space. He feels that this helped him build certain sound characters and he vividly recalls today those youthful experiences imagining space and shape when he thinks of issues concerning tone production. Another player visualizes his sound taking on the shape of the contour of his trumpet bell: "I try to spread the sound out following the contour of the bell so the sound is as broad as the concert hall" (CS).

Two musicians in the study report experiencing chromesthesia or "colored hearing" as they play in response to a musical passage:

> I love the idea, the thought of color. There's the shadings of colors from vivid to pastel to opaque. And then different colors seem to have different kinds of reactions . . . . There are all kinds of things going on mentally while I'm playing. It's not uncommon that I would think of colors and actually see them [While playing]" (WK).

One of the trombone players in the study actually sees his ideal sound in terms of color perception: "Sounds do have actual colors . . . the ideal trombone sound--you know, that nice shiny bronze or shiny gold (not too gold, not a dull gold)--has to have that shiny edge which will be the projection that I have" (NB).

Horn players in this study speak of the visual and kinesthetic image of actually "throwing" their sound out into the audience to correct for the inherent projection problems of the horn. the image here is one of the notes sticking to one another to produce continuity in the phrase. He enhances this image by imaging his fingers sticking to the valves of his horn. The variety and scope of these images is remarkable and indicates that these performers bring every sort of musical and real life experience to bear on their playing.

These players have a very strong aural concept or image of the sound they wish to produce. This aural concept is important in guiding tone production and may be associated with sensations or perceptions or images in sense modalities other than the auditory. The players interviewed for this study hear this sound in their minds and use it regularly as part of their performance process.

<u>Musical Expression and Interpretation</u>

The issue of musical expression and interpretation is a thorny one at best, but one that reaches clearly into the aesthetic of musical performance. This study dealt entirely with musicians who are interpretive performance artists participating in an esemble art experience. It is their job to interpret musical works written by others under the direction of a conductor. The interpretations of these works is personalized and individual for each player. No two players perform the same passage using exactly the same musical expression. The most significant finding here in terms of mental imagery has to do with a generalized approach that is used by many players as they practice or rehearse expressive issues. Players form images from a variety of sources, manipulate them in their minds through imaging strategies, and externalize these in some way in their playing. The players identify the primary sources of imagery used in interpretation to be the actual musical content of a passage, prior personal experiences, and extra-musical associations based on the programmatic content of a composition or on the player's own imagination. These images are realized in performance in two primary ways. The image may serve as a reference to be matched or to evoke a mood or atmosphere which becomes part of the substance of the musical expression for the individual player.

Players routinely use imaging strategies to arrive at an individualized interpretation of specific passages. One characteristic comment is made by a player who goes through a passage in his mind "to clarify a phrase. I'll go over it and I'll think about it many times and then . . . I'll try to realize [on the instrument] what I've arrived at in my mind" (PK). Other players strive to connect images of prior personal experiences to specify musical compositions to aid in creating the proper mood, feeling, or atmosphere to give them an added level of inspiration in performance. One player comments:

> Every piece we play has some [connection] like that. And if you haven't had something definite in your background for it, you have to substitute something from your imagination . . . I don't think any of us would be playing in a group like this if we didn't have that kind of resource . . . . You've got to have something here to feed into you to tell a story. (AH)

Other players rely on the programmatic content of a piece of their response to the musical content of that piece to help them or their expression or interpretation of the meaning of the work. One characteristic comment follows: "In almost every piece you can find some extramusical programmatic influence . . . and even if you put one in that's not there [as intended by the composer], if it makes you project something of that piece, it's better" (DY).

Mental Rehearsal

The great majority of players in the study regard mental rehearsal as a useful tool in practice and performance situations. Perhaps the most significant point is the way that musicians use their imagination to make practice a surrogate for performance. The majority of players use their imagination to create the atmosphere or ambience of performance whenever they pick up their instruments. One of the most convincing statements on this issue was made by a horn player who said, "I never practice, I only perform" (DC). What he means by this is that he plays his best under the stress of an important performance so he views practice as an extention of the performing atmosphere. These players visualize themselves in the concert hall as they practice--they hear accompaniments, interludes, and introductions in their minds--some see a visual image of the full score as they practice to help them hear the other parts or instruments involved. One player makes a telling comment on hearing mentally the whole of a piece based on years of orchestral experience: "I can't play a symphonic passage anymore without hearing the orchestra. The sound of what is going on in the rest of the orchestra is in my imagination" (VC).

Another player comments on the importance of this phenomenon when he states that hearing the whole of a composition as one practices adds to the musical depth of the practical experience.

Some players actually use imagery to replicate the conditions of an important recital or audition to help them deal with the extra amount of stress or anxiety involved. One player uses guided imagery as meticulously as possible as he visualizes himself in performance or audition situations:

> I try to do it as realistically as humanly possible. I try to feel everything that I would be feeling, but I do it in a very positive sense. I will try to feel very at ease playing the instrument. I'll try to feel extremely comfortable going over the more difficult passages--having them float out exactly the way I want them to happen musically--hearing it--hearing the sound (RG).

The use of mental rehearsal during performance also seems to be a significant factor in improving accuracy and consistency for many players. Musicians image the way they want a passage or phrase to sound a moment before playing it and they report that this is a valuable tool for them in performance: "I'm almost reproducing what I'm playing in my mind. It's like I'm singing along. If I don't hear it or conceptualize it in my brain, there's no way I'm going to get it--especially on the horn" (PL).

The general feeling among the musicians in this sample was that mental rehearsal has tremendous potential for them and they use it as part of their practice and performance regimen.

DANCERS/CHOREOGRAPHERS

The study on how choreographers use imagery in their work represents the initial dance/movement investigation and was limited to a sample size of six, five women and one man. The findings appear to be as rich as those of the various two studies. These six choreographers, all of whom are or were professional dancers, use mental imagery as they develop their dance pieces and as they train their dancers to perform their works. Interestingly, because the art of choreography is a creative art (in this case creating dances), but also one that results in a creation to be performed, choreographers seem to use imagery in ways that resemble both the visual artists and musical performers previously discussed. Because the initial investigation of choreographers was limited to six, case study (not the presentation and discussion of categories identified across the interviews) seems the most appropriate format. Three case studies were selected as representative. These case studies provide a sense of the artistic choreography process, demonstrate some of the emerging categories, and suggest the potential of the larger investigation currently being conducted.

As a group, the choreographers seem particularly immersed in the use of mental imagery, perhaps even more than the other two groups of artists. All the choreographers demonstrate almost total recall of early dance experiences, either as participants or audience members. As the choreographers were recalling the dances they had performed or created, they gestured wildly; during every interview, the subjects rose and demonstrated at least once, usually more than once. Not surprisingly, both as dancers and as choreographers, the subjects depend to a great extent on their kinesthetic images, but do also store and retrieve images that are auditory, visual, or tactile. Surprisingly, however, the sample was evenly divided in terms of their dependence on the here-and-now stimulation of music. Three dancers found music essential; three found music to be at odds with both internal and external manipulation within their creating process. The elements of movement--space, force, body, and time--provide each choreographer with a way to store, retrieve, and manipulate their images. Imagery also seems to be an important component in rehearsal preparation and relaxation, and in alleviation of performance anxiety.

MM: Working from the Outside In

MM is an example of a choreographer who works from the outside in. She views her dances as paintings and her stage as a canvas. Yet she feels that very little of her life outside the studio has an effect on her dance-making except when a particularly stimulating object or person in the "outside world" grabs her attention. MM can in fact trace a dance piece back to its here-and-now source; during the interview MM described particular slipcovers and pictures that stimulated some finished pieces. In describing her processes, MM often feels distant from what she does. Often she explains "my body would take me over." Also, she relates that she needs music or dancers present to get her going. And when things are slowing down, MM brings in costumes or plays the music (which, by the way, she never introduces in the rehearsal until late in the process) to help both her and the dancers "perk up."

Although she has always danced, MM did not originally study to be a dancer. In fact, she earned a B.S. degree in Anthropology from the University of Massachusetts. She studied with both Martha Graham and Erick Hawkins, both of which she feels greatly influenced her work. She has danced with major dance companies in New York. Her works have been shown in New York City and throughout New Jersey. MM is in her mid-forties, small but with a perfect trim and muscular figure, and is blond. She is internally intense, but to the casual observer appears to be extremely relaxed.

During the early part of the interview, MM describes her rich childhood fantasy life and her dance training and performance, usually in one breath. Many of her early fantasies involve rich detailed dance theatre pieces in which she played "a female Tarzan or a princess" who saved all her pets. These fantasies were always acted out for herself or for anyone who would watch: "I was always the star of these little games . . . I would get scarves and put them all over my body and dance around upstairs." Creating and performing dances has always been an important part of MM's life.

Perhaps because she feels distanced from her work, MM is able to describe all her pieces and to chronicle the manner in which she developed these pieces. When questioned about what she did as a child, or early in her career, or most recently, MM places herself into that particular moment and performs and describes what happened. Many times during the interview, MM would rise and demonstrate a pattern or a method of training. For example, early in her career, MM explains that she needed to "drag dancers through the choreographic process with me" because she had difficulty creating the piece in her mind's eye. Currently, however, MM feels she has remediated to some extent her blurry mental picture and can manipulate the dancers on the stage in her mind's eye. She describes how she sees her pieces: "I visualize what they're going to look like on that stage or in a space . . . . But they're never quite completed." MM still believes she must complete her imaging through some external manipulation with the dancers present. In describing what she wants to the dancers, MM tells them more than shows them.

MM is able to work this way in part because she allows her dancers to become part of the creative team and gives up some control to them. In a manner similar to the visual artists previously described, MM empowers her dancers to be "translators of images . . . . When I see their translation, it's better than what I've imagined." Nevertheless, there are some aspects of the dance that cannot be changed by the dancers; these aspects have to do with the strong mental image that is often discounted by MM (who believes she always works externally), yet sparks much of her work:

> It was that it didn't look like what I thought it should look like . . . . But I always would pick out when people changed things . . . . I'd never remember the steps. It was the picture. The picture wasn't right. Whatever they had done didn't fit into the picture.

When MM watches her dancers, she describes a new image that she records, one that seems to be what artists often refer to as a conceptual image: "But when I watched them as a whole, the whole dance becomes an image. I don't see it in bits and pieces." Also, MM knows when she is ready to start a new piece because she begins to pay less attention to the current dance and more to a future one: "One of the keys to me that the piece is almost ready is that I begin thinking about another piece. That has seemed to happen every time to me."

MM keeps a detailed notebook, one that is important to her work but one that she never reconsults. It seems that the act of writing helps her record her images:

> I always take the book with me and write things down . . . . I think I wrote down the title <u>Slipcovers</u> somewhere in the book. But I didn't have [a heading entitled] "new dance" and then list all these things, but I can pull up the name of the music and the costuming.

MM believes that she doesn't have a very good memory, yet describes how she is able to retrieve an image when necessary, utilize various strategies with the image, and then return her image to her storehouse for future use: "Just as I'm talking to you now, I'm taking it out right now. What I've had to do with it is push it to the back of my head because I knew it wouldn't be ready for this concert . . . . I may not be ready for June either." Most of these images are visual ones, not kinesthetic images.

Interestingly, MM describes how she is able to challenge the dimensions of time and space through her ability to work simultaneously in two places and in two times. A non-intellectual, MM could rival Einstein in her simple but profound description of her imagination relativity concept:

> I don't visually step out of myself and there's my one seeing the whole and then there's me the director of the dance. No, they're one. Yet inside they're two. I can be working with a dancer and I can also see, and it's not in my peripheral vision I don't think, but I can see what's going to happen over there. Or at least I can imagine. If I'm working with this dancer here, I'm also imagining where that dancer is going to fit in over there.

Two final imagery-related issues worthy of mention in MM's process relate to her almost total visual recall of almost every dance she's done: "I think if I were to sit quietly, I could phrase every dance that I ever did, even the ones I didn't like," and to how she feels when she watches what she's choreographed: "They do have a life of their own. Those that work, the pieces that work have a life of their own. I never get tired of watching them because of that life of their own."

MPR: Kinesthetic Imagery Shapes Her Work

In some ways MPR works very differently than MM does; in other ways they are very similar. MPR relies much more on her storehouse of kinesthetic images; her interview is filled with references to muscles and physical descriptions of style. Auditory images are mentioned during the interview as well. MPR believes that her whole life affects her work: everything she sees or experiences is stored for the purpose of making dances. Interestingly MPR shares MM's lack of ability to manipulate images internally, but she remediates this lack somewhat differently. Like MM, MPR likes to "see it on the dancers," but she also can use her reflection in the mirror to "see how it looks and feels." Like MM (and indeed like all the other choreographers in the sample), essential aspects of the stimulating image are sacrosanct and cannot be changed.

MPR studied dance since she was five, but did not earn a college degree in dance. Upon completion of college, she received a scholarship to study at the Merce Cunningham School in New York City. She has performed with several professional companies in New York and has co-founded and is principal choreographer of a professional dance company in New Jersey. MPR received a choreographic fellowship from the New Jersey Council on the Arts. Her work has been performed throughout New Jersey, Pennsylvania, Connecticut, as well as in New York City. MPR is extremely tall, with a pear-shaped body, and blondish brown hair. She is in her mid-thirties and is usually described as "quiet" or "soft-spoken."

MPR has almost total recall of her first dance experience. When asked about her first performance, MPR explains, "I remember it exactly," and stands and recreates a five year old's rendition of Ball and the Jack in charmingly accurate detail. MPR also describes the dance studio where she first studied, particularly the photos and drawings of dancers which covered the walls of the stairway. As she speaks, she stands and walks up these stairs and looks from side to side, describing each photo, one by one.

Interesting are MPR's discussions of her kinesthetic images and related kinesthetic notions: "I've had so much movement in and out of my body in the last ten years."

One of MPR's favorite turns of phrase is "muscle memory," which seems to connote how muscles have memories which are not always available to the consciousness of the choreographer or dancer. MPR describes how steps come back to her during the choreography process, even without her knowing the source or even how to call it to come to her. "That whole thing sort of starting clocking in again. There's a lot of ballet in there, and there's a lot of just--various things that pop up and I'm not conscious of doing anything."

Sometimes seeing the step executed by another dancer startles MPR and makes her aware of having seen or done the step previously: "But then when I give it to somebody and I see it, there it is again.

Another interesting kinesthetic imagery-related term used by MPR is "conscious quote," which is how she refers to the conscious imitation of one choreographer's kinesthetic style and dance patterns by another choreographer. MPR uses the term "misquotes" when referring to a choreographer's use of another's style that doesn't look right with aspects of the piece, i.e., "they're never going to look the same on people in sneakers."

MPR begins the dance creation process with a "road map," a very physical/kinesthetic idea. This road map comes from the music, more in terms of numbers of sections and nature of the passages than from the melody itself. MPR doesn't believe she is good at discriminating "tunes," but "what I do think I do hear pretty well is the impulse of the music. It doesn't need to be a specific xerox of what's going on musically." In fact, MPR's dancers often perform the final piece to an entirely different musical composition.

Both mirrors and videos are mentioned many times during the course of the interview. Because she feels she is not good at seeing visual images, and also because primarily kinesthetic images shape her creations, MPR uses mirrors and videos as "diagnostic tools." Both the mirror and the video tape help her know what the piece looks like because she believes she is unable to know from her vantage point inside herself. For similar reasons, MPR often calls in a respected colleague to view the dance piece in progress and evaluate the piece, not really in terms of its artistic merit, merely in terms of what elements of dance were used. The effect is important to MPR who makes dances "for the audience to see."

Much of MPR's interview focuses on the central-image--the one that stimulates the dance in progress and the one that is critical for the dancers in the piece to master. When communicating this image to her dancers, MPR often demonstrates and touches various parts of her dancers' bodies, unlike MM who talks to them about what to do. MPR allows her dancers to change some aspects of the dance, but is quite clear about which parts must remain: "But there are other pieces of that work and they could be very tiny, little parts, but there are certain parts that I'm just adamant about. I think those are the ones that tend to be the images I started with."

During the interview, MPR was particularly passionate about one particular moment in her recent piece:

> She's walking up the staircase and they turn around. And then she walks up the staircase and then she kind of peels off. We spend an inordinate amount of time working on that. Just over and over. But I had a very clear idea of what I wanted that to be like and I just wasn't going to turn it into something different.

The following passage describes how dancers "misquote" a choreographer's work-in-progress because they are unable to see what is being shown them in the here-and-now and pull from a repertoire of previous kinesthetic images from the past:

> Certain people just see more clearly than others. I think that's a tremendous boon to a choreographer to . . . see what you're [really] doing rather than to see it through the biases of your own technique or the last dance you were in.

MPR goes on to explain what she would say to remediate such a dancer:

> This I'm telling you because I'm the choreographer. I gave you X and you're not doing X, you're doing something that you do all the time, which is a little bit like X but it's not what I asked you to do. Now look at it again and this time do what I'm showing you.

One certainly has the sense that no one misquotes MPR's kinesthetic style.

Unlike MM, who feels (rightly or not) that her life is little affected by her work as a choreographer, MPR believes that she looks at the world entirely differently because she is a choreographer:

> Like I'm fascinated by this completely mundane thing that's probably the sort of thing that eight year olds are intrigued by. But I love it when you're driving down the street and there's somebody walking down the street towards you and you kind of get a glimpse of them but there's like a tree in between so you can't see them the whole thing . . . you're going this way and they're going that way and the tree is consistently intervening. I just love it when that happens.

Statements like this certainly suggest that MPR has developed a particularly rich way to see and record what happens, but also has cultivated an attitude that cannot help but stimulate the development of even more valuable mental imagery skills.

GD: Transforming Life Into Art

Of the three dancer/choreographers presented here, GD has had the most illustrious career to date, but she also has been working professionally at least 20 years longer than the other two. GD has enjoyed great success not only in classical and modern dance, but also in choreographing dance pieces for Broadway muscals. A native of Argentina, where she trained originally, GD has also trained in Europe and in America, where she worked with such greats at Merce Cunningham, Martha Graham, Bob Fosse, and Michael Bennett. GD has received a Tony for dances that she created. Although in her late forties, GD looks much younger; she is thin and short and dark; GD is extremely animated and intense.

GD began her professional dance training at seven; she relates how the selection process to be chosen as a student in the ballet academy was extremely competitive but exciting. Since that first exposure, GD was and continues to be compelled by the wonder and power of the dance studio:

> You look into a ballet studio, you see the mirrors, too, reflecting the mirrors, reflecting the stage. As a child, the perception is not like the adult that understands it's this big room and then a mirror. I looked at that and something in me wanted to control the stage and just go through the mirror. It was instant love.

In fact, dance and performance is so central an issue go GD's life that she carries with her "a little proscenium stage, little lights, in my head . . . . it's a tiny little thing, always there, even if I'm sitting in a house." GD overlays this proscenium on everything that she observes in the here-and-now. Everything is viewed, noted, and saved "for the purpose of calling up" for future dance pieces. Yet, GD admits that she doesn't keep a journal or even write the ideas down. Yet she believes that "when you need it, somehow it will come up, you know . . . . I think if the need is there, it will jump in the foreground if it is the right thing."

The ability to store, retrieve, and remember images is natural and easy for GD. GD moves so easily and uses imagery so naturally that while in her presence it seems as if all the world (and certainly the person she is addressing) possesses these wonderful abilities: "Oh yes, I remember many performances of dance that are so clear and fresh in my mind, it's like being yesterday . . . . Don't you?"

The mirror that GD observed during her first dance class has also accompanied her and may even be more powerful a central life image than is the proscenium stage. From the time GD was seven until she was unable to dance at about age 35, the reflection in the mirror was more important to GD than her real self. Only recently has GD re-entered herself and allowed herself to view herself and her work from inside herself. The dependence that GD describes is similar to the way in which MPR feels about her reflection, but much more intense:

> As a dancer, you start. You look at yourself in the mirror. You're seeing yourself from every single angle. So you're constantly, constantly aware of your body and your face and your everything. At thirty-five, I became a choreographer and as a choreographer, I turned away from the mirror to look at the dancers and from then on, I don't look at myself anymore. So it's always them. It's always the world . . . . Then I was the instrument of another person, another [GD]. Now I feel and Now I see.

During the interview GD described a recent experience of choreographing a piece that seemed to reach many of her goals. Among other things, the piece demonstrated the integration of a variety of musical and childhood images and the cultivation of an intensely integrated dance ensemble. It received enormous critical acclaim. GD believed that the piece had a life of its own and lived outside her, almost as a baby would. She describes its early existence: "It started saying, 'I need this. This ain't working' . . . . So the piece is telling you, 'This is not right.' It might not say what is right. You have to have the answer." GD went on to relate stage picture after stage picture; the piece seemed to exert a powerful force in the room. Then, because of some legal negotiation concerning the rights to various aspects of the piece, GD explained that the piece had to close. In her discussion of it, GD personifies the piece, framing its early closing in terms more typically used to describe the premature death of a child: "It was like it came out, breathed for six weeks, and died. Not died, was killed." Even though GD had grappled with ephemeral nature of the art of dance quite early in her career, she believed that this particular piece could be all hers, yet exist outside her, and without her, and deserved to live a longer natural existence. Without question, GD's ability to imagine that her dance piece was her child suggests the powerful imaging that goes on for GD, both in and out of the studio.

As a way of concluding the interview, when GD was asked if she needed to mentioned any final imagery-related issue of importance to her work, GD asked if she could describe a childhood game that she played with her young aunt. GD believed that this game marks the beginnings of her creative process, one that combined "music, imagination pictures, acceptance, and movement":

> When I was a young kid, about the time I was five or six years old, it must have been because I don't think I had started dancing yet--my aunt loved classical music. She used to put a record or a radio on and we used to sit on the floor or lie down on the floor. And she had a game that we would play. She'd say, "Close your eyes and tell me what you see." I'd lie there and listen to the music and say, I see a rabbit running through the fields. And that was the beginning.

CONCLUSION

In summary, all of the visual artists, musicians, and choreographers were eager to talk about their creative processes. What they talked about showed a real understanding about how imagination contributes to the paintings or dances that they create or the music they perform. In every case, these artists use general imaging strategies in creating and/or performing. They form or recall images from a storehouse of past experiences, manipulate these images through a variety of imaging strategies, and create new imagination images which can become externalized in paintings, dances, or through performance. These artists draw on a wide repertoire of experiences from everyday life as well as from their professional training and artistic careers.

Certainly the overall notion that imagination drives art-making bonds these three groups of artists together. Without question, the three groups share imagery-related strategies and procedures. Yet the dissimilarities among groups are also striking, particularly when one group is described immediately after the other, as they are here. The visual artists seem to be on a discovery search, striving to find the perfect image that can be captured on canvas forever. The brass players strive to use their instruments to match the perfect sound heard inside their heads, which represents the sublime interpretation of a composer's intent. The dancers seek to place what is inside their bodies outside their bodies so that it can be placed on and in another dancer's body and be received for a brief moment in time by an audience. When framed in this manner, what these artists do through and with their imaginations seem to be completely unrelated.

Of course, researchers who study artists, and certainly artists, would agree that it is the underlying power of art--making it and performing it--that draws artists of all kinds together. The inner and outer world at large provide art-makers and performers with the images that are the sources for art. The nature, the form, the elements, and the principles of each art form change and modify these images, but the same central image can stimulate art-making in any of the art forms discussed. The overall goals of this package of studies conducted at Rutgers, and of the future investigations already begun there, is to understand those imagery-related procedures that are the same or similar across art forms, to delineate those imagery-related phenomena that are unique to each art form, and finally, to describe the imagery-related characteristics that are unique to a single individual art-maker, more an aspect of personality than a characteristic of art form.

REFERENCES

Einhoven, J. E. & Vinacke, W. E. (1952). Creative processes in painting. Journal of General Psychology, 47, 139-164.

Lindauer, M. S. (1983). Imagery and the arts. In A. A. Sheihk (Ed.), Imagery: Current theory, research, and application. New York: Wiley.
Patrick, C. (1937). Creative thought in artists. Journal of Psychology, 4, 35-73.
Roe, A. (1975). Painters and painting. In I. A. Taylor & J. W. Getzels (Eds.), Perspectives in creativity. Chicago: Aldine.
Rosenberg, H. S. & Pinciotti, P. (1983). Imagery in creative drama. Imagination, Cognition, and Personality, 3(1), 69-76.
Rosenberg, H. S. (1987a). Creative drama and imagination. New York: Holt, Rinehart, and Winston.
Rosenberg, H. S. (1987b). Visual artists and imagery. Imagination, Cognition, and Personality, 7(1), 77-93.
Trusheim, W. H. (1987). Mental imagery and musical performance: An inquiry into imagery use by eminent orchestral brass players in the United States (Doctoral dissertation, Rutgers, The State University of New Jersey, 1987). Dissertation Abstracts International, Pub. No. 88-08237.

DREAMJOURNEYS: USING GUIDED IMAGERY AND TRANSFORMATIONAL FANTASY WITH CHILDREN

Isabella Colalillo-Kates

The Rainbow Light & Co.
Toronto, Ontario M6E 2N7 Canada

ABSTRACT

A child's early formative years are characterized by a harmonious blend of cognitive and affective learning strategies. Reverie and analysis are woven into the emerging brain processes and are not separate.

Hemispheric dominance, in which one of the brain hemispheres becomes stronger than the other, appears to establish itself, in most children, as they are exposed to people or environments where learning is highly controlled.

In the modern school system cognitive learning strategies dominate over affective learning styles. This leads us to consider whether, in fact, many of the children who do not function well in school are suffering from displaced hemispheric orientation (split brain/psyche).

There is growing evidence that learning blocks in both children and adults are rooted in an inherent imbalance between the cognitive and affective learning capabilities associated with left and right brain hemispheres.

The introduction of imagery and visualization into the learning strategies of young children and young people results in a reestablishment of contact and interaction between the two brains. Imagery techniques assist children in coping with low self-esteem, in reducing phobias and fear, in redirecting thought processes which have become stuck, and ultimately in renegotiating power for the child in terms of his/her learning. Empowerment and clarity are the natural outcomes of this type of affective learning strategy.

THE MODERN LEARNING ENVIRONMENT

The common learning environment promoted by the current definition of education, largely views learning as a process in which cognitive functions are productive and affective functions are not. A child who daydreams is considered lazy, while one who applies his/her time to ready-made information is viewed as a hard worker. Add to this the notion that a child is part of an economic system which expects to use him/her when education has stuffed the child/adult with enough information, we realize why our system of education prefers to stay with left hemispheric orientation.

The true meaning of education has been lost. Education which means to lead out, is an act of birth or midwifing the human mind into its full potential. The current application of education (for the past several thousand years actually), simply wants to produce a workable social unit which can be manipulated, controlled and submerged to the greatest "good." This kind of education is largely concerned with "exterior" knowledge, which can be codified, quantified, measured and transmitted in organized systems. Knowledge of the inner sources of knowing are left to the few "genius" types, like Einstein, who defied the system of learning and who decided from an early age to link himself with his dreaming faculties as well as his analytic faculties.

As a young child enters the school system she finds that the creative learning processes are largely left untended. The task of learning becomes the chore of accumulating a lot of facts and formulae. Self-discovery and wonder remain, however, the inner processes which secretly foster the left-brain (academic) modes of learning.

It is important to begin to recognize that left brain dominance in learning produces untold stress in young children, which eventually manifests as pronounced or subtle forms of learning blocks.

When fantasy and the creative imagination fall under the despotic control of logical structures centered in one of the brain hemispheres, it results in varying degrees of physical, psychic and emotional discomfort. These blocks have many forms and many dimensions.

In the most severe cases where this displacement of brain dominance has occurred, children are labeled slow, learning disabled, emotionally disturbed, and often "unteachable" by educators. These educators themselves practice left brain dominance strategies in teaching and measure left brain competence in clustering information.

It is my thesis that one child can learn as well as any other, no matter what their hemispheric orientation, if we as educators know how to provide the child with the learning tools and strategies best suited to the child's way of learning, sensing, perceiving and storing information.

It is not the child who fails in learning, but the educator who fails in using appropriate techniques and knowledge to reach the child.

Whole brain learning modalities are proposing new methods to diagnose, address and resolve a range of learning difficulties for children and other learners.

At the root of this work is the great need for parents, educators and policy makers to work more closely together to restructure the goals, values and methods of the educative process and call on those which highlight and "bring forth" (educate) the wisdom as well as develop the intelligence of the child. This calls for a renewed spiritual integrity at the heart of our society, particularly within the core group of parents and educators working for transformative practices.

GUIDED IMAGERY

Imagery in its myriad applications is one of the easiest approaches used in wholistic diagnosis and later in remediation of split brain/psyche conditions found in children. Imagery is, of course, also irreplaceable in working with "normal" children who are ready to expand their learning and experiencing boundaries.

Imagery is useful in the identification of imbalances, such as fears, traumas and projections, and the scope to which these have interactive relationship to the larger psyche, the physical body and the body of emotions. In addition to its diagnostic function, imagery, when used more widely and tested clinically, will prove to be a clear and effortless means of exposing learning blocks and in assisting in the transformation of the imbalances.

WHEN, WHY AND HOW TO USE GUIDED IMAGERY

Guided imagery can be used with individuals and with groups. Since this form of visualization is intended to produce a particular experience and is therefore task-oriented, it is used in a number of specific ways: to teach imagery to groups, to attain specific goals, to access a particular situation, and to define the issue more clearly, to guide the individual to a point of possibilities, choices, goals, to free the individual from the burden of self, to expand boundaries of experience which can tap the past, present and/or future, to explore trauma and dreams.

These are some and certainly not all the ways which work in using the imagery modality. Imagery in education is also used successfully to develop abstract faculties of the imagination, to promote creativity and to develop along with kinesthetic techniques, the ability to develop skills (sports, music, writing, performance, recall, etc.).

TYPES OF IMAGERY EXPERIENCES WITH CHILDREN

Stories are synonymous with children and childhood. Children love stories and respond to stories which correspond to some aspect of their own reality--whether real or abstract.

In doing imagery work with children, I have discovered countless applications for the visualization work, to which "stories" children have responded enthusiastically and transformatively.

Some examples of types of imagery work are featured and others may be filled in by the reader.

Imagery used to expand and explore the child's actual or potential creativity, using visualizations calling on meeting the inner teacher, the inner artist, the inner "whatever" which would enhance the child's self-concept and self-help strategy. At the end of the visualization, a follow-up might be drawing pictures of the experience, writing a story and sharing the content highlights with the therapist/teacher or another child. Any type of activity which deepens the meaning of the inner discovery and anchors the child to the power of the image which has been contacted will have a deep transpersonal effect on the future activities of the child.

Imagery used to deepen the child's self-understanding and to help the child come to an understanding of the totality of the self, uses such fantasies as The Greatest Me, The Inner Genius, The Magic House of Answers, The Forest of Knowing Trees, The Animal Ally. My own advice on developing these types of inner dramatizations is to allow your own imagination to link in with the child and go through the experience together.

It is also useful to allow the child whatever he/she needs to become comfortable. I often allow children to image with their eyes open, or to lie or sit in whatever way is most comfortable for them. Eventually, as I work with them more and more, I attempt to gently straighten out their bodies so their spine is straight and help to induce the below conscious state by gentle balloon breathing. This induction is not necessary for such types of imagery work as Transformational Fantasy, which I will talk about later.

Imagery is also helpful in dealing with states of fear, dread and doom, sometimes related to test phobia, fear of darkness, and so on. In this work some journeys which I have found successful are The Hero Journey, in which a favorite fairy tale can be adapted to suit the child's particular needs. The Quest is another similar journey where the child meets with and successfully dispels obstacles by ingenious means. These means can be provided by the guide or worked out by the child as the fantasy progresses. In each of these journeys the guide helps the child find magical helpers, to discover or create ("it's your fantasy, what do you want the wall to do?") their own resources, weapons, tools, or whatever is necessary to overcome the actual obstacle.

At times the guide may wish to invest the child with an object such as the Vest of Confidence, the Wand of Light, the Cloak of Light (or Invisibility). These resources serve to empower and offer protection to the child, from the beginning, so that by the time the obstacle is encountered, the child knows the effectiveness of the resource and is not hesitant in overcoming the block.

If the child has problems with nightmares, then the imagery journey can parallel the dream experience, and when the ogre or monster is met, the child can find a way to use the resources in order to turn the Ogre into an Ally. The resources which the child finds in overcoming the obstacles are actually inner resources, qualities, talents and abilities which the child accepts, owns and learns to use. Once the child can do this work in fantasy situations, it becomes easier to transfer these abilities to real life.

In my experience, children can apply these abilities to finding answers to life problems, to school and friendship issues, and many other situations where problem solving requires action.

Imagery is used to explore many kinds of blocks and other forms of dis-ease, by expanding the sensorium so that the child can deal with anger, pain, frustration and other negatively stated emotions. The Journey into the Body, The Magic Apple, The Trial, The Quest, The Anger Room, The Hallway of the Mind, The Centre of All Seeing, The Rainbow Body, The Safe Place are some of the fantasy experiences designed to search out blocks and create positive strategies to achieve degrees of balance, comfort and eventually security. Once a comfort zone is established, further explorations can be made with the goal of restoring the psychophysical body to a state of control.

Educators, parents and teachers may find other applications of imagery in working with children which I have not mentioned. Certainly the scope appears to be without limits. Goal-setting, skill building and practicing new and old skills using imagery and the kinesthetic body are some of the other ways to apply imagery to education. Since imagery work is largely intuitive, openness and trust are the desired qualities with which to enter the work.

Setting the goal, identifying the issue and being flexible throughout the imagery journey are also important. This ordered sense of purpose makes relevant the intent and magnifies the scope for the dreamer, while the flexibility in changing directions, trying new things and letting the dreamer go off on his/her own experience are essential to successful work.

Whatever happens in fantasy is okay. Infusing the experience with a sense of adventure and play creates a richer framework for the experience. Starting off with a few short but engaging visualizations, especially with a new group or person, establishes trust and confidence in the process.

If imagery does not come quickly, it is necessary to first engage one of the other senses--can you smell the roses, feel the rain, touch the door-knob, and then call in a familiar scene, photograph or visual memory. This is done by saying--close your eyes--can you feel the rain? Open your eyes. What did it feel like? Close your eyes. You are walking by the ocean. Can you see it, smell it? Feel the spray? This rapid succession of open eyes and closed eyes begins the process of expanding the sensorium in those who say they can't image.

Color, sight. sound, smell, taste and touch are all pathways for accessing images. We all have ways to contact images through one or all of these senses. This is the beginning of longer journeys. Children usually do not have many problems with imagery for they are easily connected to their visual-feeling worlds.

TRANSFORMATIONAL FANTASY

Transformational Fantasy is a modality which uses imagery as an integrated diagnostic and remedial tool, developed by John T. Shaffer. Practice of TF as a therapeutic tool for self-understanding and transformation leads the "dreamer" to experience his/her own inner sage, to become involved in the drama and to reach a resolution or undergo a catharsis of the plot, through which blocked energy is released. The physical and psychic pathways are thus cleared for change.

The influence of Carl Rogers' non-directive therapy is a feature of TF and it differs from guided imagery in the sense that it evokes the "dreamer's" imagery rather than feeds the dreamer a storyline or set of images.

The facilitator or guide, who has been trained in this process, simply directs the "dreamer" to the stage, pathway or action where the drama unfolds. The "dreamer" tells his story as the process unfolds. The dreamer can find the drama in any of the ten main staging areas, and usually decides where to begin. The right brain or the left brain stages are very basic staging areas and all dreams eventually find their links here. The guide invites the dreamer to describe the nature of the symbols, the texture of the images, the props and resources found in each area, and in the pathways which link the ten stages. If links are missing, then they will be opened up as the work progresses. An integrated being is the goal of this work.

Once the "dreamer" has become familiar with the map of her inner landscape, she is invited to "go" between and among the staging areas. In the initial stages of exploration, the guide suggests that the dreamer "be" in the area. Going is a means of attaining linkage, which results in a healthier state of body/mind interaction. Blocks and imbalances reveal the absence of links and the work then becomes that of redressing these imbalances. The "star" begins to work with the symbols, the dramas and plots within each staging area using creative approaches, so that balance can prevail.

As the dreamer enters this vast framework of the inner psyche, moving through the rich and sometimes foreboding landscape, following the route of the journey, stopping to take active part in the drama, making decisions which alter the movement of the script, she discovers the wonder of her inner theatre.

The dreamer participates in scenes and acts which recall the best and the worst of ancient and modern drama, meeting personal symbols and archetypes, which are linked to outer situations in his life. As the dreamer finds and uses a variety of resources to reshape and rewrite the old scripts, new scenes are created in which the "star" assumes greater control and responsibility for the direction and outcome of the plot or drama as a whole. As the inner imagery and events come under the control of the dreamer, the transformational process is underway. Inner changes affect outer changes.

TF is being used in treating illness, neurotic and displaced behavior patterns, reverse psychological impasses, and is currently being viewed with great interest by educators. It has the capacity to be used as a diagnostic tool of great depth in discovering the root patterns of learning blocks and disabilities.

The immediate benefits of using TF with children, especially those who are having problems in school, or in relationships, as well as better adjusted children, can be seen in ease of process--children love it and do it easily; they experience renewed energy and vitality, develop self-esteem and self-acceptance, along with greater joy of learning.

The long term benefits in terms of permanent behavior reversal or redirection, reorientation of hemispheric dominance to both sides of the brain, and the mediation of learning disabilities to achieve improved performance, remain to be tested.

TF is essentially a controlled form of lucid dreaming, and as such, puts back into the "driver's seat" the driver who, for whatever reason, seems to have lost control of the vehicle of his/her body/mind/spirit.

CHILDREN AND TRANSFORMATIONAL FANTASY

Children love Transformational Fantasy because it is like an imagination game through which they can tell their own story. Children love to tell stories about themselves and what they know, think and feel. TF gives them the opportunity to do that and more--it integrates the fantastic with the real, and so doing, it reconnects them to the core of their being, which is the faculty of the creative imagination.

Balance, creativity, openness and growth become possible.

The ten staging areas are the two brain hemispheres, the center (between the two brains), the Hallway of the Mind, the Third Eye Centre, the Crown, the Sacred Centre (outside the body), the Heart Centre, the Stomach (solar plexis) Centre, and the body.

The child/dreamer enters the drama as actor, observer, sometimes editor, and often playwright. There is no induction needed for this work, as children move easily into relaxation once they have engaged with the process. There is also no need to analyze, or deepen the experience as in guided imagery. In TF the body responds effortlessly to the changing scripts, and as in Zen breathing practice, the new changes take care of the cleansing and rebalancing.

SYNOPSIS OF A CASE HISTORY

Alexandra imagines well, though not always easily. She is open to both guided imagery and TF work. She has problems in math and often finds herself feeling lost and frustrated before tests.

When we meet, we use whatever modality suits her frame of mind. She responds well to TF when she is feeling fairly centered and open and wants to work on herself. At other times she asks for guided imagery to be used so she can ground her energy. I usually begin by asking her to find and be in a place which feels very safe and comfortable. She finds such places easily.

Her favorite "safe" place has become her center, the place between the two hemispheres and she seems to prefer the TF modality mainly because she likes to go on a journey and bring back resources and gifts into the center for future use. She has brought characters, allies and props here for conferences, and then sends them back to their own places, for she views the center as "home" base for herself. This linking function demonstrates the degree of success this work has had for her.

It is useful to experience a journey with the knowledge of having resources close by or knowing where to find them when the need arises. Alexandra has discovered that when other resources can't be used, she blows away ugly images or makes them vanish by pushing buttons (many children use buttons to move through unpleasant or finished experiences). She has also discovered that a cleared or empty space can be moved so that its boundaries are joined to a pleasant space, with good imagery.

I believe that this is one of the "transformational" functions of imagery work which promotes healing and integration.

The storage of symbols in the psyche is akin to storage disks in computers. The symbols connect the organic and abstract bodies which link the body/mind systems. Alexandra is often witness to this work as it reveals itself to her. She often shouts, "Look, look. Look at what I can see!" She watches, she listens, and she speaks. The moments of listening are precious for she becomes her own witness. The moments of telling and acting are the sound which create the passion of the drama.

The verbal expression of a preverbal reality empowers the dreamer. When Alexandra says "Look, there's a bird, crying in the cage," she has touched and been compassionate with the symbol of her own pain and feeling of entrapment.

In Zen meditation the continuous and sustained act of conscious breathing is a form of processing. If one does this long enough with enough concentration, one wanders past the images of the monkey mind to reach the deep forceful reality of deep silence. No separation. The source of reintegration and Self.

For children, this place exists, often, outside their immediate reach. Children live through the mind--the upper floor of the house of being. Imagery is the interim step leading to meditation, and both have the task of lightening the load of the mind's random input by processing and sorting.

Imagery assists us in stopping and slowing down so we can "clean" house. Dis-ease and learning blocks may be a direct expression of a runaway psyche. It is the psyche which is controlled and run by its own data overload and has forgotten how to sort, store and retrieve experience in a conscious way.

As Alexandra reflects, meets with and deals with the images of her inner drama, with its stored plots and unresolved questions, she is clearing and sorting and ultimately recreating her inner self. She is also learning to find ways to unblock where blocks exist. Imagery can then be likened to a poetic as well as a meditative act.

In children, imagery and especially TF has both sides. Alexandra has become very interested in her inner world and uses her imagining time to make herself feel better and often to do other creative work. She has discovered free access to a wide and boundless space which offers endless material for reverie and self-understanding. It is a fulfilling act.

Alexandra can now move from dreams to imagery. The Hallway of the mind, which is the storage disk of subconscious memories becomes accessible in imagery work to a more manageable degree than it sometimes is in dreamwork. Everything in the Hallway coexists and is interactive. Experiences of the past are redefined in the present and all the "rooms" are in relationship to all the other rooms and to the rest of the psyche and body centers.

The role of the dreamer in fantasy work is then to find the threads linking these experience clusters and through the creative act of conscious awareness, which is offered in TF and guided imagery, to make sense or rectify the information.

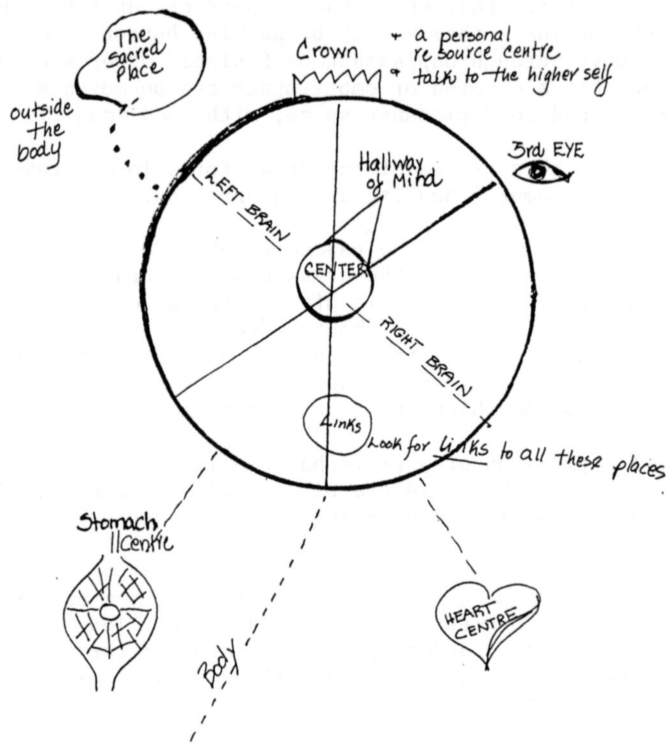

The 10 Staging areas

Left Brain
Right Brain
Centre
Hallway of the Mind
Heart Centre
Stomach Centre
Body
Sacred Place
Crown
3rd Eye Centre

- These are explored by "being" there.
- Later exploration finds or forges links, then one can "go" from place to place.
- Each person describes their personal, authentic imagery associated with each centre.

Dreamwork and Imagery work can therefore be seen as metaphors for body/mind organizing and sorting. We remove what is harmful and sustain the helpful.

Gaston Bachelard, whose fascination with the human psyche was endless, said, "I am, moreover, convinced that the human psyche contains nothing that is insignificant."

Transformational Fantasy and Imagery work have proven this to be an essential truth.

REFERENCES

Bachelard, Gaston (1969). The poetics of space. Boston: Beacon Press.

Canfield, Jack (1981). The inner classroom: Teaching with guided imagery. Holistic Education for living, A. Harris (Ed.), HOlistic Education Network.

De Bono, Edward (1985). Six thinking hats. Penguin.

Gaylean, Beverly C. (1981). Confluent teaching. Holistic Education for Living, A. Harris (Ed.). Holistic Education Network.

Grimm, Jakob, and Grimm, Wilhelm (1954). Grimm's fairy tales. New York: Nelson Doubleday.

Houston, Jean, and Masters, R. (1970). Mind games: The guide to inner space. New York: Dell.

Jacobs, Joseph. English fairy tales, 5th ed. New York: Putnam & Sons.

Katz, Isabella M. (Spring, 1987). A new age in education. Ontario's Common Ground.

Klipper, Ilse (1984). My magic garden: A meditation guide for children. Palo Alto, CA.: Pathways Press.

Miller, J hn. The compassionate teacher: How to teach with your whole self. New Jersey: Prentice Hall.

Rozman, Deborah (1985). Meditating with children: The art of concentration and centering. University of the Trees Press.

Schroeder, Lynn, and Ostrander, Sheila (1982). Superlearning. Delacorte Press.

Shaffer, John Thomas Adams. Transformational Fantasy. St. Louis: A&S Printing.

Vitale Meister, Barbara (1982). Unicorns are real: A right brain approach to learning. Rolling Hills Estates, CA.: Jalmar Press.

Zen Buddhism: An introduction with stories, parables and zen koan riddles told by Zen Masters (1959). Peter Pauper Press.

NOTIONS OF CONSCIOUSNESS AND REALITY

Imants Baruss

University of Regina

Robert J. Moore

Campion College
University of Regina

> Once we admit that the ways of reasoning vary with the ways of the reasoners, the scope for common ground seems too narrow to escape relativism, and the admission marks the fact that there are different institutions, different practices and different styles in approaching the world. Tolerance we may have, but no claim to universality for our own ways. (Newell, 1986, p. 101)

The researcher approaching the study of the nature of consciousness for the first time is often bewildered by the plethora of viewpoints and lack of consensus in this area of study. Why does this situation exist? The problem appears to lie in the disparity and incompatibility of firmly held ideas about the nature of consciousness and the manner in which it is to be studied. Many of these ideas are defended by their proponents, not only as the only legitimate ideas about consciousness, but as the only existent ones. What apears to be accepted in theory, but fails to be appreciated in practice, is the recognition that these various versions of consciousness are correlated with a given person's purported experience and their personal beliefs about the nature of reality. After briefly demonstrating the disparity of views concerning consciousness, an empirical study examining the nature of the relationship between notions of consciousness and beliefs about reality is described.

DISPARITY OF VIEWS CONCERNING CONSCIOUSNESS

It has frequently been remarked that the area of consciousness studies is in a state of confusion (e.g., Roberts, 1984; Toulmin, 1982; White, 1988). This can be demonstrated by considering some examples of statements about consciousness which illustrate the disparity of views concerning consciousness that contributes to this confusion.

James has said, "breath moving outwards, between the glottis and the nostrils, is, I am persuaded, the essence out of which philosophers have constructed the entity known to them as consciousness" (1904, p. 491). While James, at times, argued for the somatosensory reduction of subjective experiences, he nonetheless emphasized the importance of the stream of consciousness. That was not the case with Watson (1919), who dismissed consciousness altogether from the domain of scientific investigation as something that was ill-defined and unimportant. There are those who currently hold a position similar to that held by Watson, such as the eliminative materialists, who have maintained that consciousness is an archaic concept that should disappear and that all discussions of mental events should be in terms of neurophysiology (Churchland, 1983).

Most contemporary psychologists prefer to discuss consciousness in terms of information-processing (Mandler, 1985). For example, Klein has said that "equating consciousness with information dissipates the mystery associated with consciousness seen as an entity" (1984, p. 175). As an emergent property of information processing systems, consciousness is sometimes perceived as having downward causal effects (Hofstadter, 1979; Sperry, 1986, 1987).

There are also, however, more radical versions of consciousness that have consistently appeared in the literature. These versions have stressed the importance of consciousness as that which endows human life with meaning and allows for an expanded understanding of reality (Chang, 1978; Walsh, 1980). For example:

> I found myself at once identical with the Voidness, Darkness, and Silence, but realized them as utter, though ineffable, Fullness, in the sense of Substantiality, Light, in the sense of Illumination, and Sound, in the sense of pure formless Meaning and Value. The deepening of consciousness that followed at once is simply inconceivable and quite beyond the possibility of adequate representation. (Merrell-Wolff, 1973, p. 37)

Clearly such transcendent versions of consciousness conflict with the more conservative ones.

RELEVANT EMPIRICAL STUDIES IN THEORETICAL PSYCHOLOGY

There was some precedent for an empirical examination of notions of consciousness and reality. Harvey, Hunt and Schroder (1961) have discussed conceptual systems as experiential filters that serve to evaluate sensed events of the external world and that account for differences in reactions to the same situation. Coan (1968) has factor analysed the major tenets of the writings of various theorists in the history of psychology in order to uncover the underlying dimensions of their conceptual systems. Krasner and Houts (1984) expanded on Coan's work by surveying groups of psychologists with regard to their theoretical orientations, epistemological beliefs and values. Using a different instrument, similar work was carried out by Kimble (1984). Unger, Draper and Pendergrass (1986) developed an Attitudes About Reality Scale which they used with a group of college students to determine their beliefs about reality.

The literature also revealed that physicalism versus transcendentalism is a salient dimension of belief systems within the western intellectual tradition. For example, both Frank (1977) and Coan (1968) have discussed such a dimension. Osborne (1981) has stated that physical versus transcendent views of reality are reflected in approaches to consciousness.

AN EMPIRICAL STUDY OF NOTIONS OF CONSCIOUSNESS AND BELIEFS ABOUT REALITY

The present study was carried out in order to determine the correlation between notions of consciousness and beliefs about reality. This was accomplished by developing an original questionnaire and distributing it to members of the academic and professional community who would, in principle, be in a position to write about consciousness in the academic literature.[1]

The questionnaire itself was developed in three stages. In the first stage, 150 articles and books were read which contained discussions of consciousness. This led to the development of a 158 item Preliminary Questionnaire comprised of statements about consciousness reflecting the literature reviewed. This questionnaire was then administered to a small sample of faculty and students in order to determine which statements about consciousness were meaningful to an academically sophisticated population.

On the basis of an analysis of the responses to the Preliminary Questionnaire, a Pilot Questionnaire was constructed for use in the second stage of the research. This questionnaire contained, in addition to a number of the statements from the Preliminary Questionnaire, items that would assess a person's belief system about the nature of reality. These included statements from the following categories:

1. Epistemological beliefs: the extent to which a person felt that consciousness could be understood through a process of scientific investigation and whether they would be willing to consider alternative methodologies.

2. Ontological beliefs: the material-transcendental dimension, mind-body problem, determinism versus free will and the status of reality.

3. Religious and parapsychological beliefs.

4. The importance of meaning.

5. Values: values and attitudes toward life and death, the role of values in scientific investigation, ethical concerns in general.

6. Extraordinary experiences: whether or not a person believes that they have had inexplicable, mystical or out-of-body experiences.

7. Intolerance of ambiguity.

Extensive analysis of the results of a Pilot Study with 72 academics, students and mental health workers led to the development of a Survey Questionnaire to be employed in the third stage of the study.

The final version of this Survey Questionnaire was distributed widely to academics and professionals in Canada and the United States. Forty-two percent of 334 respondents who completed the Survey Questionnaire identified themselves with the discipline of Psychology, 12 percent with Physics, and six percent with Philosophy. In smaller numbers, respondents who indicated affiliation with Computer Science, Psychiatry and Religious Studies, as well as other disciplines, also participated.

RESULTS OF THE SURVEY OF NOTIONS OF CONSCIOUSNESS AND BELIEFS ABOUT REALITY

The data from the completed Survey Questionnaires were cluster and

---

[1] Details of the development and implementation of the questionnaire, as well as the results, can be obtained from the authors.

factor analyzed, with factor scores being calculated for each of the factors and used in bivariate analyses with demographic data and endorsed statements about consciousness. These analyses resulted in the identification of three major positions or aggregates of beliefs regarding the nature of consciousness and reality: a materialist position as well as positions of conservative and extraordinary transcendence.

The materialst position is characterized generally by a physicalist-scientific approach. Adherents of such a point of view were less likely to be religiously affiliated, more inclined to think that only that exists which is physically real, and that science is the only way to acquire knowledge concerning reality. The notions of consciousness articulated within this position represent consciousness as an emergent property of sufficiently complex neural systems, or define it in terms of information processing. In addition, consciousness is characterized by intentionality, that is, consciousness is always of or about something.

Two separate constructs define the position of conservative transcendence: religiosity and meaning. Persons exhibiting this position emphasized the importance of religious beliefs, such as the belief in a Creator or belief in life after death, or would contend that meaningfulness in life cannot be accounted for solely in physical or scientific terms. Such people indicated an affiliation with the traditional religions of Judaism or Christianity, with a dualist perspective on the mind-body problem and a belief that human knowledge is not exhausted by scientific inquiry. Consciousness is characterized by subjectivity and is that which gives meaning to life as well as evidence of a spiritual dimension within each person.

The extraordinarily transcendent position entails three constructs: extraordinary experiences, extraordinary beliefs, and inner growth. Individuals exhibiting such a system of beliefs were more likely to claim to have had extraordinary experiences such as mystical or out-of-body experiences and to have changed their ideas about life dramatically in the past. Extraordinary beliefs included beliefs in a universal consciousness and reincarnation. Inner growth was indexed by an aggregate of statements that emphasize introspection and personal transformation. Persons tending towards this position were more likely to have their own religious beliefs, to believe that physical reality is an extension of mental reality, and that insight into the nature of reality can be achieved through extrasensory perception and modes of understanding that are superior to rational thought. This viewpoint is associated with a stress on altered states of consciousness, the contention that consciousness is an unbounded, transcendent reality, and that it is the key to personal self-transformation.

CONCLUSIONS AND IMPLICATIONS

There are a number of comments that one can make about these findings. To begin with, it is clear that the disparity of notions concerning consciousness is not a superficial phenomenon, but one which reflects a heterogeneity concerning deeper, more fundamental beliefs about reality generally. While such differences of opinion are not of vital importance in many areas of research, they are pivotal in the study of human consciousness in that they lead to radically different versions of consciousness. Because of this, a specific investigator's beliefs about reality must explicitly be taken into account in any research concerning consciousness.

A second comment concerns the incidence and impact of extraordinary experiences. Of the total number of respondents, 53 percent claimed to have had experiences that science cannot explain, 47 percent indicated that they had had transcendent or mystical experiences, and 23 percent that they had had out-of-body experiences. These proportions are not inconsistent with the high incidence of extraordinary experiences found within the general population (e.g., Greeley, 1987). While it is known that claims to mystical experiences subsume a variety of actual experiences (Thomas & Cooper, 1980), the consequence of such experiences for any given individual appears to be the same: an inclination towards a transcendentalist position concerning the nature of reality. As Ring has noted for the particular case of near-death experiences:

> NDErs almost universally allege to have lost all fear of death <u>and</u> to be convinced that the end of life is anything but. Death, they say, as in a single voice, is but a transition into a higher, transcendental realm of being. There is no death. (1987, p. 172)[2]

It seems that those who claim to have had unusual experiences are sufficiently convinced of their validity in order to alter their beliefs about reality.

As a final comment, this study extends and further clarifies previous empirical work in the psychological literature. Conceptual systems such as those discussed by Harvey, Hunt and Schroder (1961) could be identified in this study. Consistent with the ideas of Frank (1977) and Osborne (1981), the physical-transcendental dimension turns out to be central in understanding the range of positions with regard to consciousness. This same dimension, found by Coan (1968) and suggested by the results of the studies of Krasner and Houts (1984) and Kimble (1984) within the psychological community is supported by this research in that such a dimension is revealed here to be operative for a more general academic and professional population. The present study also extends aspects of Unger, Draper and Pendergrass' (1986) work in two ways: (a) the Survey Questionnaire had a more thorough set of items concerning philosophical issues than Unger, Draper and Pendergrass' Attitudes About Reality Scale; and (b) the subject population for this study consisted of highly educated academics and professionals rather than college students. As in the case of Unger, Draper and Pendergrass' work, the results of this study demonstrate that factors involving the personal are correlated with ideological positions.

AUTHORS NOTES

This research was carried out by the first author at the University of Regina in partial fulfillment of the requirements for the degree of Doctor of Philosophy in Psychology.

Financial support was received from the Faculty of Graduate Studies and Research, University of Regina, and from King's College, University of Western Ontario, for the first author, and from the University of Regina, President's Fund, and Campion College, University of Regina, for the second author.

The authors gratefully acknowledge the assistance of Dr. P. Herman and Dr. R. Morecock in the distribution of the Survey Questionnaire, and Lea Nevett in typing the final draft of the manuscript.

The first author is currently a Lecturer in Psychology at King's College, University of Western Ontario. The second author is an Associate Professor of Psychology at Campion College, University of Regina.

---

[2] A NDEr is a person who claims to have had a near-death experience.

REFERENCES

Chang, S. C. (1978). The psychology of consciousness. American Journal of Psychotherapy, 32, 105-116.

Churchland, P. S. (1983). Consciousness: The transmutation of a concept. Pacific Philosophical Quarterly, 64, 80-95.

Coan, R. W. (1968). Dimensions of psychological theory. American Psychologist, 23, 715-722.

Frank, J. D. (1977). Nature and functions of belief systems--Humanism and transcendental religion. American Psychologist, 32(7), 555-559.

Greeley, A. (1987). The "impossible": It's happening. Noetic Sciences Review, 2, 7-9.

Harvey, O. J., Hunt, D. E., & Schroder, H. M. (1961). Conceptual systems and personality organization. New York: Wiley & Sons.

Hofstadter, D. R. (1979). Godel, Escher, Bach: An eternal golden braid. New York: Basic.

James, W. (1904). Does "consciousness" exist? The Journal of Philosophy, Psychology and Scientific Methods, 1(18), 477-491.

Kimble, G. A. (1984). Psychology's two cultures. American Psychologist, 39,(8), 833-839.

Klein, D. B. (1984). The concept of consciousness--A Survey. Lincoln: University of Nebraska.

Krasner, L. & Houts, A. C. (1984). A study of the "value" systems of behavioral scientists. American Psychologist, 39(8), 840-850.

Mandler, G. (1985). Cognitive psychology--An Essay in cognitive science. Hillsdale, N.J.: Lawrence Erlbaum.

Merrell-Wolff, F. (1973). The philosophy of consciousness without an object--Reflections on the nature of transcendental consciousness. New York: Julian.

Newell, R. W. (1986). Objectivity, empiricism and truth. London: Routledge & Kegal Paul.

Osborne, J. (1981). Approaches to consciousness in North American academic psychology. The Journal of Mind and Behavior, 2(3), 271-291.

Ring, K. (1987). Near-death experiences: Intimations of immortality? In J. S. Spong (Ed.), Consciousness and survival: An interdisciplinary inquiry into the possibility of life beyond biological death. Sausalito, CA.: Institute of Noetic Sciences.

Roberts, T. B. (1984). The concept state-of-consciousness and an SOC model of psychology. Unpublished manuscript, Northern Illinois University, Department of Learning, Development & Special Education, DeKalb.

Sperry, R. (1986). The new mentalist paradigm and ultimate concern. Perspectives in Biology and Medicine, 29(3), Part 1, 413-422.

Sperry, R. W. (1987). Structure and significance of the consciousness revolution. The Journal of Mind and Behavior, 8(1), 37-65.

Thomas, L. E. & Cooper, P. E. (1980). Incidence and psychological correlates of intense spiritual experiences. The Journal of Transpersonal Psychology, 12(1), 75-85.

Toulmin, S. (1982). The genealogy of "consciousness." In P. F. Secord (Ed.), Explaining human behavior. London: Sage.

Unger, R. K., Draper, R. D., & Pendergrass, M. L. (1986). Personal epistemology and personal experience. Journal of Social Issues, 42(2), 67-79.

Walsh, R. N. (1980). The consciousness disciplines and the behavioral sciences: Questions of comparison and assessment. American Journal of Psychiatry, 137(6), 663-673.

Watson, J. B. (1919). Psychology from the standpoint of a behaviorist. Philadelphia: J. B. Lippincott.

White, P. A. (1988). Knowing more about what we can tell: "Introspective access" and causal report accuracy 10 years later. British Journal of Psychology, 79, 13-45.

THE METAPHOR OF PARTS OF SELF: FINDING REAL SELF AND EMERGENT IDENTITY

Don D. Rosenberg

Family Service of Milwaukee

ABSTRACT

Without fully considering its implications or possibilities, clinicians use the metaphor of "parts of self." This metaphor is useful for understanding clients with a chameleon-like self-experience of not knowing which identity represents the real self. The purpose of this paper is to explore the implications of using this metaphor and to present insights on the use of the metaphor with clients, especially those who experience rapidly shifting states of identity. In addition, a theory of emergence of self rather than the integration of self is suggested. Winnicott's concepts of true and false self and Erikson's concepts of identity and identity diffusion are used in order to examine the meaning of parts of self. Much of the data for this paper derives from the "Multiple Selves Exercise" developed by the author. This exercise and some "Identity Maps" resulting from it are explained.

Clinicians using the metaphor "Parts of self" need to know its implications and possibilities. Therapists may clarify ambivalence about suicidal thoughts: "Part of you is suicidal; part wants help." They may clarify conflict: "Part of you wants your parents' love; part is enraged with them." "Parts" can describe chameleon-like self-experience in which one cannot find a central identity separate from "parts," to know "Which self is ME?" This commonly occurs in abused children, borderlines, adolescents, children of alcoholics, and many others. "Sub-personalities" is a concept related to "parts." This paper explores a use of this metaphor based on the "Multiple Selves Exercise" (MSE) and "Identity Maps" developed by the author. Concepts of true self, false self, identity, and identity diffusion are used to explain emergence of "real self."

MEANING AND METAPHOR: TWO CONSIDERATIONS

The Significance of Part Versus Whole Self

Clinicians disagree on the importance of parts vis-a-vis the whole self. Schwartz (1987) emphasized the parts, noting different contexts bring out different competencies, affects, and ideas. For instance, "Many of us have had the experience of returning home for a family visit after a long absence and finding . . . that being with our family again shifts our whole conception of ourselves, and we're back in an old personality" (p. 27). Schwartz suggested valuing all selves, not to see only that one dimension of personality most significant to family problems. For instance, the distant side of father may be crucial to a family problem, but father's emotional side is not seen in the clinical context.

Assagioli (1965, 1974) emphasized the central self. He described "identification of the self with these changing and transient contents [of consciousness]. Thus, if we are to make self-consciousness explicit, clear, and vivid, we must disidentify ourselves from all these contents and <u>identify with the self</u>" (1974, p. 11).

Jung's (1959) "Persona" (Mask) also emphasizes the self rather than the sub-identities. The self sacrifices itself in favor of roles so that the persona is not real.

> It is a compromise between individual and society as to what a man should appear to be. He takes a name, earns a title . . . In a certain sense all this is real, yet in relation to the essential individuality of the person concerned it is only a secondary reality, . . . [in which] others often have a greater share than he. (p. 138)

Experience with the Multiple Selves Exercise confirms this emphasis on the importance of finding the "real" self, defined as the central core self, experienced as the emergent "me." It is not an integration of the false selves or the identities within a persona. It emerges from behind false selves, as if from behind a wall of defenses. It acquires an identity of its own, separate from the identity of the part or false selves. For many clients it is rarely exposed.

<u>The Prescriptive Implications of Using Metaphor</u>

Using this metaphor, the therapist needs to understand the client's self-experience and the prescriptive implications of "parts of self." Does this metaphor encourage internal unity? Does it emphasize multiplicity of selves or the central real self?

First, therapists need sensitivity to the <u>implicit prescription</u> that one part is preferred. Obsessives or borderlines provoke one into taking sides with their ambivalences or splits (i.e., different identities) over highlighting the real self around which the parts revolve, one can avoid siding with ambivalence or with one part of self against the rest. Further, one then facilitates development of the real self.

Second, the metaphor is valuable for labeling persona and bringing forth real self. For example, Phil's mood was upbeat; he cited examples of progress. Next session he was depressed, without a sense of previous success. Such a regression is often caused by a narcissistic injury, usually an error in empathy (Kohut & Wolf, 1978). The therapist had insufficiently mirrored Phil's joy in his successes. The fragmented, narcissistically wounded self of childhood was the Depressed One, labelled Hurt Little Phil. Labeling Phil's experience helped him to recognize his switch from his mirror-hungry self to his regressed self, to be in control. Partializing assisted individuation.

Third, some clients are adversely affected by such metaphors. For example, the therapist said Alice used her intellect, not her feeling side, to resolve conflict. She experienced this as a scolding rejection of her brighter identity. This fit her fear that women could not act smarter than men. Here was another male putting down women. So partializing the self had that meaning for Alice. When he emphasized the unity of the self, accepting the bright self, she was able to expose her needs and to trust the therapist as a constant holding object accepting her needs.

Fourth, consider that the metaphor may be a reified artifact or that metaphors protect therapists from swings in state, from identifying with client's helplessness. These linguistic, theoretical, or counter transference concerns must be kept in mind in the form of healthy skepticism. Regardless, client self-experience changes when described in terms of parts of self protecting a hidden real core self, as described below.

DEVELOPMENTAL THEORY OF REAL SELF

Successful Self Development

A developmental view expands the concept of parts. Self-representations develop from the primitive undifferentiated matrix of self-and-object in infancy to cohesive self with stable identity at the mature end. Body image, sense-of-self, and self-representations are integrated on the "self" side. Object constancy, identity, and mutuality are developed on the "object" side. Inner and outer, real and imaginary, past and present, I-and-you are all discriminated. One learns to tolerate love-hate feelings. In adolescence, identity emerges as self is experienced in relation to the broadened object world. Drive satisfactions strengthen the self with positive experiences of pleasure within the self and for its needs (Winnicott, 1960. A corollary is that excessive frustrations, intrusive parents violating boundaries, and excessive stimulation threaten the self and lead to distortions in self development known as "false self."

Unsuccessful Self Development

Two concepts describe incomplete development of identity, namely, "false self" and "identity diffusion." Winnicott's (1960) concept of "false self" describes the outcome in which real, core self is hidden behind defenses. Erikson's (1963, 1968) concept "identity diffusion" describes the outcome in which self-representations fail to coalesce around a core sense-of-self. Below, these concepts are examined in turn and used to describe observations of clients grappling with self-experience.

1. True and False Self

Winnicott (1960) defines "true self" in terms of early body ego experiences.

> Only the True Self can be creative and only the True Self can feel real. Whereas a True Self feels real, the existence of a False Self results in a feeling unreal or a sense of futility . . . . The True Self comes from the aliveness of the body tissues and the working of body-functions . . . . [It is not] reactive to external stimuli, but primary. (p. 148)

Parenting can either force true self underground behind false self defenses or can permit its expression. This leads to a view of parenting as observing the pace, schedule, communicative style, needs, and energy level of the baby, and to accept them, to work with qualities the child brings to life, to avoiding preconceptions of what the child needs to be, how much it needs to eat, or how soon it should count. True self comes alive through

> repeated success in meeting the infant's spontaneous gesture or sensory hallucination . . . . In the first case the mother's adaptation is good enough and in consequence the infant begins to believe in external reality . . . . The True Self has a spontaneity, and this has been joined up with the world's events . . . . In the second case, . . . the mother's adaptation to the infant's hallucinations and spontaneous impulses is deficient, not good enough . . . . The infant remains isolated. But in practice the infant lives, but lives falsely . . . seduced into a compliance, and a compliant False Self reacts to environmental demands. (pp. 145-146)

In neurosis, false self performs a defensive function of protecting the true self, which withdraws, isolated behind the false self organization. "The false-self organization may thus carry on a high level of adjustment and involvement with reality, but the true self remains hidden and withdrawn" (Meissner, 1982-83, p. 36). False self "forms a substitute way of relating to objects and dealing with the external environment that is both fallacious and unreal, and fragile . . . and may serve as a source of inner desperation and hopelessness" (p. 35). It is associated with rigid but needed defenses. "Its typical anxiety affect is threat of annihilation and its pervasive defense mechanism is staying dissociated and hidden, not repressed" (Kahn, 1972, p. 98).

Some degree of false self is inevitable. Winnicott (1960) outlined a dimension from least to greatest health. At one end, false self is identified as if real, the true self being totally hidden. At the healthy end, false self contains socially adaptive, polite, and mannered behavior, plus the organization which helps the self forego primary process and narcissistic omnipotence.

This conception of self respects the richness of identities uncovered in the Multiple Selves Exercise and the fragility and freshness of real self-experience. Further, it fits the observation that when real self appears in therapy, it is often weak, exposed, scared, and vulnerable while also omnipotent. It must resume its maturation, now re-exposed to the object world.

2. Identity

Defining Identity--The concept of "identity" overlaps the self-experience of the emergent, real self (a term here preferred to "true" self). Identity is a sense of sameness of character, of being the same person as oriented to the external world, a person with a continuity of goals and memories. Identity is more than the sum of identifications (Erikson, 1963), while false self is more or less identifications. The identity of real self cannot come from outside or from roles alone; it must emerge, unfold, as more of a given, not a thing conditioned by social relations. Real self identity is the amalgamated experience of real self-in-the-world.

Identity and Roles--Assagioli (1965, 1974) defined identity in terms of more mutable qualities which he labeled contents of consciousness, namely, the body, emotions, intellect, and roles. He designed an exercise to dis-identify from these functions and roles, and to identify with self as the experiencing consciousness. "We are dominated by everything with which our self becomes identified. We can dominate, direct, and utilize everything from which we disidentify ourselves" (1974, p. 211). In his self-identification technique, people practice these statements: "I have a body; but I am not my body. I have emotions, but I am not my emotions. I have a mind, but I am not my mind. I recognize and affirm that I am a center of will." This paper differs somewhat from Assagioli. "Identity" is not synonymous with roles or functions, but is a more inclusive concept than Assagioli defined. Further, the real self is defined as a more complete living entity than is Assagioli's self-as-consciousness. As far as it goes, however, Assagioli's exercise fits the outcome of the Multiple Selves Exercise. Clients detach from their social identities. But to say they are detaching from body, emotion, mind, and roles is insufficient to describe the broad character structures or identities from which they are individuating, here labeled false self identities.

Recently Dixon and Sands (1983) noted that peak experiences had a solid sense of identity. But Dixon and Sands moved away from the real self and emphasized psychosocial roles at the center of identity. Observations discussed below suggest the real self emerges from within and is not defined by roles. These authors are writing about the false self identities, not the real self. Like Assagioli, Dixon and Sands describe the problems of identifying with roles (i.e., false self). An identity founded on unstable identity structures is prone to identity crises. People defined

> in terms of their jobs lose a significant means of self-identification when they are unemployed. Moreover, the loss of work may suggest a greater loss reflective of the symbolic meaning of work--adulthood, responsibility to others, and status, for example. These meanings form the contours of a person's identity. (p. 227)

In summary, identity is more inclusive than psychosocial roles. False self identities can be based on identifications and roles. But real self emerges; it is not an integration of false selves, sub-personalities, roles, functions, or identifications. False self makes one unstable, crisis-prone.

Identity Diffusion--The adolescent experiences new behavior-of-the-self in relation to a more independent world, heterosexual experience, vocational activities. However, many people never finish adolescent tasks of experiencing a personal continuity in which skills, competencies, and achievements across varied contexts are seen as manifestations of self, coalescing into "identity." They have chameleon-like identity; shifts in state occur, leading to the question, "Which way I behave is really me?" People who have this difficulty feel different in different situations and wonder "Who am I?" Erikson termed this "identity diffusion." Whereas real identity is a whole, a gestalt, in which the previous parts are no longer recognizable separate gestalts, when the separate parts or identities are maintained as diffuse identities, then they function as defensive character structures (i.e., false selves). We want to reconnect the client with the center.

One addendum: often identity formation is incomplete during adolescence. It seems only in the optimal case is identity actualized. It seems that a central, unified identity--the term "unified" probably is closer to experience than is "integrated"--may take one well into the third decade or later to solidify.

3. Emergence Rather Than Integration

Identity emerges as experiencing of the continuity of real self, a recognition that the rest of the parts are not real, but are in a sense "unreal" like Jung's persona, Winnicott's false selves, Erikson's diffused identities. Clients often refer to former identities as unnecessary. Mostly, false selves are not needed in the final personality outcome (other than Winnicott's healthy false self). Jill, for instance, wanted to keep her Coquette false self. But later her real self succeeded with men in more gratifying ways than the Coquette; so she could even drop that vestige of false self.

In addition, the real self encompasses the total functions and competencies of all self. It contains self-perception, autonomous ego functions, ego awareness of drive states and needs, openness to inner and outer experience, motility and expressivity, as well as other ego and superego functions. The real self which emerges seems to amalgamate features which seem at once to be grandiose and idealized, actual and ideal, innate and learned, past and future. It is as if the real self were experienced as "me as I am most deeply, me as I wish I would let myself to be, and me as I envision my best possibilities."

"Individuation means becoming a single, homogeneous being, and, insofar as 'individuality' embraces our innermost, last, and incomparable uniqueness, it also implies becoming one's own self" (Jung, 1959, p. 143). So emergence of real self facilitates the resumption of individuation. The separation-individuation phase is when most character disorder problems arise. Exposing real self resumes development from that point (Mahler, 1972). On the other hand, since false selves contain active identifications with significant others, they maintain childhood objects, maintain conditions under which real self became hidden in the first plce. Thus, false self prevents individuation.

FOUR DEVELOPMENTAL LEVELS OF FALSE SELF IDENTITIES

"Parts of self" applies differentially along a developmental line of the self, so for different levels of self maturity and self-realness, the metaphor has different meanings. This hierarchy falls on a dimension described by the factors of needs, traumata, availability of loving objects, and internalization of loving objects.

1. Mixed feelings--One might say, "Part of me is angry at you; since you're my friend, I overlook that." Part here means only a feeling or idea out of a context of a whole attitude towards someone. The metaphor is simply symbolic language for explaining oneself. For individuated people with a sense of personal identity, "part of self" is experienced as a metaphor useful for highlighting feelings, impulses, or ideas.

2. Neurotic ambivalence--Two examples are, "Part of me is excited to be at the podium, but part is scared and wishes I were not here"; "Part of you wishes you were dead, but part of you wants to be rescued." Obsessives often assign one side of ambivalence to someone else and the two people act out the sides. For example, a therapist argues why Gill should take a job; Gill is doubtful. He projects his ambition into the therapist, who identifies with it before recognizing what is happening. Thus, Gill defeats his own threatening competitive ambitions by arguing with the therapist.

This is the common use of the metaphor of parts of self. It may be counterproductive if it defines the positions rigidly. The client needs to know both sides belong within self. Also, the therapist needs to locate the false selves who distract one from the vulnerable real self whom they protect.

It is useful to help the client own impulses as acceptable reactions. For instance, the therapist told Jane:

> The Depressed One (a false self) takes over; it is suicidal. That keeps the Hurt One from being empty and angry. You fear

she might get your Real Self rejected. When that Depressed One comes out, I comfort you; fear is soothed, and you can be real again. That sequence of Real, Hurt and Angry, Depressed, Soothed, then Real happens over and over to protect the Real Self.

The conflict between anger and fear of rejection is solved by turning against the self depressively; but these positions are solidified into false self states.

3. Fluid internal states, multiple identities--Here are mostly character disordered people aware of the split-off real self, but with many false self identities wondering "Which one is really me?" These are the ideal candidates for the Multiple Selves Exercise.

4. Dissociated selves, splitting of self--For these less individuated people, "part of self" is no mere metaphor, but a description of inner self-experience. Their splitting of the self maintains injured parts as they were at points of trauma, fixation, splitting-off, dissociation. Here we recognize the borderline, the schizoid, and many chronically sexually abused victims. It helps to locate parts of self with these people, but not to have them renounce the false selves, without which they feel overwhelming anxiety. All the fragments need holding, appreciation, acceptance until a sense of wholeness of self and objects (constancy) is sufficient to enable dis-identification of the false self parts.

For example, Mr. Poe tapped into Peter, his child self, abandoned by his family at age four, never revealed again due to his intense demands, painful aloneness, and fear of badness. Pete is a later socialized self, struggled to please his foster parents, while always feeling it was a game, never real. Pete protected Peter by denial and dissociation. Big Pete is a still later protective childhood self, embodying rage and macho toughness. Even a hint of disapproval of Pete or Big Pete aroused annihilation anxiety, the threat of Peter's demise. Then Big Pete resorted to alcohol abuse and other risky behavior. Only recognizing all three as essentially damaged children in need of soothing, wholeness, and constancy permitted Mr. Poe to remain stable and safe, to trust the positively introjected therapist-object, and to amalgamate the three selves into a real self, William, who eventually felt strong and real. Holding all the selves rather than dis-identifying from them was required here.

DIFFERENTIATING FALSE SELF FROM OTHER DISORDERS

False self identities differ from multiple personalities. The criteria for Multiple Personality Disorder (American Psychiatric Association, 1987, DSM-III-R code 300.14) require two or more personalities recurrently taking full control of the person. Each personality has unique memories, behavior, relationships. False self cases, however, do not dissociate to the point of distinct personalities, lack amnesia, do not rest control in a single part. Testing would not reveal differences among false selves, but real self and false selves might differ on mood and personality tests. False self types and multiple personalities may differ in degree or in quality.

The criteria for Identity Disorder (of adolescence, 313.82) overlap false self, yet the latter is more inclusive than the former. Criteria include distress (and social impairment) regarding uncertainty about issues relating to identity, such as long-term goals, career choice, friendships, sexual orientation, religion, moral values. Here is the person with self-doubts, asking, "Who am I?" Real self, however, does not feel such doubts.

Some false self types may have borderine qualities wherein identity confusion may be substantial and where splitting of self into good and bad occur. Self divisions are so profound (e.g., Alice, Mr. Poe) that we must work to pull selves into one; dis-identification or detachment processes are contraindicated initially. This corresponds to level four on the hierarchy above.

TECHNIQUE: MULTIPLE SELVES EXERCISE (MSE)

Goals of Exercise

The MSE helps via role playing, action, use of space, memory, and imagery to accomplish several goals:

1. Experience and label complexes of history, emotion, and behavior experienced as separate identities.

2. Heighten the unifying function of emergent real self, the unexposed self of inner self-experiencing.

3. Distance or dis-identify from regressive, neurotic selves, dropping them from the defensive pantheon, so defense of the real self is less necessary.

4. Overcome projection of part-self-images.

5. By follow-up on the exercise, solidify one's real self in all interactions.

6. Uncover the history of false self identities.

7. Understand defensive functioning as a sequential appearance of the several false self identities in moment-to-moment interaction.

Technique: Mechanisms of Change

Some ideas about why the exercise works are:

1. Pattern change, inner life is exposed rather than hidden, new interpersonal experiencing of self.

2. Kinesthetic imagery experience of self in its many facets, for "self-experience is intimately related to body-ego" (Kahn, 1972, p. 101), separating parts spatially, a multisensory experience of change.

3. Connection with real self in safe holding setting, making it safer to expose true self and experience life from within it.

4. Images of identity created from troubling experiences, lower anxiety, thus to be safe to be real.

5. Detachment from unproductive, rigid modes of operating with others.

6. Identification with the therapist.

Technique: Procedure

These are steps in the Multiple Selves Exercise:

1. Clear area. "Stand here. Imagine a circle around you. I will

ask you to step onto the circle. When you step to a spot on it, be one of the identities that is you, any one, any part of you. Step there."

2. "Who are you there in that place?" "What name shall we call you?" "Describe yourself. Talk for yourself as you are, there, now, not about that person; be that you." "What is important to you." "How old were you when you first appeared?" "How old do you feel?" "Your main thoughts? Feelings?" "What can you remember hearing? Seeing?" [Make it multisensory.] "Who are you most like?" "Most unlike?" "Who most involved with?"

3. "In the center is a special you, the self that is most real, perhaps seldom exposed. Step into the center." "How do you feel different there than there on the circle?" "How long have you hidden?" "For what reasons?" "What happened?" "What is your name?" "Tell about yourself, your unique feelings, thoughts, specialness." "Who protects you the most?" [Generally, increase discrimination of real self from the identities on the circle. Be supportive.]

4. "Pick another spot on the circle. Step there." [Explore with same questions as step #2.]

5. "Leave that you on the circle. Step into the center, the real you." "How are you different?" etc.

6. [Continue repeating until no more identities can be located. You may suggest the client consider some you have observed who have not been discussed yet. End up in the center.] "Now step out of the circle and look back at it. Be real. How do you feel now, over there?"

7. Follow-up in subsequent sessions. Examine experiences which brought each self into existence and the sequential appearance of false selves. Re-use the map. Amend it.

Make a visual experience: put an Identity Map with names and quotes on the circle on a blackboard. Look at problems, anxieties, regressions as defenses against exposing real self: "What pulled you from your real self; let's get you centered again." Keep comments accepting, supportive, empathic, and positive. Talk to each identity as if it were a person in its own right. Write down everything said. Quote as much as possible. Point out obvious differences in affect and bearing from self to self as a way to heighten discrimination. Modulate your voice to match the characters. Ask each if it has any symptoms or problems. The directions on the circle could represent past or future, conscious or unconscious axes; or they could represent reality, ideals, impulse, conscience, with ego in the middle. Reserve such speculations since they are outside the frame of reference of the MSE.

While many clients have an immediate experience of differentness and a change of focus, remember the map may only be an artifact; it cannot be treated as totally accurate. What is more important is the experiencing of real self and detaching from false self.

Clinical Examples

Following are two descriptions of client identities. The pre-post measures are the Beck Depression Inventory, the Profile of Mood States (POMS), and the Index of Self-Esteem. The former two are well-known. Depression scores above 10 are significant. POMS scores have a mean of 50, standard deviation of 10. The Index of Self-Esteem measures self-evaluation. A score of 30 is the cutting score of a clinically significant problem. The range is 0 to 100.

Debbie is 25, twice married, in the 52nd month of therapy. She terminated nine sessions (four months) after the MSE. She was tested at the time of the exercise; post-test is four months later. Presenting complaints were panic disorder and marital problems with her alcoholic husband. Her history includes incest.

Her score on the Depression Inventory fell from 30 to a normal 4. Her Index of Self-Esteem fell from 78 to an insignificant 9. Her POMS anger score fell from t = 74 to t = 51, Tension-Anxiety from t = 59 to t = 46, Depression from t = 65 to t = 40, Confusion from t = 63 to t = 46, Fatigue from t = 66 to t = 48. Vigor went up from t = 58 to t = 67. All changes are consistent and noteworthy, despite possible demand characteristics.

Debbie's map included the real self and nine false selves arrayed around her: Affectionate One, Perfectionist, Anxious One (Out of Control), Slut, Dependent One, Frightened One, Weak One, Bitch, and Insecure One (Critic). The Real Self

> feels good about herself, smart, calm, nice, willing, honest, humorous. I need to learn to recognize and take care of the Frightened One. I have to learn to deal with emotions one at a time. I am motivated to relax and get in control. I realize I am normal, just that I have more emotion than others.

This is a remarkable picture for a woman with panic anxiety disorder, an illness she assigned to the Anxious One, who said, "I'll go crazy, without a brain, can't breathe, can't sit still, can't concentrate and listen." This self appears after, and defends against, the affect of the Frightened One, "A little girl self, frightened about my health, my appearance, that I'm stupid and different and incompetent. I am always depressed, even if I'm pretending not to be." This self was prominent in the second marriage, envies women, never feels adequate. Mother gratified her need to cling, but frustrated her by running away, separating from father impulsively. The Weak One, who embodies an identification with mother, has no energy, feels lonesome and helpless. "I am nobody. I am sick like Mom, weak, sick, sad, needy." The Bitch hides her by being "angry, touchy. I blame others. Snap at them. I think everybody treats me bad. I'm sick of trying. I can't cope with life." this one identifies with rejection by mother and abuses her own children as well as her inner selves. The Slut acts out sexually, then fears she will lose her loved ones. The Insecure One also worries about loss, "I am clingy. Mother will leave me. I don't think people like me." Once all the themes of rejection, self-worth, loss, and dependency were assigned to their selves, then the sequence of appearance and traumatic birth-point of each self was specified. Debbie's real self position was maintained at a five-month follow-up.

Mary Ann is 44, in her second marriage. The exercise was done in the seventh session. Two months later she terminated at the fourteenth. Pre-test was before the exercise, post-test at termination. The presenting complaints were stress, lack of direction, career choice, crisis of disappointment with family, overweight, and drug abuse. Her Beck score dropped from 26 to 1, Self-Esteem dropped from 36 to a normal 10. POMS Anger changed from t = 60 to t = 47, Tension-Anxiety from t = 62 to t = 32, Depression from t = 57 to t = 38, Confusion from t = 55 to t = 37, Fatigue from t = 66 to t = 34. Vigor increased from t = 40 to t = 78.

Mary Ann identified a Center ("mature, accepting, strong, assured, capable, contributing") and eight false selves, Therapist ("loving, caring"), Ann ("wants to run an empire"), May (intellectual), Sister ("selfish as hell"), Like to Be ("diamond rings, ermine coat"), Mary ("martyred mother"), Annie (drug-using child, impulsive, smacked down), Irresponsible ("to hell with it all"). Mary Ann had a reaction a week after the exercise. She recognized she had achieved real self prior to her marriage and questioned whether her new husband would tolerate her real self. After several weeks of trying it out, she was able to balance both marriage and real self.

CONCLUSION

The author developed the Multiple Selves Exercise to help clients discriminate false, defensive parts of self from real self by using multisensory experience to facilitate maximal discrimination and to highlight the real self. The Identity Maps resulting from the Multiple Selves Exercise have been used to augment the exercise. Clients label and interrupt false self functioning. They contact and learn to stay within real self, a gratifying and liberating result. The real self seems to coincide with stable, unitary identity.

It appears the concept of an integrating identity may be inaccurate. The implication of integration is that disparate elements are brought together, into a single synergistic entity. In the case of identity, integration implies various psychosocial experiences and roles can be brought together with endowment, body ego, self-image, and sense-of-self into a whole, a new gestalt which is a reorganization of those elements. The observations in this paper suggest that such experiences may be "unified" into a collective, rather than integrated, and the collective entitites appear as false self organizations. But they are never totally unified into a single final product. However, there seems to be a central, core, true, REAL self, separate from any unified entities. It comes into focus by emergence. Any effort to integrate false selves is doomed to be limited. The essence of growth and a sense of inner reality of self is emergence of the real self.

REFERENCES

American Psychiatric Association. (1987). Diagnostic and statistical manual of mental disorders (Third Edition, Revised). Washington: American Psychiatric Association.

Assagioli, R. (1965). Psychosynthesis. New York: Viking Press.

Assagioli, R. (1974). The act of will. Baltimore: Penguin Books.

Dixson, S. L., & Sands, R. G. (1983). Identity and the experience of crisis. Social Casework, 64, 223-230.

Erikson, E. H. (1963). Childhood and Society (2nd ed.). New York: Norton.

Erikson, E. H. (1968). Identity: Youth and crisis. New York: Norton.

Jung, C. G. (1959). The basic writings of C. G. Jung. New York: Basic Books.

Kahn, M. M. (1972). The finding and becoming of self. International Journal of Psychoanalytic Psychotherapy, 1, 97-111.

Kohut, H., & Wolf, E. S. (1978). Disorders of the self and their treatment: An outline. International Journal of Psycho-Analysis, 59, 413-425.

Mahler, M. S. (1972). A study of the separation-individuation process and its possible application to borderline phenomena in the psychoanalytic situation. Psychoanalytic Study of the Child, 26, 403-424.

Meissner, W. W. (1982-83). Notes on the potential differentiation of borderline conditions. International Journal of Psychoanalytic Psychotherapy, 9, 3-49.

Schwartz, R. (1987). Our multiple selves: Applying systems thinking to the inner family. Family Networker, 11 No. 2, 24.

Winnicott, D. (1960). Ego distortion in terms of true and false self. In The maturational process and the facilitating environment. (1965). New York: International Universities Press.

USE OF IMAGERY IN GRIEF THERAPY

Mary S. Cerney

Staff Psychologist
C. F. Menninger Memorial Hospital

> From a fringe, even questionable existence, imagery has risen to be one of the hottest topics in cognitive science. (Block 1981, p. 1)

Loss and its companion, grief, are life's inseparable pair. To grow and move forward, we must let go of the past and accept the resulting pain of loss. This process begins at our birth and does not end until our death. Denying loss may temporarily ease the pain, but not its effect. Such pain continues its impact on life until it is faced and integrated into one's total personality.

Although grief is a natural process with its own internal rhythm, we may not always be able to face this pain at the time it occurs, particularly when death deprives us of a loved one. Even with anticipated deaths, a period of initial numbness generally lasts from two to four weeks (and often longer). Sometimes the reality of a loss is so traumatic that the bereaved person cannot face its meaning, and the natural rhythm of grief is temporarily blocked. The blocks that prevent grief's natural movement toward integration can become fixed and may require professional help. Therapists faced with such problems will often find that imagery can be a powerful resource. Shorr (1978) states

> Imagery, unlike other modes of communication, usually has not been punished in the individual's past and is therefore less susceptible to personal censorship in the present. Because of this, imagery provides a powerful projective technique resulting in a most rapid, highly accurate profile of the individual's personality and conflicts. (p. 96)

Although grief is a component of many kinds of loss, and what will be discussed herein may also apply to these losses, this chapter will focus on loss caused by death. This chapter examines how imagery can enable bereaved persons to process grief. We will look first at indicators for the various degrees of imagery. then we will examine the characteristics of successful grieving, including the role of so-called resistances in the grief process. Finally, we will study the phases of "letting go" that are necessary for successful integration and healthy adjustment.

PRELIMINARY CONSIDERATIONS FOR THE USE OF IMAGERY

Imagery will not always be the appropriate treatment of choice for everyone. When a death has been recent, individuals need to talk about their feelings and their loved one. Forcing imagery at this point could be experienced as an intrusion--an attempt to take the loved one away, thus ending the grieving process prematurely.

When death is sudden and unexpected, the survivors need time to assimilate what has happened. People "let go" in bits and pieces, and they cannot and should not be rushed through the process. Imagery may be helpful in facilitating the flow of the grieving process without eliminating it for certain individuals. Imagery's greatest effectiveness and most striking results, however, seem to be with grief that is commonly termed pathological or atypical, that is, grief that has gone on too long, with too much or too little affect, and whose presence is frequently camouflaged in apparently unrelated problems.

Unexpected Death

When death is unexpected, there is so much unfinished business in our lives. The last parting may have been in anger or self-righteous indignation. Plans may have been changed abruptly; schedules may have been altered; but, most of all, there may have been no opportunity to say a final good-bye. Even if a good-bye was said, the individuals might not have known that it would be the last good-bye.

The suddenly bereaved person is flooded with usually unplanned for, but necessary arrangements: funeral preparations, the visitation of relatives and friends, and often painful legal and financial decisions. Everything feels rushed, without sufficient time to think through what must be done. Even burial rituals, which can be comforting, often seem incomplete, not quite the tribute that the bereaved person would have wished to have had for the loved one. Sometimes there is no physical body to lay to rest, as when the person dies in military duty or overseas, or as the result of a fire, explosion, or similar catastrophe. Sometimes there is no funeral ritual, or the bereaved person is prevented from attending the funeral rites.

The feelings that well up within the bereaved person need to be expressed somehow. Yet who is willing to listen without sermonizing or without becoming uncomfortable? Even supposedly best and most trusted friends may not be able to tolerate the expression of such sorrow. A therapist may be the answer, but a therapist should not come with a preconceived plan of how a particular individual should grieve. At this point the bereaved person may be more comforted by sounding off with righteous indignation at the turn of events and at supposedly unsympathetic others rather than by saying good-bye. It takes time to prepare for a final good-bye.

How can a therapist help such an individual? To know how to proceed, the therapist might listen to the patient. The patient will give the direction.

> Jane, a 63-year-old activity therapist, made an appointment to see a therapist at the suggestion of her physician. Just one month before, her 65-year-old husband had collapsed and died of a heart attack as he waited for her outside her office. No amount of CPR or emergency service could revive him, and he was pronounced dead on arrival at the hospital. At Jane's married co-workers were extremely uncomfortable with loss and

her obvious grief. If her spouse could die so quickly, so could theirs--and they didn't want to be reminded of that fact! But Jane needed to express her pain and outrage. Her first words were: "I need to talk and to cry. Don't tell me I have to say good-bye. I will, but I'm not ready yet.

Not every patient will be so clear, but patients will let their therapists know what they do and do not need--if the therapists would only listen. Therapists should strive to be alert to their patients' messages about the use of imagery. As Horowitz (1983) cautions, imagery is not just a technique used in isolation to assess patient's needs:

> Image formation is one kind of thinking, a mode that is close to emotion. A psychotherapist listens for image experiences, but any exclusive focus on image formation is an unbalanced approach. Image techniques should be related to a larger, well-formulated plan for how a patient may change. This should include attention to how the therapist's intervention influences the patient's immediate train of thought and views of the relationship with the therapist. (p. 305)

If Jane had made the same comment, "I'm not ready to say good-bye," five years after her husband's death, then the therapist would need to explore why Jane had not been able to say good-bye. One month after the death, however, may be too soon for such an exploration, particularly because the numbness that sets in after such a shock enables the bereaved person to handle the immediate necessary details surrounding a death but ususally begins to wear off within a month after the event.

When individuals are reluctant to let go of grief, life comes to a standstill: this may be the reason for holding on to grief. As long as the bereaved person does not come to terms with the death of the deceased, the implications of life without that individual can be avoided.

> In the final semester of her senior year of high school, Susan often felt overwhelmed by grief over the sudden tragic death of her sister and father in a car accident two years earlier. She had nightmares and withdrew from her friends. Her attendance and participation in her high school classes declined until she was in danger of not graduating at the end of the semester. Therapist revealed that Susan's grief was an unconscious effort to protect her from facing the apparently tragic consequences of leaving home. An older brother had left home after an angry interchange with their mother; still not on speaking terms, they communicated through Susan. Susan's younger sister, Janet, also had quarreled with their mother and had gone to live with their father. She was returning to her mother's home when she and her father were killed in the car accident. In this family, leaving was fraught with tragic consequences. Susan responded well to the use of imagery to examine many issues concerning her father and sister. She was then able to face what it meant to leave home. Examining this issue directly enabled her not only to leave home appropriately, but also to remain on good terms with her mother. (See Cerney, 1985)

Jane, the widow mentioned earlier, was having similar difficulty coping with independence. She and her husband of more than 35 years had been discussing retirement and making plans to travel. Now Jane had to face that time ahead of her alone. Not yet aware of all the implications of her husband's death, she needed time to process this sudden change.

She did know, however, that the summer trip she had planned would have to be made without her husband.

To face life without a certain loved one requires the ability to stand alone and to function without that individual. The bereaved person who does not possess the ego strength to function independently cannot allow awareness of a loved one's death to penetrate consciousness. Before we can let go of our loved ones, we must develop our own inner resources.

> Peter's father had died one month before Peter, now 26, graduated from college. Although Peter was able to go on and graduate, he was never able to stay with any employment longer than a few months. Although he was the oldest child, he was unable to assume the responsibility that he had seemed to handle quite appropriately before his father's death. Peter became a concern for the entire family, but particularly for his mother, who was overly solicitous about him. His life seemed to resolve around attempting to start a job and spending time at home where his mother ministered to him. Although Peter responded to imagery, and worked through many issues concerning his father, he could not say good-bye and indicated the potential for disorganization when pressed to consider his father's death.

Therapy with Peter centered on understanding his inability to hold a job, his attachment to his mother, and how his illness gave his mother's life meaning and purpose. As Peter began to understand the role his illness had played in the family dynamics, he struggled with the fear that his mother would die if she did not have him to care for. In some ways, his fear was well grounded, and much family work was needed before his mother could deal with the death of her husband, letting go of her son, and looking at what her life could be without the two of them. Peter's mother had nursed her husband during his final illness and she continued her nursing care now with their oldest son. Thus occupied, she could allow her other three children to move out of the home to develop lives of their own.

As Peter saw his mother begin to cope with her grief and rebuild her life, he was able to examine himself, his own strengths, and his own needs. In his efforts to let go the bonds that held him to the past, Peter was supported by his mother, his siblings, and the beginning realization of his own talents and abilities. Eventually, Peter was able in imagery to say good-bye to his father. Instead of experiencing guilt that he was abandoning his father, Peter reported that he felt as if a huge burden had dropped from his shoulders, and he felt the comforting presence and support of his father within him.

The Support System

Peter's support system--his family, his treatment team--facilitated his acknowledgement of his own inner resources and his letting go of the past to face the future. Support systems are essential for most individuals in times of stress. A support system that allows bereaved persons to share their unique pain is probably a necessity in successful grieving. The bereaved person needs to experience the support of others who acknowledge that no pain is, ever has been, or ever will be as unique as the pain the bereaved person is now experiencing. That is a true statement. Pain is individual; no two people experience pain the same way. No two people possess the same constellation of experiences, resources--physical and mental, and psychological developments that interact with each other and the current experience. But a support system may not always be available, and friends may not always be supportive.

Facing Profound Grief

Sometimes even close friends cannot tolerate a bereaved person's grief because it brings up the possibility that they, too, could experience the same loss. Such individuals should speak honestly and directly to the bereaved person, explaining why they cannot be available and supportive, rather than just leaving the bereaved person bewildered and wondering why one's friends would react so hurtfully. There is no pain like that caused by a trusted friend's failure to give support, not only by abandoning the bereaved person in a time of need, but also by becoming actively hostile and rejecting. Such behavior multiplies one's losses. Not only must the loss of a particular loved one be faced, but also the loss of a trusted friend must be dealt with. Those individuals so betrayed describe chest pain "like being stabbed over and over" whenever they hear the hostile rejecting words or experience the rejecting behavior of their supposedly trusted friend. At a time when they are most vulnerable, they must accept that they have trusted someone too immature to value a friend's need above personal feelings of comfort. To let go of a trusted friend is difficult under any circumstances, but it is especially painful at such a time of need.

PSYCHODYNAMIC CONSIDERATIONS IN GRIEVING

The Role of Resistance

Resistances permit a time-out from reality, a time to regroup and catch our breath. Even so-called normal, well-adjusted individuals are not able to face reality one hundred percent of the time. "The patient is resisting" is not the patient's problem in fighting treatment, but rather the therapist's problem of understanding that the approach to this particular issue is not correct or timely. Patients cannot always speak directly to their problems and their needs, but they do communicate. Therapists can understand the message by keeping preconceived conclusions from interfering and by being sensitive to nonverbal as well as verbal modes of communication. Even verbal communication may not be that elucidating with meanings concealed and couched in complicated metaphors. Freud (1905/1953) discovered that

> When I set myself the task of bringing to light what human beings keep hidden within them, not by the compelling power of hypnosis, but by observing what they say and what they show, I thought the task was a harder one than it really is. He that has eyes to see and ears to hear may convince himself that no mortal can keep a secret. If his lips are silent, he chatters with his finger-tips; betrayal oozes out of him at every pore. And thus the task of making conscious the most hidden recesses of the mind is one which it is quite possible to accomplish. (pp. 77-78)

Resistances are messages to the therapist that the patient is not ready to deal with a particular issue; some preparatory work must be done first.

> Ruth's compulsive handwashing had become increasingly problematic in the last year. Medication alleviated the behavior somewhat but did not help as much as Ruth and her therapist had hoped. Her therapist, suspecting some unresolved grief issues, referred her for grief therapy. In the imagery session, Ruth readily imaged her father who also suffered from compulsive

handwashing and had died when she was six years old. In her imagery he would only smile at her, never answering her or saying anything to her.

When an image does not respond that is a clue that the patient's feelings about the individual are usually angry; these must be worked with before the grief process can continue. Ruth, for example, would become frustrated with her imagery work because of her father's lack of response, which she was unable to explain. A technique from hypnosis, "The Three Dreams," was helpful in approaching this problem. Ruth imaged herself in a restful place where she would fall asleep and have three dreams. The first dream would give a clue to what was keeping her father from speaking; the second dream would give a resolution of the difficulty; and the third dream would give an even better resolution to the problem.

Ruth reported that nothing came to mind for the first dream. My response was, "That's fine, now have the second dream which will give a resolution to the problem." Again she reported that nothing came to mind. Again I said, "That's fine, now have the third dream that will give an even better resolution of the problem."

"Therapy, that's all that comes to mind, she reported.

Again I responded, "That's fine," and then proceeded to explore the meaning of "nothing." Did she feel like a "Nothing" and that there was nothing she could do about it? Ruth immediately exclaimed, "That's exactly how I feel!" We then proceeded to explore Ruth's feelings about herself. To look at the source of these feelings, I used a variation of a technique from hypnosis, "the rope": I asked Ruth to make those feelings of nothingness into a rope and to slide along the rope to where the feelings all began. Ruth reported that she was going back and wasn't stopping. I asked her if she was frightened or wanted to stop. "No," she responded, "I want to get to the root of this problem." Ruth did finally come to a stopping point where she said she was under a curse, the same one her father was under. The curse was "handwashing," a punishment for something she had done, but she didn't know what. She then spoke of her feelings about the birth of a younger brother. Ruth reported other feelings and memories centering on her father and mother and the jealousy she felt from her mother.

When Ruth was five, her parents had talked about divorcing and they did separate for a while. She was told that she could live with whichever parent she wished, and she chose her father. After a short time, her parents reconciled, and a few months later, her father died. Ruth had been close to her father, who had been close to his mother who died a few months after he did. Furthermore, Ruth's mother had been close to her father who died when she was a child. These and other issues emerged before Ruth was ready to say good-bye to her father. She also considered what it would mean not to have excessive handwashing as part of her daily routine. Handwashing had been a way to keep men in her life. After the death of her father, there was a succession of stepfathers. Ruth became close to one of them who died within a month after her brother died of cancer when Ruth was 16. Not able to hold on to fathers, Ruth seemed to adopt handwashing--the curse--which kept her in a psychological bond with her natural father and with her husband, who often had to take care of certain household duties or to act as an authority to stop her handwashing rituals. Whenever he told her to stop, she would.

All these issues were clues to the path to follow in working with Ruth's grief over her father's death. Ruth's father finally spoke to her in imagery after these problems were confronted. She then could tell him how much she had missed him and how disloyal she had felt as she searched for him in stepfathers, particularly the one for whom she had cared so much. She told him about her concerns and her fears. When she could finally say good-bye to him at age 36, she also said good-bye to her handwashing.

Anger and Guilt

What blocks many a grieving process is our reluctance to acknowledge anger. Whether the anger is realistic or unrealistic in nature, it needs to be recognized and resolved.

Unrealistic anger: Unrealistic anger is most difficult to confront because it threatens our perception of ourselves as kind and loving individuals. We need to realize and accept that we all are selfish, self-centered individuals and that we do not like to have our established routines altered and our sources of nurturance changed. But that is only one part of us. We are also loving, concerned individuals who frequently are willing to sacrifice our own welfare for others. We do not appreciate loss, even while knowing it can afford an opportunity to grow. Death or loss of a relationship forces us to change, to alter our routines, at least temporarily, and we must seek other sources of nurturance. Just recognizing this fact usually is sufficient to relieve considerable pressure within the bereaved person.

But what about realistic anger? I have referred to the one who died as "the loved one," but that individual may not be loved. We hold ambivalent feelings toward most individuals. Sometimes "love" is the dominant feeling, and sometimes "hate" or a related feeling is the dominant feeling.

Realistic anger: Realistic anger can have many sources, such as real uncaring behavior toward the deceased.

> Bill seemed unable to mourn his wife, Mary, who had died rather quickly after a brief illness five years before he sought therapy. They had been married for 27 years. Bill currently had a beautiful relationship with another woman, but he could not bring himself to marry her and he was in danger of losing that relationship. Tears flooded him in the first therapy session. In imagery, Bill told Mary how much he loved her and how he wished she were still with him. He told her about his current relationship, which he would give up in a minute if Mary could come back to him.

As Bill's use of imagery continued, other important facts emerged. Mary had been in therapy prior to her illness and was in the process of leaving Bill when she became ill. Mary would have divorced him, but death intervened. As Bill got in touch with his anger at her for considering divorce, he began to realize why she had done so. Bill had not been the most sensitive husband, and his domineering ways had kept Mary dependent on him until she began to make progress in her therapy.

> In imagery, Bill told Mary that he had never realized how his behavior had affected her. As Bill and Mary talked, Bill appeared to be filled with new insights. He recounted incident after incident in which he scrutinized his behavior, finally understanding what he could not understand before: how lacking he was in sensitivity and concern for Mary. Bill shed copious tears of sadness and repentence. The blinders had been removed from his eyes, and he saw himself differently. Mary consoled him and forgave him for the hurt she had suffered, and he

forgave her for leaving him before he had the chance to change their life together. Mary told him that he did have another chance--with a wonderful woman--and that he "should not blow it." Bill laughed at that and told Mary about Marcia and how, in many ways, they were much alike. Mary smiled enigmatically and said, "She's the one I thought would be perfect for you. Now don't let the lessons you learned with me be wasted." Bill and Mary embraced and bid farewell. He watched as she slowly moved out of sight. With one last wave of the hand, she blew him a kiss and was gone.

When Bill returned to the present, he sighed, "I feel as though a heavy weight has been lifted from my shoulders. Mary was a wonderful woman with a great sense of humor. I know she'll be with me, helping me to make a success out of my marriage to Marcia. I do have a second chance."

The bereaved person may also experience realistic anger toward the deceased because of injustices that have not been atoned for, wrongs that have not been righted in the eyes of the bereaved person. This form of angry grief is frequently concealed by other more acceptable grief.

> Alice's maternal grandfather had molested her from age 4 to 6. It was "their" secret, and she had been afraid to tell her parents because she feared they would not believe her or would blame her. Alice never did tell her parents, both of whom had died within the past year. Now, at age 36, she regretted her silence and found that it interfered with her ability to mourn her parents. Using imagery, Alice shared her secret and received from them the comfort and support she had longed for over years.
>
> But Alice's real problem was her inability to mourn her grandfather who had died when she was 8, She hated him with a vengeance, but she also felt guilty as if her hateful thoughts and wishes for his death had actually cased his death.

Unrealistic Guilt: Troublesome guilt emerges not from realistic behavior, but from sources deep in the unconscious, with roots in early childhood before conceptual thinking was part of the thinking repertoire. At that level of concrete thinking, thought takes on a life all its own, with little or no difference between thought and action. To a child, wishing someone dead is the same as killing the person. Children often assume responsibility for deaths, divorces, and catastrophes that disrupt their lives. As a consequence, they suffer untold guilt, which is frequently expressed in a self-defeating or rigid perfectionistic lifestyle. Such individuals have difficulty allowing themselves to get in touch with their anger. At some deep level, they fear the destructive potential of anger that they experienced in childhood. Even if they allow only a little to emerge, they fear they will lose control and become raging maniacs, destroying all around. These individuals frequently must struggle to get their images to speak to them. Before they can mourn their current loss, they must work through those early losses for which they, as children, felt responsible. This type of mourning is frequently done in stages as a constrictive, punitive superego softens through much work around the person's childhood rage and terror.

Letting Go

Murray Bowen's (1978) concept of making peace with one's family and learning about one's family also applies to dealing with guilt and anger. The questioned behavior must be placed in context. By going back in time to what it felt like to be a child experiencing death, divorce, or some other family crisis, individuals can get in touch with their underlying guilt and can understand that their former self--the child--is not guilty and does not deserve punishment. When they can forgive the child, the burden of guilt will be lifted from their shoulders, and they will be freer to face the other guilts that have plagued their lives.

> Susan, who had never been close to her father, felt guilty about the closeness she felt toward her stepfather. When Susan asked her father in imagery why he had never been close to his children and had never allowed them to be close to him, he responded, "I never learned how; my father was also very distant when I was growing up." Susan exclaimed, "He didn't know how! He didn't know how to show his love!"

Susan reported that her anger toward her father melted when she realized that he really did loved her; he just didn't know how to show that love.

Philip recalled a similar experience. His father had teased him as a child, often reducing him to tears. Suddenly, in one of the imagery experiences, Philip exlaimed, "That was the only way he could show his love. My father never learned to show love because that was the way his father showed his love to him." Philip's father was still alive. At the next session, he reported the difference that he experienced in his relationship with his father. Now they both were teasing each other in a good-natured way and enjoying a relationship that Philip had only dreamed of. This change in attitude and relationship also affected Philip's current life. He reported considerable improvement in his relationship with his wife and his own children. Furthermore, Philip, a minister, had never felt comfortable accepting a pastorate of his own. Now he found that he was able to request the kind of pastorate he wanted. At follow-up five years later, he was an administrator and supervisor in his religious organization, and he spoke of what a difference the change in his relationship with his father had made in both of their lives and in his own family, especially for his children who loved their grandfather.

Anger Toward Self

As anger toward others disappears, the bereaved person must face the individual he or she is really angry with: the self. But why are we angry with ourselves! We "should" know better; we "should" be able to avert the difficulty or do something about it. Such demands infer omnipotence and omniscence, which are characteristic of children's concrete thinking when children feel that they either directly cause an event or that an event occurs through their negligence. As individuals accept their humanity with its imperfections, they can let go of their anger and their unrealistic guilt. Removing the "shoulds" allows the love and care to surface and allows us to become more altruistic and more concerned about the needs of others. The bereaved person can then let go of the deceased one.

But some wrongs are wrong in whatever context. Sexual and physical abuse are difficult to understand, even when we recognize that the perpetrators may also have been abused or that perhaps the victims may have felt some pleasure (difficult to admit) in the experience. Such experiences are more complicated to work through but they are possible. Alice reached a point in imagery where she was able to tell her grandfather how his "touching" had affected her life. He hung his head and cried, as he told her how sorry he was. She knew that he had been ill and that he had been arrested shortly before his death. Alice was able to separated her experience of abuse from her earlier love for her grandfather and in forgiving him, she could say good-bye. Alice's life subsequently changed quite significantly. She lost weight and her relationships with men improved. Eventually she married, and now reports that she is happy and has two chldren of her own.

IMAGERY SESSION PROPER

Induction: Setting the Stage

The induction of imagery does not generally have to follow hypnotic induction techniques. It should flow naturally from discussion that precedes the induction. For example, Susan (the patient mentioned earlier whose father and sister were killed in a car accident) spoke of nightmares about her father's car accident in which her father, terribly mutilated, approached her. I suggested that she close her eyes and dream about her father coming to her. For the vast majority of individuals I have worked with, such a triggering suggestion is all that was needed.

Frequently I just ask the bereaved to imagine and describe the individual who needs to be mourned. The description indictes whether a preliminary stage is necessary before beginning the actual dialogue. If the individual is described as being dead in a casket, then I suggest that we heal the individual, breathing life and health into the body. We then help that individual out of the casket. Such a healing of memories appears to be a prerequisite for dialogue with the individual. You cannot talk to a dead body and get an answer, although even that may be possible in imagery.

Imagery works on a preconscious, concrete level where there is no distinction between what is real and what is not real. Therefore, everything is possible. Klinger (1980) states, "Experiencing something in imagery can be considered to be in many essential ways psychologically equivalent to experiencing the thing in actuality" (p. 5). He is not alone in this view (Kosslyn, 1980; Neisser, 1976; Sheikh & Shaffer, 1979). According to some studies (John, 1967; Leuba, 1940; Perky, 1910; Segal & Fusella, 1970), imagery and perception are experientially and neurophysiologically comparable processes that are intrinsically difficult to distinguish.

On occasion some individuals cannot image the deceased person or the other individual with whom they need to communicate. Such blocking, which speaks to the need for other preliminary work, is similar to the problems that prevent an image from speaking.

> Susan described her father as badly scarred from the car accident that had killed him and her sister. I suggested that in her love she could heal him, which she did immediately. She then asked, "What will I do about his arm? He doesn't have one." I suggested that there was an arm beside her chair. At first she didn't see it, but I asked her to look again. Immediately, she responded, "Oh, here it is!" and she attached it to his body. She then said, "He has no shoes." I told her they were on the other side of her chair. She saw these with no hesitation, picked them up and handed them to her father.

The therapist must set the stage for the dialogue that will enable a patient to deal with the unfinished business that blocks mourning. There are important diagnostic implications in this initial phase. The therapist must decide whether the mourning issue is more complicated than simply needing to say good-bye. Images may not respond, as noted earlier; they may be too painful to look at due to injuries and the ravages of illness. Confronting the image rather than avoiding it is essential to coming to terms with the loss, but timing is of the essence.

Susan's sister had been so mangled that the family had not been permitted to view her body. When Susan imaged her sister, the sight frightened her, but she courageously looked and with her love healed her sister. In gratitude, her sister smiled and thanked her. Susan said that until then her sister had not seemed dead because they had not been allowed to see her in the coffin.

Early Stage of Grief Resolution: Dealing with the Negatives

I then ask the bereaved person to talk to the loved one. Some facilitation may be necessary, such as, "What does your father say? Don't put words in his mouth; just whatever comes to mind." After the preliminaries, the bereaved person may need help to get in touch with and express anger for the abandonment that the death caused. It is difficult to be angry with someone who died. We generally think the person couldn't help dying, except perhaps in suicide or careless living. Sometimes the bereaved person can be helped through such facilitating statements as, "Not having--here has changed your life. It was so good to depend upon--and now--isn't here." Such encouragement is usually sufficient to initiate the expression of discomfort and annoyance with the loss.

At any stage in the imagery, other issues may emerge that need to be dealt with when they occur. They may speak to the need to delay the grief work proper until other issues are resolved. The therapist should follow the patient's lead facilitating what the patient may not have words to say, but not doing the work for the patient. Helping a patient get in touch with anger does not lead the patient but rather facilitates getting in touch with the block to the grieving process. The leadership of the therapist is expressed in knowing what must be accomplished, but not forcing it. A patient who will not follow the lead should not be forced to pursue it. Instead, other avenues will need to be explored and either also abandoned or pursued, depending on the therapist's clinical judgment. Patients must not be pressured into letting go or saying what they are unable to acknowledge; generally speaking, they will not follow a direction that would be hazardous for them. However, they can succumb to excessive pressure.

Middle Stage of Grief Resolution

After patients have worked through their anger and guilt and ambivalent feelings toward the deceased person, they need time to "speak" with the loved one. I frequently suggest that they have a quiet talk which need not be reported to me. This quiet time usually lasts 5 to 15 minutes, but on occasion it has been shorter or longer. When the patient lets me know that the talk is over, I ask again, "Are you ready to say good-bye?"

If the patient says, "No," I respond, "That's fine. You don't need to say good-bye until you are ready." I then ask what would help to say good-bye. With patients who do not have a ready answer to this question, I will use the three-dream technique described earlier to get an indication of what is still needed before the bereaved can bid their loved one farewell. Usually something is unfinished. Sometimes, since this reluctance to say good-bye is often expressed near the end of the hour, I just suggest that patients bring themselves back to the present when they are ready. We talk about their experience, and I usually suggest that they rest afterward because the experience can be quite taxing emotionally. In such instances when we repeat the imagery in a later session, we quickly pass through the initial stages to handle what is left undone so the bereaved person can say their good-byes.

The Place of Ritual

Some individuals express keen regret that they could not prepare their loved one's body for burial or attend the funeral services. Yet these ceremonial activities can be enacted in imagery.

> Clara had been ill in the hospital when her 20-year-old son supposedly committed suicide with a drug overdose. The verdict of suicide was uncertain because he had spoken to his mother the evening before and had planned to visit her the next day. After visiting his mother, he had planned to accompany the youth group on an outing later that afternoon. He was a diabetic and had been depressed, but authorities hypothesized that perhaps he had accidentally taken additional medication, forgetting that he had already taken sleeping pills. Medical complications due to his diabetes may also have contributed to his death.
>
> In imagery, Bill's mother had him tell her what happened. He explained that he couldn't sleep and wasn't feeling well. He had forgotten to eat, and he thought it had been a long time since he had taken the earlier medication. Clara was quite relieved. After she spoke at great length with her son, she expressed the wish to prepare his body for burial. Her son liked purple. She dressed him in a white suit and a light purple shirt with a dark purple tie, and she laid him in the casket with a purple flower in his lapel. She arranged purple flowers around the casket and orchestrated the funeral service. She heard his favorite prayers, musical selections and hymns, and she herself sang Malotte's "Our Father" for him. She rode in the funeral cortege to the cemetery, and saw the casket being lowered into the ground. She then drew his spirit from the grave, allowing it to be with her. He was free and no longer a captive in his diabetic body. As she left the cemetery she had imagined, she decided to plant a tree on his grave, which she later did in reality.

Leave-taking rituals enable bereaved persons to give to their loved ones and to bid farewell in a concrete manner. Sometimes going to the grave in imagery can have an important healing effect. Attending to leave-taking rituals may be the unfinished business.

SAYING GOOD-BYE

When bereaved persons are ready to say good-bye I suggest that they encircle the deceased in white light. If relatives or friends have preceded these loved ones in death, I suggest that these others will greet the newly deceased. Depending upon the bereaved's religious belief system, I might suggest that they place their hand in God's hand and go with God (see Cerney, 1988). Otherwise, I might simply say, "Say good-bye and allow your loved one to walk away. When he or she is gone, let me know."

When the bereaved person reports that their loved one is gone, I then suggest allowing the presence of the loved one to be in the mourner. Many individuals report this experience on their own, and few appear to have difficulty in experiencing this oneness with their beloved.

> Betty had great difficulty saying good-bye to her mother and father who had died many years before. She didn't want to let them go. Yet they pleaded with her to do so. They needed to go to get on with their new life, and she needed to get on

with hers. Finally, Betty, who was deeply religious, said good-bye and saw her parents go with God. Betty was quiet for a long time. With obvious relief, she suddenly exclaimed: "They're here with me. I feel their presence within me. and I feel closer to them than I have ever felt."

Karen, age 19, also had great difficulty saying good-bye to her father, who had died six years before she entered therapy. Her two grief sessions were separated by a nine-month interval. At the initial session, she had been unable to say good-bye. Using the three-dream-technique, we found that Karen's reluctance to change was blocking the farewell and her progress. She first had to make a decision to change and then face the implications of change. During the interim, she worked with her psychotherapist and made significant progress. Finally, she asked for another appointment when she felt ready to deal with her father. Her appointment fell on the anniversary of her father's death.

Karen still had difficulty saying good-bye. Suddenly she opened her eyes and said, "He was with me all along!" She reported that she just couldn't let her father go, even though she knew she should. Then it seemed like a force within her pushed her to let him go. When her father disappeared from sight, she felt his comforting presence internally. It was such a wonderful feeling! Karen was on cloud nine and practically floated out of the office at the end of the session.

Internalization

When individuals have been able to let go and say good-bye to their loved one, they often report feeling the presence of their loved one within themselves. Freud (1917/1963) said that identification with the lost one is necessary to complete the mourning process. Internalization is a way to keep the person alive without denying that he or she is gone. Whenever others touch our lives, we are changed for better or worse; they leave their mark on us, and we are never the same. In therapy I frequently tell or show the picture story of "Little Blue and Little Yellow" by Leo Lionni (1959), because it captures how others change our lives. They add color and life to our existence, which can never be taken away, even through death.

After successful imagery work, patients usually speak of feeling peaceful and relieved, as well as permeated by a deep pervading fatigue. It is the kind of tiredness that comes after setting down a heavy load. I usually encourage my patients to rest after such a session, because some integration occurs during rest or sleep and because they need time to assimilate what has happened. We discuss the experience only briefly, for they generally do not want to talk much. The patients usually are able to speak about their experience in a follow-up interview.

Ending the Imagery Session

If patients do not spontaneously bring themselves out of imagery by opening their eyes when they are finished, I say, "When you are ready, bring yourself back to the present." I then wait for the patient to speak as some time is needed to reorient to the present. If the patient does not speak, I say, "How do you feel?" Their response will indicate how much additional work is needed. Some individuals might report a sense of peace; others might report feeling troubled. If that is the response, the reason for that feeling will need to be explored. Such a response usually indicates additional work is needed and that some aspect of the anger block still remains.

Follow-up to Good-bye Session

As follow-up, a second session or more can help the individual to process the leave-taking. The second session can be used to review the work to determine whether all that needed to be done was completed in the first session or in the session in which imagery was initiated. The bereaved person may be unable to image the loved one in a subsequent session, but that is not a problem. Not being able to image as one did before may indicate it is no longer needed because the needed aspects of the loved one have been internalized. At times, the bereaved person may be able to image only the face of the deceased one. I have found this to indicate that the work is partially completed. When this happens, we repeat the imagery session to determine if there is anything that is unresolved that needs to be discussed. This second session often brings to light issues that were not in the bereaved's consciousness and ability to recollect in the first imagery session. The patient may have needed to resolve certain issues before others could be tackled. In the second and later sessions, any issues obscured by the unresolved grief will emerge. These issues are generally related to major alterations in the bereaved person's life that may have been too threatening to be faced alone and too colored by mixed feelings toward the individual who is gone.

CONCLUSION

Imagery is a powerful technique that can be most helpful in facilitating the letting go that is part of every mourning process. However, imagery must be sensitively approached; timing is of the essence. The letting go and integration that is necessary to successful grieving may not be possible in one session. Imagery sessions must be titrated according to the patient's ability to handle them. For some individuals, one session may suffice; for others, two or a few more; for still others, imagery may need to be used intermittently.

The use of imagery must be integrated with a full diagnostic assessment of the particular patient's issues and the best approach to similar problems. In using imagery, the therapist must never lose perspective of what is best for the patient. As Horowitz (1983) noted earlier, "Image techniques should be related to a larger, well-formulated plan for how a patient may change" (p. 305).

The effectiveness of imagery seems almost miraculous. Many individuals make significant progress in only a few sessions. The intricacies of why and how it works so effectively are not known, but Meichenbaum (1978) suggests that three psychological processes explain the effectiveness of all imagery-based therapies. Sheikh (1983) summarizes these as:

> (1) the feeling of control which the patient gains as a result of the monitoring and rehearsing various images;
> (2) the modified meaning or changed internal dialogue that precedes, attends, and succeeds examples of maladaptive behavior; and
> (3) the mental rehearsal of alternative responses that lead to the enhancement of coping skills. (p. 423)

REFERENCES

Block, N. (Ed.) (1981). Imagery. Cambridge, MA: MIT Pres.
Bowen, M. (1978). Family therapy in clinical practice. New York: Jason Aronson.

Cerney, M. S. (1985). Imagery and grief work. In E. M. Stern (Ed). Psychotherapy and the grieving patient. New York: Haworth Press.
Cerney, M. S. (1988). Is that all there is?": Religious belief and the grieving process. Submitted to Psychotherapy: Theory, Research, Practice, Training.
Freud, S. (1953). Fragment of an analysis of a case of hysteria. In J. Strachey (Ed. and Trans.), The standard edition of the complete psychological works of Sigmund Freud, Vol. 7, pp. 6-122. London: Hogarth Press. (Original work published 1905.)
Freud, S. (1963). Mourning and melancholia. In J. Strachey (Ed. and Trans.), The standard edition of the complete psychological works of Sigmund Freud, Vol. 14, pp. 243-258. London: Hogarth Press. (Original work published 1917.)
Horowitz, M. J. (1983). Image formation and psychotherapy. New York: Jason Aronson. (Rev. ed. of Image formation and cognition, originally published 1970; 2nd ed. 1978).
John, E. R. (1967). Mechanisms of memory. New York: Academic Press.
Klinger, E. (1980). Therapy and the flow of thought. In J. E. Shorr, G. E. Sobel, P. Robin, & J. A. Connella (Eds.), Imagery, Vol. 1: Its many dimensions and applications. New York: Plenum Press.
Kosslyn, S. M. (1980). Image and mind. Cambridge, MA: Harvard University Press.
Leuba, C. (1940). Images as conditioned sensations. Journal of Experimental Psychology, 26, 345-351.
Lionni, Leo (1959). Little blue and little yellow. New York: Astor-Honor.
Meichenbaum, D. (1978). Why does using imagery in psychotherapy lead to change? In J. L. Singer & K. S. Pope (Eds.), The power of human imagination: New methods in psychotherapy. New York: Plenum Press.
Neisser, U. (1976). Cognition and reality: Principles and implications of cognitive psychology. San Francisco: Freeman, Cooper and Co.
Perky, C. W. (1910). An experimental study of imagination. American Journal of Psychology, 21, 422-452.
Segal, S. J. & Fusella, V. (1970). Influence of imagined pictures and sounds on detection of visual and auditory signals. Journal of Experimental Psychology, 83, 458-464.
Sheikh, A. A. (Eds.)(1983). Imagery: Current theory, research, and application. New York: John Wiley & Sons.
Sheikh, A. A. & Shaffer, J. T. (Eds.) (1979). The potential of fantasy and imagination. New York: Brandon House.
Shorr, J. E. (1972). Clinical use of categories of therapeutic imagery. In J. L. Singer & K. S. Pope (Eds.), The power of human imagination: New Methods in psychotherapy. New York: Plenum Pres.

THE EXISTENTIAL QUESTION AND THE IMAGINARY SITUATION AS THERAPY

Joseph E. Shorr

Institute for Psycho-Imagination Therapy
Los Angeles, California

> For it was not so much by the knowledge of words that I came to the understanding of things, as by my experience of things I was enabled to follow the meaning of words. (Plutarch)

How does the world look to a man or woman who is sad, furious, happy, aggressive, sexual, guilty, conscience-stricken, loved, fat, ugly, etc.? And how does the world look to a man or woman in his house, at work, on vacation, in sexual situations, alone, with members of the same sex, in school, in crisis, in war, with nature, with people close to him, etc.?

In short, how does man view his "lived" world? The phenomenology of man aims at the description of the experience of the individual in a situation. This viewpoint holds that man is best comprehended in the light of that which is unique to him and in reference to his concrete situations in the actual world. Existentially to understand a man, he must be considered as existing now in a certain way, with the awareness that he is constantly engaged in becoming something different as the result of relating to his past, present and future.

This paper proposes two techniques, namely, the Existential Question and the Imaginary Situation, to be used to understand him and hopefully to change him. Perhaps the simplest way is to ask the man how he views himself in certain human encounters involving others. Still another way is to ask him to imagine himself in certain situations and then to assess his individual reactions.

The theoretical basis to asking the Existential Question, as proposed in this paper, is best stated by Laing:

> One is in the first instance the person that other people say one is. As one grows older, one either endorses or tries to discard the ways in which the others have defined one. One can decide to be what it has been said one is. One may try not to be what, nevertheless, one has practically inevitably come to assume one is, in one's heart of hearts. Or one may try to tear out from oneself this "alien" identity that one has been endowed with or condemned to, and create by one's own actions an identity for oneself, which one forces others to confirm. Whatever its particular subsequent vicissitudes,

however, one's identity is in the first instance conferred on one. We discover who we already are.

The Existential Questions are designed to ascertain how he has been defined by others, what he still endorses about himself or is trying to discard in the "here and now." Equally important are the revelations of the "unconscious strategies" that the patient uses within this context. As Laing states it, "Thus every relationship implies a definition of self by other and other by self." The author attempts to get at this definition of self and of others by the use of a question or an imaginative situation. If I were to ask a patient, "How do people take advantage of you?" I may find out how he defines himself and others. And if I were to ask him to imagine himself being short-changed in a cafeteria, I may find out even more about how he defines himself and others.

Perhaps a definition of an Existential Question could be stated as the question that elicits how a person views himself and how he feels others view him, and best demonstrates to the patient and therapist the strategies by which he defines others and how others define him. It must be emphasized that we are interested in knowing not only how he views the world, but also the "unconscious strategies" by which he copes, manipulates, repeats, controls, sustains neuroses, deceives himself, increases anxiety, reduces anxiety, justifies himself, punishes others or himself, etc. Take, for example, the wife whose unconscious strategy is to provoke her husband into hitting her so that "he would know I'm alive," or the businessman who constantly becomes involved in schemes for wealth which invariably end in failure and self-deception, or the mother who does so much for her daughter in order to infantilize her, and keeps her that way by pronouncement of "ungratefulness." In short, we are interested in knowing who defines the relationship between any two people and what stake each person has in either sustaining or changing this definition.

It is our hope that by the combined method of the Existential Question (EQ) and the Imaginary Situation (IS), we may get to know how the patient becomes undermined, what strategies he employs to defend against this, and, hopefully, what he can do about it. The basic assumption is that man has the capacity for self-awareness. He has the capacity to know what he is doing and what is happening to him. As a consequence, he is capable of making decisions about these things and of taking responsibility for himself.

ILLUSTRATION

Existential Question

1. Call you anything, but never refer to you as what? (This is an open-ended question. Caution should be exerted not to give any hints as to possible answers on the part of the therapist.

Examples: Henpecked; a failure; unethical; unfair; a lady; a homosexual; old; weak sister; selfish; without feelings; a whore; etc.

Imaginative Situation:

Henpecked - Imagine you are home with your wife in a kitchen with lots of unwashed dishes

Whore - Imagine that you are drunk at a party where there are lots of men

Stupid - Imagine that you are participating in a TV quiz show

Phenomenological Intent

It is hoped that by this approach, the worse possible way in which the individual thinks others might regard him can be viewed. It may be possible, also, by the combined method of the Existential Question and the Imaginative Situation to determine the particular defenses that the patient uses. Experience also indicates that many times, associative experiences may be recalled and reactivated. An example of this was offered by one patient who, in response to the Imaginative Situation of the TV quiz participant, recalled a high school situation where a harsh teacher had humiliated her.

As can readily be seen, the flexibility and skill of the therapist must be called upon in these instances to take the patient to the point that clinical experience and assessment of the unique individual he is dealing with may require.

Needless to say, since no one can always predict the answer to the Existential Question, the therapist must be able to use his knowledge of human psychology to set up any one of countless Imaginative Situations to help determine the patient's "view of his world."

It must be remembered that the suggestions made in this chapter are not, in themselves, all of therapy--but, hopefully, are definitive aids to sharpen the focus of the patient's world. The suggestions herein presented are not in lieu of support, persuasion, suggestion, advice, dream analysis, free association or any other specific measure the therapist may be using, but are offered as additions to the armentarium of the therapist.

I cannot overemphasize that both of the methods presented are part of a genuine lived interpersonal experience on the part of the therapist as well as the patient. When asking an Existential Question that elicits a strong, meaningful response from the patient, the therapist must have the plasticity to transpose himself into the world, however alien, of the patient. I try to answer the questions as they affect my being-in-the-world. When asking the patient to imagine himself in certain situations, I try to imagine my own reactions to the very same situation. In fact, it is my own previous emotional experience that leads me to "invent" new situational possibilities.

THE EXISTENTIAL QUESTIONS

Let us now examine the first of the two proposed methods, namely, the Existential Question. With the necessity of seeing the patient in his world, the author has developed certain flexible, but tangible, Existential Questions. These are not presented as test questions, but more as part of a natural conversational dialogue. Examples of a partial list of such questions are as follows. Following each question will be some typical illustrative responses. The presenting order is a matter for the clinician to decide in the therapeutic process.

1. Call you anything, but never refer to you as what? One patient who was in competition with a favored brother regarded his brother as strong, and responded to the question with, "Never call me a weak sister." It indicated his attitude towards himself in relation to other males in the world. Other responses are never call me bitch, whore, a nuisance, lonely, stupid, an ass, short, fat, insensitive, sexy, etc.

2. Did (Do) you ever make a difference to anyone? (Sometimes stated, "Did you ever come first with anyone?") This question resulted in a very

strong reaction on the part of a mother who had left her husband and children to become a writer in another city. She was actually hoping to make a difference to somebody, if only to an anonymous reading public, since she felt she had never come first with her parents, husband or children. One of the most frustrating experiences possible is to have full discharge of one's sexual impulses in the absence of having made any difference to the partner.

3. Did (Do) you know where you stood with (Father, Mother, Boss, or anyone the conversation may indicate as appropriate)? One young lady in response to this question stated that as soon as she felt her mother liked her, her mother would change to a negative attitude towards her. There were times when her mother remained fairly constant in one state or another, only to suddenly shift states with no predictability. In short, the young lady never knew where she "stood."

4. Were (Are) you ever believed? Or, Did anyone listen to you? A young man constantly confronted me with the statement that he thought I did not feel he was telling the truth, no matter how I approved or confirmed his remarks. After I asked him "if he were ever believed," he reacted with a huge amount of associative reactions to his life experiences in which not being listened to by others was very strongly presented.

5. Did (Does) anyone acknowledge your existence? How? Great emphasis has been given by Tillich and others to the concept of "confirmation of a person's existence." One example of this was presented by a patient who was raised in an orphan asylum. Repeatedly, Sunday after Sunday, he had waited at visitors' hour time for his mother to arrive--only to be disappointed except on rare occasions. To the question, "Did anyone acknowledge your existence?" he understandably burst into tears and talked at length about his orphan asylum and present-day experiences where acknowledgement of him did not occur.

6. How do (did) you get people to become aware of you? When I have asked patients how they made people become aware of them, they oftentimes have reacted startled. The implication that they had been involved unwittingly in strategies to elicit attention surprises them. Further, inquiry usually reveals a host of methods like: getting angry, temper tantrums, act intellectual, show interest in Mother's clothes, be silent, etc.

7. What choices were (are) generally open to you? To the question of choices, most patients respond readily. Examples are: none, only if I worked, if I sided with my father, or I got anything I wanted too easily, etc.

8. How much space do you take up? It is not uncommon for very tall, husky men to feel that they take up just a tiny part of space. One patient said she felt like a "grain of sand" because her mother had pounded into her the concept that "we are all like insignificant grains of sand."

9. How much time could you call your own? "There is no time I can call my own" is often heard from patients. I usually add that it seems to me that they are in a "time-struggle." One patient reported that he was always ten minutes late and this was the way he fought coercion or being obligated to anyone. Perhaps the term "obligation-struggle" might be appropriate.

10. Do (Did) you feel close or intimate with anyone? The responses to questions of intimacy are quite revealing to me since, on numerous occasions, patients have reported feeling most intimate and close to: dogs, school chums, uncles or aunts, and to various inanimate objects like dolls, trees and certain books.

11. What could (can) you call your own? The responses to this question have ranged from literally nothing, my own thoughts, only my bicycle, my bath, the time away from home, to everything materially but nothing of love.

12. What do (did) you hope for more than anything else? This question may develop in two directions. If the past is emphasized by the patient, he may indicate qualities in himself he wishes to have developed, but couldn't because of parental strategies. If the present is emphasized by the patient, the responses are usually geared to missed vocational opportunities. However, the past and present tend to jell as the patient proceeds in his discussion and, quite often, the parental values and social standards are delineated. The degree of the patient's acceptance or rejection of these standards, and the struggle he may still be in, are in evidence. "They wanted me to be a dentist so I'd be the first professional man in the family" is one good example.

13. What did (do) you feel most sorrow over? Here I find many of the acts of omission stated. Some examples are: I wish I had stayed on in college; I wish I had been kinder to my kid sister; if only I hadn't received that dishonorable discharge; I should have stayed in newspaper work; or that I left my wife, etc.

14. No matter how much you do, it's not enough. (Or, Do people underestimate you?) Presented at the appropriate time to patients who have used unrewarded hard work as an unconscious strategy to deal with others, this can have quite a marked reaction. One screamed, "Yeah, it's like shelling mounds of walnuts and soon as you shell one mound, there comes another." Another said, "I'm always taken for granted--I am tired of being so good."

15. What are you dedicated to? This question oftentimes shows the degree of commitment the patient will allow himself to people, situations, or causes, as well as how much of a feeling of belonging with others he feels he has. It is possible to get feelings of disappointment and being let down by various people and situations. "I donated five years of my life to __________ Corporation, and then when they got research grants for other things, they promptly closed my department without so much as consulting me," etc.

16. How do (did) you prove you are worthy of love and respect? Typical answers are: there are none, I guess; if I worked hard; if I had a serious discussion with my dad and didn't read comic books; if I remained a little boy to my mother; by buying her gifts until she can't possibly believe I'm not sincere; by getting my doctorate; etc.

17. What was (is) your experience with sharing? Instant responses are: hell; nothing; everything absolutely equal, so I'm still afraid to ask for a larger share; my father ate first while we watched and then if there was anything left, we ate it; my mother was a hoarder; we were taught to share everything but love; we only shared as a family if someone got married or something; the truth is, I'm pretty damn selfish; I act generous, but it's usually an artful act; etc.

18. How much energy is devoted to justifying your existence. Many a patient has responded as if they had been shot in mid-air, just nodding with agreement that a great deal of energy is spent this way. Once in awhile a patient will ask the therapist to be reminded if he acts like he's justifying his life, stating, "I don't want that kind of feeling." The many kinds of rationalizations are particularly clearly indicated here.

19. In what way would you raise your children differently than you

were raised? This question gets into the game of opposites. Depending on the degree of insight a patient has, he will usually indicate his view of the lacks and attacks of his childhood. He may very well be indicating a direction for himself in therapy.

20. What was (is) your mother's fantasy about you? This question invariably causes a great deal of thought and nearly always elicits an answer involving grunts of "ahs" of insight. For example, one patient said, "Ah, I know--I was supposed to be her husband. I was her shrine, like a religious faith. I was everything to her and I have to pretend I am 'it' to feed her fantasy." Another offered by a patient was "to marry a wealthy man to help my mother into wealthy social circles."

21. What was (is) your father's fantasy about you? "Well, my father wanted me to be a successful pharmacist so he could come to have ice cream sodas at my fountain and tell everyone that he is my father," said one man. A woman patient said, "He wanted me to be on a silk and lace pillow so that everyone could admire me." Still another man said, "To be his hunting partner." And another man said, "To be practically the wife to him that my mother wasn't." "My father wanted me to be loved by everyone," said one young lady, etc.

22. What qualities did your parents endorse in you? Responses common to this question are: none, goodness, intelligence, my musical ability, my honesty, the fact that I was so religious, hard work, my education, that I stayed away from girls, that I read a lot, my compliance, I only remember my mother complimenting me once when I saved the dog from drowning.

23. What qualities did they deny in you? Often I have heard the patient respond, "They denied I had any feelings," or "They never thought I had enough intelligence to come out of the rain." Other responses include: "I was denied a place in my family," "They denied me the right to be an artist," "They denied the existence of sex," "They denied me the right to disagree," or, "She denied me in her presence and acknowledged me when others were around."

24. What qualities are you endorsing or discarding in yourself? In this question, we are probably going to get answers that relate to the struggle of how successful the patient is in freeing himself from parental definitions rather than being engulged by it. Patients will invariably respond with, "I now feel I'm not so stupid after all," or "I have feelings even they didn't have," etc.

25. What were your mother's unconscious strategies with you? One man answered as follows: "To stand up to father but never cut him down." Another respondent said, "Have nothing to do with other women." Still another was "Silence to make me guilty." And another: "Never be smarter than my mother; taught me that nothing should ever bother me, like water off a duck's back, so I always neglected anything serious." And often patients say "gratefulness."

26. What was your father's unconscious strategy in dealing with you? Typical responses are: silence, the strap, lengthy lectures, moral persuasion, just plain fear of other people, telling me to act responsible, mother will explain it to you, talking to mother about me in front of me as if I weren't there, etc.

27. What was your strategy in dealing with your mother or father/? "By doing what she or he said and hating it," is one answer. "Pretending not to hear her or him" is another. "By getting sick a lot" might be still another. Other responses are: "Being a good boy." "Working hard."

"Flattering her or him." "Screaming at her or him until I got what I wanted." "By keeping out of her or his way."

28. What was your father's strategy in dealing with your mother? "He just withheld money from her, that's all," one patient said. "He'd always greet her with how tired he was and how rough things were," is another response. Additional responses are: silences, pretense at listening to her, making her account to him about everything, accuse her of flirting with every man she met, delay plans for fun or vacation until it was too late.

29. How would you drive someone "out of their mind?" This question usually shows the most undermining features of the patient's own life. "By telling them one thing and meaning another," or "By completely suppressing the individual every time he wants to express himself, by ignoring them and never knowing they are alive, by expressing pity and hopelessness that the poor bastard is just born that way, by never disciplining or loving him."

30. Who defines the relationship between you and (anyone the patient may be emotionally involved with)? This question has often turned out to be quite a thought-provoker. Sometimes a patient may quite meekly say, "He does, I guess." Or another might say, "I define it with women, but never with men." Another woman said, "I make him think he does, but I guess I really do." This question can be quite a "starter" to any of the Existential Questions and may lead, as has happened in the therapy sessions, to three or four or more to be asked and reacted to consecutively.

To demonstrate the limitless nature and the impossibility of capturing the total cosmos of any one man, some additional Existential Questions are shown:

1. Whom do you account to?
2. Do you ever win an argument?
3. Do you ever know what other people are thinking?
4. Do you ever see other people reacting like you?
5. How can people take advantage of you?
6. Do you fear being surpassed by other people?
7. What kind of challenges do you respond to?
8. How do you get even with people?
9. How do you punish people and how do they punish you?
10. Do you pity yourself?
11. What's your best defense against being taken over by another?
12. In whose presence do you feel the greatest loss of identity?
13. What are your peak experiences?
14. Do you feel that there are two parts of you at war?
15. What kind of criticism can you take the best?

16. How do you deceive others and how do you deceive yourself?

17. What is your fantasy about marriage (or work, fun, etc.)?

18. Are you ever taken for granted?

19. Can you simultaneously be your mother's son (or daughter) and your father's son (or daughter)?

20. What are you becoming?

A word of caution must be injected. First, this list of Existential Questions is a partial list. Other questions may occur to the therapist that may even more accurately describe the authentic inner man. On this, we rely on the skill, experience and flexibility of the therapist. Certainly, not all the questions need be asked.

Second, many existential positions of the patient's world may be stated clearly without interrogation by the therapist. He may just simply tell you.

Third, we must re-emphasize that these questions (and others) should be asked as part of the general therapeutic dialogue and not as the attorney for the prosecution.

THE IMAGINATIVE SITUATION

In the author's opinion, equally as important a method as the existential inquiry in determining the patient's "view of the world" is the use of the "Imaginative Situation." When the patient is asked to imagine himself in certain structured situations, responses may be elicited that accurately bring into the "here and now" states of feeling that have their roots in the past.

Moreover, it may be desirable to combine the Existential Question with an appropriate Imaginative Situation. (For an example of this, the reader is asked to refer to the earlier Illustration.)

Since the possible number of Imaginative Situations are legion and new possibilities are constantly occurring to the author, a list of such possible situations can only be partial. It must be added that patients themselves offer spontaneous images that relieve the therapist of structuring one of his own. In fact, experience indicates that when patients become aware of the therapist's Imaginative Situation approach, they may come up with Imaginative Situations of their own away from the therapeutic hour and offer them to the therapist.

Other writers have suggested the use of such imaginative techniques. Some of these have been included in the list to follow. However, the bulk of examples arose out of the day-to-day experience with patients.

Sometimes the responses to the Existential Question may in themselves be deemed sufficient. While it may be theoretically correct to assume that an Imaginative Situation could be matched to an Existential Question response, from a practical standpoint, it may not always be possible for the therapist to spontaneously come up with an appropriate Imaginative Situation. Sometimes it is possible that, in presenting an Imaginative Situation, an Existential Question, perhaps even previously unsuspected on the part of the therapist, may emerge. An example of this was the response of one patient in imagining whispering to his father. No matter how he was encouraged to react, he could not imagine whispering anything into the ear of his father. From this reaction, the therapist was able to ask the Existential Question, "Were you ever close to anyone?" with the suspected and highly predictable emotional response.

Let us now examine the Imaginative Situation technique itself. In this particular technique, the therapist may include the Imaginative Situation as part of the conversational dialogue, weaving and connecting this response with the Existential Question response. It may be that the therapist will wish to concentrate for a prolonged period on the Imaginative Situations. Experience indicates that certain Imaginative Situations may lead to associative images leading to further images, etc. The only guide, as far as the author can judge, is the meaningfulness of the images to the patient and the therapist.

If the patient's responses are constricted, narrow, or blocked, the therapist may "push" or "encourage" more affect. The therapist, using clinical judgment as to the readiness of the patient to face himself, may attempt, at certain times, to test the "limits" of the patient's ability to imagine himself in particular difficult (for the patient) situations. The resistances and defenses of the patient may possibly never become clearer than in "testing" the limits.

In Children of Sanchez, Oscar Lewis gives a fine example of the individual differences in imagination that members of the same family would offer in viewing the identical object:

Part 2 - Consuelo:

> If someone gave Manuel a common stone, he would hold it in his hand and look at it eagerly. In a few seconds, it would begin to shine and he would see that it was made of silver, then of gold, then of the most precious things imaginable, until the glitter died.
>
> Roberto would hold the same stone and would murmur, "Mmmmm , , , What is this good for?" But he wouldn't know the answer.
>
> Marta would hold it in her hand for just a moment, and without a thought, would throw it away.
>
> I, Consuelo, would look at it wonderingly. "What might this be? Is it, could it be, what I have been looking for?"
>
> But my father would take the stone and set it on the ground. He would look for another and put it on top of the first one, then another and another, until no matter how long it took, he had finally turned it into a house.

The theoretical purpose of using Imaginative Situations is based not only on seeing how the patient views his world, but also being able in time to "open up" the "closed system of internal reality." Fairbairn describes this internal world as a "static internal situation" which is precluded from change by its very nature so long as it remains self-contained. It is my contention that the better able the patient and therapist are to see this "tight little inner world," the easier it will be to deal with the whole of the patient and his world.

A partial list of Imaginative Situations follows:

1. Imagine that you have a power machine in front of you and that by pressing a button, you can get anyone in the world, past or present, to appear in front of you. Who would it be? Now have a dialogue with him or her.

2. Picture yourself in a department store after hours--you are all alone, you can go anywhere and take anything undetected. What would you do?

3. With what you now know living in 1989, in what past would you have liked to live in? Explain.

4. Imagine you are next to the ear of (some significant person in the patient's life), and whisper something. What would you whisper?

5. Imagine you are in front of a mirror. Describe what you see. Have a dialogue.

6. Would you rather have extraordinary sight, hearing, smell or touch? Why?

7. Imagine you are in a prison cell.

8. Imagine you are being blackmailed. How would it be done? Explain.

9. If a bus driver stopped for you with an empty bus, where would you sit?

10. Imagine you are in an old hotel lobby.

11. Imagine you hear the name of some man or woman. Describe him or her.

12. You see your name on a huge theater marquee.

13. How does it feel to walk in a meadow?

14. Can you get the image of some festivity?

15. Imagine you are being interrogated by a board of inquiry for some wrongdoing.

16. Imagine you are a phantom and can go anywhere unnoticed.

17. You come across an old trunk and you open it.

18. You look through a hole in the wall into another room.

19. You are attending your own funeral (or the funeral of somebody significant in the patient's life).

20. You are part of a circus. What do you do?

21. Imagine putting your arms around somebody.

22. You walk up to a house and open the door. Use your imagination.

23. You walk along a road and meet Diogenes.

24. You have an expensive car. Who would you have as your chauffer, assuming you could afford one?

25. You are having a tug of war with someone. Who is it and what happens?

26. Walking down a road, you meet Father Time.

27. You are a servant to a millionaire.

28. You are fighting an octopus, shark, lion or tiger with a huge sword.

29. You see a woman or man go by on a bridge at night. Twenty seconds later you hear a splash. Instantly you know he or she has jumped. However, you keep on walking.

30. Two men are holding you and another man is hitting you unmercifully. What would you do?

31. You run over a child with your car. You keep on driving.

32. Imagine that you have been falsely accused of murder. Accuse those who are falsely accusing you.

33. Imagine that nobody can see, hear or touch you, and try as you might, you go unrecognized.

34. Imagine you are an innocent fugitive "on the run" from the law.

35. Imagine you are molding a figure of somebody out of a block of wood. Who would it be? Describe.

36. You are to imagine that you have a feeling of "universal benevolence and goodness."

37. Teach a class of high school students on "how not to feel guilty about sex."

38. Be a prison warden. Explain your role.

39. You come up to a cave and, upon entering, find an old witch or old sorcerer (present one or the other at a time).

40. Imagine you have a 24 hour camera on (somebody significant in the patient's life).

41. You are in the bathroom and some man or woman comes in unexpectedly.

A CASE HISTORY DEMONSTRATING THE COMBINED METHOD OF THE EXISTENTIAL QUESTION AND IMAGINATIVE SITUATION

John is a 35-year-old man, divorced father of three, illustrator and artist. He presented a long history of situations in which he was physically self-destructive, bordering on suicide. On two occasions, he actually planned suicide and nearly carried this out successfully. He appeared schizoid, withdrawn, intelligent, and Hamletian. He would pause on occasion and say he was in a "state of confusion." He was an excellent voice imitator of prominent personalities and realized that his real self was safe behind this facade.

His father was a Navy pilot who was killed in flight when John was nine. John was taught by his grandmother to glorify his father. His father gave John the impression that he was a God before he died and that he expected John to be God someday. John blamed himself for his father's death--since his view of the world was to be "responsible" for everyone and everything around him. His mother wanted social station for him, preferably by being a successful businessman. Little affection came from his mother.

A governess named Catherine was his only source of affection and concern. His father, unable to stand the competition of Catherine, fired her. Before she went, however, she approached John and told him that if he didn't attempt to change his father's mind, she would join a convent. She subsequently did join a convent and John blamed himself for this.

In the first few sessions, John reported that sometimes he felt Christ-like and other times he felt like committing suicide.

In answer to the Existential Question, "Never refer to me as what?" he answered, "Businessman." Moreover, to the Existential Question, "What was your mother's fantasy about you?" he answered, "To be loved and accepted on a high social level, preferably marrying into Bostonian prominence." He strongly rejected this direction for his life--although he had been in business, he never bothered about the business and allowed his business partner complete control.

I made him imagine (IS) having lunch with his mother in a fashionable restaurant. Here is the verbatim dialogue out of his imagination:

MOTHER: You can't be out of work too long, John, you know.

JOHN: Yes, Mother (sarcastically).

MOTHER: Why don't you start another business?

JOHN: You are a bitch, bitch, bitch; leave me alone! He screamed).

At a later time he responded to the question (EQ), "How do you make yourself aware to anyone?" by, "Well, I did with my father by letting him hit me with a ball in my eye, after I noticed that he had missed the ball I threw to him."

I asked him to imagine (IS) being the "servant to a millionaire." He imagined he pushed the "old son of a bitch down the steps." In the Department Store (IS), he went to the gun section to "get some guns to kill my father."

In the Power Machine (IS), he brought in Shakespeare, Dostoyevsky and Freud. But in all three situations, he could not talk to them except from a distance, and then only in an abstract way. "I can't reveal myself to them," he said.

At another session, he answered that he could not really call any time hs own (EQ). He guessed he was in a "time-struggle" with his mother.

From the dreams he had reported (where I had him imagine being the people and things in the dream in the tradition of Gestalt therapy), my own clinical judgment told me that before we could uncover the "unconscious strategies," it was first necessary to dispel his fear of insanity. It was not until the thirtieth session that I was able to ask him to "imagine driving someone crazy." His verbatim reply was:

> By covering up feelings of hate with false feelings of love, dedication and trust. But never understanding or listening to you. By teaching false values. By placing your identity in jeopardy if the truth is spoken.

A few sessions later, I had him imagine (IS) he was in a meadow. His verbatim account is as follows:

JOHN: A hurricane wind comes up. I see the edge of the forest. I run for cover and there is none. I see a great big eye behind me. It's a blue eye. It's frightening. I am afraid.

THERAPIST: Whose eye is it?

JOHN: It must be Catherine's eye. I know it is. It's Catherine's eye.

THERAPIST: Imagine you have a spear and throw it at the eye.

JOHN: I do, but the spear hits it and falls away.

THERAPIST: Imagine you are in a tank and you are running over the eye.

JOHN: Man, that's hard. I'll try. It's getting a little easier; I can crush it.] Makes arm motions as if he is crushing something] [A long silence; he has tears in his eyes] You know what?

THERAPIST: What?

JOHN: The eye was Catherine's eye. It was my guilt, my obligation to her, my responsibility. When I crushed that eye, something lifted. I guess I don't feel guilty about Catherine anymore.

In another session, I had him imagine (IS) that he had a fever. His verbatim account is as follows:

I'm in grade school, and I threw up into my hands because I couldn't tell the teacher I felt sick. After I threw up, my teacher sent me home and I rode home on my bicycle. As I drove up to my house, my father pulled away. I called after him, while I almost passed out. He did come back. I was guilty over my sickness, over not being a "good soldier." I didn't want to draw attention to me. If I couldn't be a "good soldier," I'd be like a raging little girl. Like Eloise in the comic strip. Now I get it! My mother made me feel that, left to my own devices, I'd be an idiot.

I then asked the EQ, "How do you justify your existence?"

JOHN: I always justify because left to my own, I'd do something terrible.

THERAPIST: The only way out is to be perfect and good.

JOHN: I see. If I accept blame or I'm less than perfect, I'll turn into a headache.

I asked him to imagine (IS) that he was facing a board of inquiry.

Adopt a Joan or Arc attitude. Answer all questions clearly, looking them straight in the eye. Basically, I'd say "Love me even if I did wrong." Then I'd collapse.

I urged him to (IS) accuse the accusors, since I said, "What the hell did you do wrong?"

> All right. [Pause] I'd look at them, like my mother. You don't listen, you don't hear me, you're foreign to me. Only through fever can I get any attention from you.
>
> I'd turn to the father. I don't want to be a soldier, some Boy Scout pledge, with old ladies hail-fellow-well-met I don't know what, but I don't want that and I don't want to be a chip off the old block, but an individual! [Long pause] You know I couldn't make an honest mistake.
>
> I feel better now. I feel like Zorba. I don't want to be Eloise or Joan of Arc, because so long as I am, I give up any chance for being loved or having fun.

Within a few weeks he found he could go back to work again. this represented quite a breakthrough because, in the past, he would stay in his room illustrating and painting for months, unable to get himself in a job situation. A few weeks later he reported feelings of wanting to walk off the job, but he said, "I know better now. I just feel guilty. I don't know about what, but I feel real guilty."

I asked him to imagine (IS) he was a prison warden. His verbatim answer is as follows: "No, I'd rather not, because that's my mother's role and she can have it."

This avenue of exploration indicated to me the possibility that his present work problem ("Never call me a businessman") might have another direction. I asked him (EQ) if he felt others would pass him by, leaving him standing alone? He then proceeded with his own association, stating: "That old man of mine was a saint. How can you ever be better than a saint?"

I interspersed the question (EQ), "No matter what you do, it's not enough?" He seemed not to respond to this, repeating over and over, "How can you beat a saint?" I asked him to (IS) imagine himself going up to St. Francis. His account of this (IS) was simple and immediate.

JOHN: I'd hand him a cigar and say, "Be a man like me." [Long pause] My father never was a man; he made the pretense of being a man. He never did anything wrong. He was spiritual.

THERAPIST: What was your unconscious strategy in dealing with your father?

JOHN: To make him think he was the man, the saint, the perfect one.

THERAPIST: What does this have to do with work?

JOHN: I am angry at my bosses. Gee whiz. I hope they understand it, because I projected onto them this spiritual superiority of my father and I am angry because I am sick and tired of protecting his fucking image.

At the next session he reported that work had been a lot easier and the guilt had seemed to lift. (EQ) "How can people take advantage of you?" I asked. "They can't, if I don't protect their fucking image," he replied. He spontaneously presented an image of:

Shitting in a pot, in a pot next to Freud, and we can talk about anything personal we want to . . . . Then I think of you and I going to a football game and we are both eating hot dogs and we are watching the game and enjoying it very much . . . Wow.

At best, the above illustration is only a partial one. While it may be argued that this particular man is adept at imagination, and therefore was amenable to this specific kind of approach, my own experience indicates that nearly everyone responds as readily as if it were usual conversational dialogue.

DISCUSSION

My own thoughts based on my experience with the combined method as therapy lead me to some tentative conclusions.

1. The combined method as therapy gives Sullivan's term "participant-observer" a dimension of intensity that I hadn't encountered in using the usual methods of therapeutic techniques. It seemingly takes more of the resources of the therapist and patient. There are fewer "dead" spots in the therapy session. The therapist not only listens, but also experiences the patient's communications at many different levels.

2. The therapist has greater opportunities for creativity, seeking the kinds of Existential Questions or Imaginative Situations to stimulate the patient to responses and reactions. Instead of the patient trying to fit into a prescribed theory of therapy, the therapist is trying to gauge and assess the unique system of the individual.

3. Not unlike other approaches, the assessment of the "ego strength" of the patient is extremely important. In the combined method, this necessity may even be heightened.

4. The marriage of the Existential Question and the Imaginative Situation may be quite a harmonious one at some instances. At still other times, each may act as independent partners in the marriage. If it is a "shotgun marriage," the therapist may be on the wrong track or the patient may be resisting. Time and experience will bear this out.

5. My experience indicates that, very often, either no interpretation or very little interpretation is necessary in using the combined method as therapy. Patients usually offer a host of their own interpretations as a result of the experience.

6. When a patient expresses hopelessness and despair, the combined method has a great possibility of "jarring him loose" and breaking the "log jam."

7. After rapport has been reached between the patient and therapist, I found that practically all patients could become involved in the combined method as therapy. If a patient does remain uninvolved or angry at having to imagine, it provides us with another avenue of exploration and therapy.

REFERENCES

Shorr, J. E. Psycho-imagination Therapy: The integration of phenomenology and imagination. New York: Intercontinental-Medical Book Corp., 1972.

Shorr, J. E. (1973). In what part of your body does your mother reside? Psychotherapy: Theory, research and practice, 10(2), Summer, 31-34.
Shorr, J. E. (1974). Shorr imagery test. Los Angeles: Institute for Psycho-imagination Therapy, 1974.
Shorr, J. E. (1975). The use of task imagery as therapy. Psychotherapy: Theory, research and practice, 12(2), Summer, 207-210.
Shorr, J. E. (1976). Dual imagery. Psychotherapy: Theory, research and practice, 13(2), Fall, 244-248.
Shorr, J. E. (1977). Group Shorr imagery test. Los Angeles: Institute for Psycho-imagination Therapy.
Shorr, J. E. (1977). Go see the movie in your head. New York: Popular Library.
Shorr, J. E. (July 1978). Imagery as a projective device. Imagery Bulletin, Los Angeles: American Association for the Study of Mental Imagery, 1(2).
Shorr, J. E. (1978). Supplementary Shorr imagery test. Los Angeles: Institute for Psycho-imagination Therapy.
Shorr, J. E. (May 1979). Imagery as a method of self-observation in therapy. Imagery Bulletin, Los Angeles: American Association for the Study of Mental Imagery, 2(2).
Shorr, J. E. Shorr parental imagery test. Los Angeles: Institute for Psycho-imagination Therapy. (In press.)
Shorr, J. E. Shorr couples imagery test. Los Angeles: Institute for Psycho-imagination Therapy. (In press.)
Shorr, J. E. (1980). Discoveries about the mind's ability to organize and find meaning in imagery. In Joseph E. Shorr, Gail E. Sobel, Pennee Robin, and Jack A. Connella (Eds.), Imagery: Its many dimensions and applications, Vol. 1. New York: Plenum Press.
Shorr, J. E. (1981). The psychologist's imagination and sexual imagery. In Eric Klinger (Ed.), Imagery: Concepts, results, and applications, Vol. 2. New York: Plenum Press.
Shorr, J. E. (1983). Psycho-imagination therapy's approach to body imagery. In Joseph E. Shorr, Gail Sobel-Whittington, Pennee Robin, and Jack A. Connella (Eds.), Imagery: Theoretical and clinical applications, Vol. 3. New York: Plenum Press.
Shorr, J. E. (1983). Psychotherapy through imagery. New York: Thieme-Stratton, Inc.
Shorr, J. E. (1986). The use of imagery in group psychotherapy. In Milton Wolpin, Joseph E. Shorr, and Lisa Krueger (Eds.), Imagery: Recent practice and theory, Vol. 4. New York: Plenum Press.
Singer, J. L. (1966). Daydreaming: An introduction to the experimental study of inner experience. New York: Random House.
Shorr, J. E. (1971). Imagery and daydream techniques employed in psychotherapy: Some practical and theoretical implications. In C. Spielberger (Ed.), Current topics in clinical and community psychology, 3. New York: Academic Press.
Stampfl, T. G. and Leavis, D. J. (1967). Essentials of implosive therapy: A learning theory based on psycho-dynamic behavior therapy. Journal of Abnormal Psychology, 72, 496-503.
Sullivan, H. S. (1953). The interpersonal theory of psychiatry. New York: Norton.
Szalita, A. B. (Spring 1968). Reanalysis. Contemporary Psychoanalysis, 4(2), 83-102.

POINTS OF VIEW: WORKING WITH SPONTANEOUS IMAGES IN GROUP PSYCHOTHERAPY

Mark F. Ettin

Private Practice, East Brunswick, New Jersey
Adjunct Associate Professor, Department of Psychiatry
UMDNJ, Robert Wood Johnson Medical School

Amidst the complexities of the psychotherapy group, it is possible to see the way clear. Within the free flow of the group dialogue, mental images of abiding lucidity often arise spontaneously, figuratively following the twists and turns of interaction and literally leading towards sequences of meaningful exploration. Such emergent metaphoric and symbolic word-pictures serve to depict individual and interpersonal dynamics, while aptly characterizing the collective's thematic patternings, resistances, and impasses (Ettin, 1986). Unlike the fixed motifs of Desoille (1965) and Leuner (1969, 1984), or the standard situations of Shorr (1978, 1983, 1986), and Ahsen (1981), these creative configurations often arise unbidden or unplanned (Horowitz, 1970; Ettin, 1982). Suddenly a mental picture comes to mind in direct response to the group's timely need for concrete representations of its more abstract processes. By carefully attending to and following such portending images, members are helped to personalize meanings and clarify interchanges, while the group itself can both analyze its current trends and make necessary adjustments to its progress (Ettin, 1985).

THE GROUP AS A CULTURAL PHENOMENA

Any particular emergent image, while an immediate product of its creator, is also a synergistic event born up from the raw material of the group involvement. Such images serve a collective and communicative function as soothsayers for the shared experience. The contributor of an image, whether a member or the leader, serves as group spokesperson, that participant most sensitive, expressive, or vulnerable to the presenting affect, issue, or theme. Firth (1973) suggests that transfer of meaning from the private to public domain is evident when symbols are seen to have a social or an organizational effect on the conglomerate. In these cases, private reveries transform into public statements. As such, the individual contributor's authority comes to surpass that of idiosyncratic experience, and in a real sense he or she talks to and for the group.

> The significance of private symbols may be thought to lie in the degree to which they express experiences or feelings of what may be called the audience . . . the initial visionary acts as a trigger for the . . . [group]--one might say a catalyst. (pp. 236-238)

In the normal course of the group life, members become more attentive and responsive to each other and to their common culture. They discover universalities of experience, similarities and differences of perception, empathic resonances, and a diversity of approaches to the group's shared tasks and goals. These intimate, intricate, and often subtle experiences together can be manifestly expressed in the form of creative configurations. The group's overt realities, as well as its latent potentialities, can be so depicted. The group comes to develop a language expressible in symbols of interaction and in self reflective images. The arousal of these mental images can bring members together, stimulate formative energies, foster insightful recognitions, and move the shared process to richer levels of engagement.

The group therapist's task, here, is to actively listen and watch for those spontaneous images which arise as collective representations (Durkheim, 1974, Levy-Bruhl, 1985), bearing immediate relevance and specific cultural import. The therapist explicates the evolving therapeutic context and equilibrates the group process by working within the linguistic and perceptual frame set up by the emergent image form. Thereby, group themes, affects, developmental issues, and focal conflicts can be identified and worked through (Whitaker & Lieberman, 1964). Ultimately, it is the individuals in the group that must be treated. It becomes critical to alternately work between the general and the specific, and from universal to particular levels of imagistic elaboration and decoding.

This distinction between private and public symbols, and the varying attentions required at covariant levels of meaning, is finely elucidated by Firth (1973):

> An anthropologist is concerned to find out what a given symbol corresponds to in the general understanding and operations of a body of people. He seeks if not consensus at least the highest common factor in referents. He does this because he is looking at symbols as bases for or expressions of common action; the element of communication of meaning is dependent upon the possibility of shared understanding. A psychologist . . . may be interested in this too, but he is also interested in the departure of the symbol from the consensus, with the cues it offers to individual development. (p. 208)

GENERAL COMMENTS ON THE ELABORATION OF EMERGENT IMAGES

The initial emphasis in working with emergent images is to stay within the confines of the word-picture itself. Interpretive and reductive conclusions are resisted, while attending to the image content and its inherent transformational potentials. By elaborating the image, various member's creativities and psycho-imaginations are brought into play (Shorr, 1983). Suggestions may be made to change or sharpen the mental picture so as to better reflect the affects and circumstances eliciting its occurrence. By circumambulating or walking around the image to see its various sides, shades and contours, a more encompassing perspective becomes possible (Mattoon, 1978). What does the image look like to the various members? What differing perspectives can be shown about the image? Members are then able to readjust their personal positions and perceptions to account for these other points of view. By extending the image in a process of active imagination, implications are drawn out, and the symbolic content is allowed to develop, to change, and to transform in response to the group's projective, interpretive, and assimilative needs (Hannah, 1981). Can participants add anything new to the developing picture? What is happening in the image? What is about to happen as a consequence of the developing scenario? How do members feel about the way the picture is evolving? An intuitive sense of implication is gained by seeing how the symbol evolves.

By amplifying the image, comparisons and similarities can be drawn to known cultural, mythical, and historical forms and antecedents (Jung, 1976). What motifs, scenarios, collective or universal concerns does the image suggest? What contexts or metaphoric implications are brought to mind? Here, various hidden agendas and predetermined cultural patternings can be elaborated. Closely following a Jungian position, the emergent creative forms are viewed as "living symbols," able to reflect, guide, and ultimately change the ongoing group process. The image content itself, treated as a fully descriptive presentation, becomes the mercuric message to be recognized and headed?

Within such an open ended and phenomenological exploration, the psychotherapeutic process takes on poetic license. By staying within the metaphoric confines of the presenting image, linguistic embellishment becomes central to the analysis and the further construction of meanings. How does this image explicate, talk about, and depict the many aspects of the current group scene? What sensual qualities of the image touch the experience being reflected? By taking the image and its symbolic significance seriously, we can also take each experience as far as possible, exploring and exploiting various subtleties and sequences, various plots and potencies. By working within the presenting image, we can push the creative relation as far as language and common sense will allow. The analogy implied within the image can reach asymtotic limits, so that the emergent talk approaches the essential tale. The purpose, then, of constructing symbolic relations, and the impetus for images spontaneously arising from within the flux of experience, is the need to impose grammatical order on a mass of seemingly unconnected experiences. The occurrence of an organizing image creates a framework, an appearance of coherence. It is as if to say, by seeing our experience in this way, we can make sense of our goings on together.

The last step in the explorative process looks to the formative past for etiological antecedents, and to the anticipatory future for ameliorative transformations. Following Freudian understandings (Freud, 1964; Horowitz, 1970), the processes motivating image formation now come under specific therapeutic analysis. The urges, motives, defensive structures, object relations, memories, fantasies, or group level transferences which provide source material for the arising image are probed. What in the group process has caused this image to arise? What spurred this expressive change? What are the inherent qualities of the image, i.e., aggressive, compliant, remorseful, etc.? What conflicts are implied? What overdetermined personal experiences or adjustments account for this particular image form? What changes in individual patternings or in group adaptations are needed to resolve the presenting problem or impasse? What directions are suggested for working through? Through free association, secondary elaboration, and subsequent interpretation, the therapist relates the emergent imagery to the group's focal conflicts and to the individual member's intrapsychic and interpersonal life adjustments. The imaging process, itself, treated as a fully motivated dynamic, becomes the messenger to be halted, frisked, and relieved of its overdetermined meanings before being sent on its symbolically unencumbered way.

EXPECTED SEQUENCE IN WORKING WITH SPONTANEOUS IMAGES

While images arise spontaneously, a regularity in the process of image formation and elucidation can be outlined. The working sequence is generalized as follows:

1. An individual, interactional, or group level problem or conflict is presented or enacted.

2. The presence of resistance, impasse, or dysfunctional problem solutions leads to frustration, confusion, chaos, demoralization, and/or disequilibrium within the group.

3. The sudden emergence of a metaphoric or symbolic image characterizes heretofore diffuse, abstract, and unorganized energies and trends; and the group intuitively recognizes the relevance, power, and prescience of the image.

4. The group is encouraged to actively develop the image through a brainstorming process which includes psycho-imaginal elaboration, circumambulation, active imagination, amplification, and poetic license to call out the inherent metaphor by particiularizing its essences and implications for the current situation or problem.

5. The symbolism of the image and its evoking circumstances are generalized by the therapist and related to common situational, developmental, groupwide, or universal concerns, which the members are then encouraged to discuss and explore within this wider context.

6. Members are now engaged in free association, secondary elaboration and interpretive analysis of the phenomenology and etiology of the original problem, impasse or resistance with one eye toward the formative past and one eye on the transformative future.

CLINICAL VIGNETTES

Quick Sand

Cassie, a 36-year-old woman, suddenly had her engagement broken off by her fiancee. She is stunned, enraged, and depressed. With an air of desparation, Cassie talks about all the dreams that have gone down with the relationship, and of everything she is doing to quickly get over her dysforic feelings. The group is very responsive to Cassie's sadness and her anger at her ex-fiancee, but has difficulty relating to her efforts to stay afloat. Whenever Cassie exposes her losses and her floundering self-healing plans, the group remains silent and members appear cringingly uncomfortable. The therapist suggests that there is something about the quality of Cassie's sadness and restorative attempts that makes it difficult for the members to respond empathically to her. The group members are encouraged to explore their paucity of reaction by expressing how they actually feel when Cassie demonstrates her sadness and distress. The group's imagery is cultivated by asking, How do you picture Cassie at these times? How do you see her? Paul, an obsessive young adult, identifies a sense of paralysis and helplessness in Cassie's demeanor. With sudden intuitive force, Rosa suggests that "its like Cassie is in quicksand." The more she struggles, the sooner and the faster she seems to go down.

The group is reluctant to engage with Cassie, within this desperate thrashing, for fear of being grabbed and submerged within her grief. They suggest that her various frantic attempts to remain on the surface of her feelings just engender panic, and push her down faster and further. The members also begin to realize that Cassie is blaming herself and the group for the failure of her relationship, and acts as if to drag everyone down with her. With the quicksand image as a guide, the group helps Cassie look at her paralogism of misappropriated projections and activities, which ultimately result in her remaining emersed, stuck, and sinking within her own depression. They can now reach a hand toward a member who has had the ground come out from under her.

Through Cassie's experience and its encapsulation in imagery, other members are able to grasp their own sinking and suffocating reactions to hurt and loss. Rosa suggests that perhaps facing the feelings and just waiting them out would be a better strategy than struggling so. Paul wonders if maybe the work that needs to be done now involves developing internal supports rather than grasping for external handholds. The group goes on to expressly explore Cassie's and their own responsibility for the drowning of her relationship. They look into Cassie's pattern of relating with her ex-fiancee, and with the group, which leads to dangerous and quixotic disappointments.

A Glass of Acid

Some sessions later, Rosa appears very shaky. She reluctantly relates that she has just taken her comprehensive exams for her master's degree, and is unsure if she has passed. The group queries Rosa about the test, encouraging her to explain the relevant details and to talk about her concerns. Rosa is very tentative, and the group becomes impatient when she is not more forthcoming. Rosa appears on the verge of crying, but tries resolutely not to let loose her tears. The image occurs to the therapist that Rosa is holding her feelings and fears like "a glass of water filled to the brim." If she moves forward she might spill.

Kevin develops the image further by suggesting that if, in fact, it's water that's contained, what's the danger? He says, "It's more like she's carrying sulfuric acid." The therapist encorporates this elaboration by suggesting that Rosa is crossing the threshold to her profession. If she is carrying her fears with benign liquidity, spilling and failing the comprehensives will just be water under the bridge. She will take them again. If, however, she is full of turbulent acidity, any overflow may seem to corrode her chances of traversing from the present into the future. She may fear that "bridges will be burned and there may be no other way across."

The other group members associate to the glass of acid image by relating to the risk, terror and vulnerability of crossing difficult transitional bridges in their own lives. What are they facing? How do their feelings come across? What are they holding in for fear of ruinous alchemical reaction? With the glass of acid image as a guide, Rosa and the group are more able to speak directly of the churning anxieties inherent in being put to the test. Rosa can recognize and explore the extent of her vulnerability, as well as her attempt to repressively contain her fears lest they destructively spill out of control. The group can explore with Rosa the origin, meaning, and current utility of this self-contained stance. Rosa can see how holding in her feelings eats away at her, and she can experiment with other ways to soothe her turbulent insides. The image also suggests that Rosa needs a milk-based lining to neutralize her anxieties. Using the water/acid/milk image as a symbolic guide, the group can explore with Rosa if lapses in mothering contribute to her lack of confidence and fears of change.

The Marathon

A long-term therapy group in its fourth year was struggling with a number of members simultaneously considering terminating. Wanting to exit yet stay attached, Harmon asks for a six month leave of absence to concentrate on his graduate studies. Lisa discusses her impending move to marriage and a new geographic area. Of late, she had been steadily moving away from the group. Yet she appears afraid to make a formal break.

Group members consider these matters in muted tones and with an evident lack of energy and involvement.

Amidst obvious dependency issues, Lisa expresses her concern that even after moving, she will need the group. Jokingly, she suggests that the other group members might see her jogging back across country to attend a session. June quickly quips that she can easily picture Lisa as "a group marathon runner." With the presentation of the marathon image, the group spirit begins to lift as preconscious recognitions dawn. The marathon, as a modern event, carries many ready connotations of fitness, perseverance and determination. In ancient Greece, the messenger reaching Marathon signals a Persian invasion, thus preparing the polis by giving them time to secure their defenses and battlements. The runner, upon completion of the task, terminates. The city group, with proper prewarning, is preserved. In this image, Lisa, who speaks of leaving, is actually seen running toward the group. In dual symbolic significance, she works out her last gasp of participation, while serving the collective function of mobilizing the remaining members for reengagement and a continuance of their therapeutic struggles.

The therapist highlights the emergent image by suggesting that "this long-term group effort, at times, assumes marathon proportions." Who will finish this race? Who will drop out? What are appropriate grounds for leaving? What pace is required in order to stay involved? What does it feel like to tire and work through fatigue? How does one know if, in fact, their therapy race is run? The symbolic resonances inherent in the marathon image energize the group, while stimulating an in-depth exploration of the current dynamics around ending or moving on.

Harmon and Lisa, now, directly consider the meaning and timing of their impulses to leave. One of Harmon's continuing complaints is lack of available energy. His compulsive and single-minded strivings often lead to mental and physical exhaustion, and subsequently result in failed mastery and goal attainment. With the marathon image as a guide, the group helps Harmon realize that he is approaching graduate school in the same driven manner that led to his dropping out of medical school in a heap of demoralized debility. He springs where a steady job is more the required pace. Suggestions are made that perhaps a more metered approach might be advisable, and if so, members wonder if Harmon really needs to leave group to succeed in his studies.

Lisa, on the other hand, is encouraged to consider the anachronistic fears which impede her from cleanly cutting the umbilical stretching across the finish of her time in the group. In the course of this discussion, she comes to realize that despite her anxiety about moving on with her life, she is doing quite well and feeling much better. The group points up the strides Lisa has made in her time here. In fact, on exploration, Lisa realizes how little she currently relies on the group, on the therapist, or for that matter, on her parents for security and direction. The path of the group discussion now turns toward the sadness of taking leave, the inherent loneliness of the long distance runner. Over a number of sessions, plans are made for cutting the chord in a formal termination.

Listening to Lisa and Harmon talk of leaving initially proves demoralizing and contagious for the remaining members. The other, now, wonder expressly if they can stay the course. Working within the symbolic scenario of the marathon image, the therapist encourages various group members to assess where they are in their own therapy progress. "How do you feel about how far you've come? How much farther do you need and wish to go? What landmarks and milestones remain to be passed?" As the various group members explore their commitments and reservoirs of available energy, necessary adjustments are made to carry themselves toward completion. New leaders quicken their participatory pace and come to the forefront as the reformed pack moves on together.

The sudden appearance of the marathon image, and its supplementary forms, tangibly help the group focus, hold, and work through this transitional period in its common life. Expressive junctures or turning points in the group are often "marked by ritualistic signs" (Whitaker & Lieberman, 1964, p. 117). Such a sign may, in fact, be the occurrence of a particularly striking image or figure of speech. Like a key symbol in a dream series or a resounding cultural production, the marathon image, with its symbolic implications, guided this therapeutic process for some time through a sequence of crisis, termination, and renewal.

SPONTANEOUS AND A PRIORI IMAGES

Levi-Strauss (1988) proposes a structural approach to symbolic understandings. Each image presents a way of depiction couched in particular codes, paradigms, or systems of expression. In symbolic relations, a superimposition takes place, a layering of forms, as one expressive display comes to stand in for another set of experiences. Providing an imagistic term from an alternate descriptive system instills creative tension and opens up metaphoric possibilities. "The metaphor rests on an intuition that these terms connote the same semantic field when seen from a more global perspective" (p. 194).

This is exactly the process that takes shape in the group. An image arises, appropriated from a pertinent parallel paradigm to describe an otherwise undecipherable set of circumstances. The emergent image carries within it an inherent set of forms, terms, relations, and transformations. Each word-picture evokes motifs and scenarios suggestive of progression or regression, danger or triumph, evasion or enhancement. Each image holds its own natural extension or diminution. The image, within pictoral confines, presents a panorama of functional and compositional qualities for combination, elaboration and analysis. When working with any particular image, it is preferable to stay within its perceptual language. For in psychotherapeutic dialogue, as in other creative expositions, it is not helpful to mix and match metaphors.

Supplying an image for a group, proforma, may not provide the most expressive or timely symbolic paradigm. Attending and developing emergent images has the advantage of flexible occurrence, the right picture for the right circumstances. Bachelard (1969), in pointing out the prescience and phenomenological potency of fresh images, suggests,

> Because of its novelty and its action, the poetic image has an entity and a dynamism of its own; it is referable to a direct ontology. . . . By its novelty, a poetic image sets in motion the entire linguistic mechanism. The poetic image places us at the origin of the speaking being . . . [for] the image has touched the depths before it stirs the surace." (pp. xii, xix)

Within the ongoing group process some degree of organization is already straining to form up and materialize. Less than conscious processes are already subliminally equating experiences and prefiguring in concrete and expressible representations. Letting a key image arise from within the group's experience makes use of these existent formative processes. As such, the group moves along by way of its own images and symbolic codes. The ultimate referrent for the group experience becomes the semantic and experiential field itself, which, by definition, requires linguistic expression, elaboration, and metaphoric transposition. Within the interactive matrix of the group, the unspeakable is spoken, the literate arises from solecistic, and order comes out from chaos. Working with spontaneous images truly allows the psychotherapy group to develop many and varied points of view.

REFERENCES

Ahsen, A. (1981). Eidetic group therapy. In Gazda (Ed.), Innovations to Group Therapy, Springfield, Il.: Charles C. Thomas.

Bachelard, G. (1969). The poetics of space. Boston: Beacon Press.

Desoille, R. (1965). The directed daydream. New York: Psychosynthesis Foundation.

Durkheim, E. (1974). Sociology and philosophy. New York: Free Press.

Ettin, M. (1982). Imagery in client-therapist communications. American Journal of Psychoanalysis, 42(3), 229-237.

Ettin, M. (1985). Private eyes in a public setting. Journal of Mental Imagery, 9(3), 19-44.

Ettin, M. (1986). Within the group's view: Clarifying dynamics through metaphoric and symbolic imagery. Small Group Behavior, 17(4), 407-426.

Firth, R. (1973). Symbols: Public and private. Ithaca, New York: Cornell University Press.

Freud, S. (1964). New Introductory Lectures on Psychoanalysis, Vol. 22. New York: International Universities Press.

Hannah, B. (1981). Encounters with the soul: Active imagination as developed by C. G. Jung. Cambridge, Mass.: Sigo Press.

Horowitz, M. (1970). Image formation and cognition. New York: Appleton-Century-Crofts.

Jung, C. (1976). The symbolic life. Collected works, Vol. 18. Princeton University Press.

Leuner, H. (1969). Guided affective imagery: A method of intensive psychotherapy. American Journal of Psychotherapy, 23, 4-22.

Leuner, H. (1984). Guided affective imagery: Mental imagery in short-term psychotherapy. New York: Thieme-Stratton, Inc.

Levy-Bruhl, L. (1985). How natives think. Princeton, N.J.: Princeton University Press.

Levi-Strauss, C. (1988). The jealous potter. Chicago: University of Chicago Press.

Mattoon, M. (1978). Applied dream analysis: A Jungian Perspective. New York: John Wiley & Sons.

Shorr, J. (1978). Clinical uses of categories of mental imagery. In J. Singer & Pope (Eds.), The Power of Human Imagination: New Methods in Psychotherapy. New York: Plenum Press.

Shorr, J. (1983). Psychotherapy through imagery. New York: Thieme-Stratton, Inc.

Shorr, J. (1986). The use of imagery in group psychotherapy. Scandanavian Journal of Psychology.

Whitaker, D., & Lieberman, M. (1964). Psychotherapy through the group process. Chicago: Aldine.

USE OF "THREE BOXES," A PSYCHO-IMAGINATION THERAPY SPECIAL IMAGE, WITH A SCHIZOPHRENIC POPULATION

David Tansey

Clinical Psychologist
Private Practice
San Diego, CA

ABSTRACT

The Three Boxes, a special image developed by Joseph E. Shorr (Shorr, 1983), and used as a projective test item, was administered to 27 schizophrenic residents at Hanbleceya, a therapeutic community established for the treatment of schizophrenia. The results were used in the following two ways. First, to confirm or deny from quantitative data the premise that conflict, as measured by The Three Boxes, and their associated sentence completions, would be reduced as residents moved through the phases of the program toward a non-psychotic way of relating to others. And second, to provide qualitative descriptions of how three of the modal members of the population want to be seen, feel about themselves at core and their defenses and coping mechanisms, as revealed by interpretations of their responses to the test items.

INTRODUCTION

Psycho-Imagination Therapy (Shorr, 1983) includes the use of imagery as a psychotherapeutic and diagnostic tool. Through imagery, therapist and client may discover together how the person feels defined, or misdefined by others, whether and to whom they are making a difference, and at what price. Imagery allows the therapist to share the phenomenology of the client. Phenomenology here means a shared perception of how each views the world, self and others. The therapist must see inside of how the client sees the world, must know the other as the other is. This empathic sharing of world view, in the sense of inclusion (Friedman, 1985) "imagining the real" leads to trust; trust growing out of the client's sensing the understanding and acceptance of the world as seen, felt and felt about by the client, in the therapist. And it is the trust growing out of this professional emotional involvement of client and therapist that is the <u>sine qua non</u> of change.

The Three Boxes is one items from The Shorr Imagery Test (Shorr, 1976). This instrument has most routinely been used as a projective measure of individual personality. It can be quantitatively scored for degree of conflict and it can be used qualitatively for personality description. This paper uses both the qualitative and quantitative facets to examine the personalities of the 27 individuals on their journey through schizophrenia.

The Three Boxes, and their associated sentence completions, seem consistently to reveal the following. From the large box, the person's style of interaction with the social environment or the outer projection of personality is portrayed. From the small box, the person's inner core or the central aspect of their personality is reflected. The middle box shows aspects of the barriers inside or the mechanism of coping between the large box and the small box or the personality defenses.

The residents of Hanbleceya consist of a group of individuals embarked on their healing journey through psychosis. Issues are worked on in depth in an atmosphere of community loving confrontation. Many of these individuals have been labeled chronic and at times out of touch with the world of reality as it is understood by the general population.

At Hanbleceya (Fitzpatrick, 1985), relationship is seen as a vehicle for growth and transformation, reconciliation and healing. The therapeutic community is a safe place where the healing journey of each is the concern of all. Meeting, with relationship, is the medium for the journey. In a responsive, loving community, this allows for feeling of self and therefore feeling of existence to occur. A loving trusting community creates space for meaningful dialogue, confrontation, and working through issues. Hence, the purpose of Hanbleceya is to provide a safe environment for the healing journey of the residents and reconciliation amongst family members. Healing occurs in the between, to use Buber's (Friedman, 1985) term, of the relationship of client and therapist, client and family, and client and community, within the culture. For healing to occur there must be trust, and confirmation of otherness. It is believed that for a resident to trust, the resident must accept the culture, and the commitment and the love of the therapist.

It is also believed that the journey from insanity can be broken into four major phases. Phase One requires the resident incorporate concrete structure. This takes place in a totally loving confrontive environment where the tasks of the resident are to learn to focus, is to pay attention and to be able to shift attention appropriately, and to bond to the community and a therapist. Phase Two encourages less structured semi-independent living where the tasks of the resident are to develop intimate relationships based upon trust, love and acceptance. Phase Three's major task is independent living where old issues recur and the resident deals with separation from the therapeutic community, their primary therapist, and their family. Phase Four allows part time participation in the community in addition to work or school and the tasks of the resident are acceptance, forgiveness and taking care of unfinished business both with the therapeutic community and the family.

Given these conceptions of imagery, therapy and schizophrenia, it was considered that visual imagery, with its ability to avoid censorship in more normal individuals, might also give insight into the world view of these schizophrenics in spite of their often incoherent thinking. This utilization of imagery could facilitate dialogue with a high level of intimacy and empathy without the therapist having to sacrifice reality or clear thinking. It was further considered that conflict scores derived from the imagery might be correlated with the developmental stages of the subjects in the treatment program to see if the level of conflict revealed in the residents would be reduced as they moved through the program.

METHOD

Subjects: the subjects were 27 residents of Hanbleceya, a therapeutic community established for the treatment of schizophrenia. They were asked to participate, but were told that participation was voluntary and they could withdraw at any time.

Procedure: the test items were administered by the subjects' usual therapist. The therapists were unaware of what the imagery might reveal or how the instrument was to be scored. The therapists were trained in standard administration by the author. The author was familiar with all of the subjects but scored and interpreted the protocols blind after they were obtained by the therapists for this study. The resultant data were used in the following two ways.

1. Conflict Scores

Each of The Three Box images, together with their associated sentence completions, were scored for degree of conflict according to the standards of the SIT (Shorr, 1976). The conflict data were then compared between phases and against the results from the standardization population.

2. Modal Subjects

Procols of three subjects were selected where their conflict scores on each box matched the average of subjects from their phase. Qualitative personality descriptions were developed based on these responses.

RESULTS

Conflict Scores: The table below presents mean degree of conflict reflected in the protocols of subject and standardization samples for The Three Boxes item.

The Three Boxes

Mean Conflict Score

Population	Number	Score
Standardization	118	8.39
Phase I	15	8.93
Phase II	9	10.56
Phase IV	3	7.33

Note: There were no Phase III residents available to be tested at the time the research was done.

There were no significant differences found between the small test populations in any pair of phases or between any of the phase populations and the standardization sample. These results were rather surprising because it had been predicted that a continuous decrease of the degree of conflict as the residents proceeded through the phases would occur. There is a trend toward more conflict evident in the imagery of phase two residents than there is in phase one residents. It may be speculated that phase two residents are more in touch with their internal conflicts than are the phase one residents. By phase four, there is a trend toward showing the level of internal conflict has been reduced.

Modal Subjects: Representative responses of residents from three phases of treatment, together with an interpretation and with their conflict scores, are presented below.

E., Male, 20, Phase I

Imagine three different boxes. One is large, one is medium, and one is small. (Pause.) Now imagine seeing something in each box. (Long pause.) Now tell me what you see in the boxes.

LARGE BOX IMAGE: Like a wooden stick, bigger than a broom stick, shorter, bigger diameter. A bunch of sticks, color like salmon, about that dark, not really pink.

SPEAKING AS IF YOU ARE THE IMAGE, FINISH THE SENTENCE: I FEEL irritated because I were (sic) so cooped up and can't get out.

THE ADJECTIVE THAT BEST DESCRIBES ME IS . . . I don't know . . . wooden like.

I WISH someone would take me out of this box and build something with me.

I MUST use the bathroom.

I SECRETLY desire to be part of the house.

I NEED some fresh air.

I WILL take a walk around the room.

NEVER REFER TO ME AS useless.

Conflict Score--Medium (3).

Interpretation: Wants to be seen as useful, but instead is incapacitated, dependent, agitated, unable to maintain focus.

MEDIUM BOX-IMAGE: cotton balls

SPEAKING AS IF YOU ARE THE IMAGE, FINISH THE SENTENCE: I FEEL sad.

THE ADJECTIVE THAT BEST DESCRIBES ME IS soft.

I WISH I could be of use to someone rather than just sit here.

I MUST make myself useful to someone.

I SECRETLY desire to clean up messes.

I NEED to be helpful

I WILL get out of this box.

NEVER REFER TO ME AS sedentary.

Conflict score - Low (2).

Interpretation; copes by being useful in an overadaptive way.

SMALL BOX-IMAGE: Oreo cookies. Not any different from any other cookies, just sitting by themselves.

SPEAKING AS IF YOU ARE THE IMAGE, FINISH THE SENTENCE: I FEEL sad.

THE ADJECTIVE THAT BEST DESCRIBES ME IS tasty.

I WISH someone would eat me.

I MUST bring pleasure to someone.

I SECRETLY want to roll down hill.

I NEED to be eaten.

I WILL get out of this box.

NEVER REFER TO ME AS not being tasty.

Conflict score - High (4).

Interpretation; at core, undifferentiated, inadequate, rebellious, needing symbiosis.

J., Female, 30, Phase II

Imagine three different boxes. One is large, one is medium, and one is small. (Pause.) Now imagine seeing something in each box. (Long pause.) Now tell me what you see in the boxes.

LARGE BOX-IMAGE: Bundle of clothes. A lot of T shirts that my brother brought me back from Italy. They are colorful and come with a card.

SPEAKING AS IF YOU ARE THE IMAGE, FINISH THE SENTENCE: I FEEL fine.

THE ADJECTIVE THAT BEST DESCRIBES ME IS lost.

I WISH I were back in the store.

I MUST find a sweather to match.

I SECRETLY want to be on you.

I NEED your body.

I WILL get close to you.

NEVER REFER TO ME AS dirty clothing.

Conflict Score - Low (2).

Interpretation: Wants to be seen as attractive, if sort of out of place, needing connection in an overt way.

MEDIUM BOX-IMAGE: Dead flowers. One dead flower is a rose that Moira gave me in the Institute. More flowers are from my home, my garden. Other flowers were from a garden that - a big garden - that you can see - miles and miles long. I went there, somewhere near San Francisco. More flowers are from the Wild Animal Park.

SPEAKING AS IF YOU ARE THE IMAGE, FINISH THE SENTENCE: I FEEL hungry.

THE ADJECTIVE THAT BEST DESCRIBES ME IS smelly.

I WISH for some soil.

I MUST HAVE the sky, the sun.

I SECRETLY deserve the rain.

I NEED your love.

I WILL get back at you.

NEVER REFER TO ME AS those things.

Conflict score - High (4).

Interpretation; defends herself by trying to be beautiful, but rejecting while needy.

SMALL BOX-IMAGE: Pieces of flesh, all corroded, different colors, bloody.

SPEAKING AS IF YOU ARE THE IMAGE, FINISH THE SENTENCE: I FEEL absent.

THE ADJECTIVE THAT BEST DESCRIBES ME IS odd.

I WISH I were home again.

I MUST find my true self.

I SECRETLY want to kill you.

I NEED to kill you.

I WILL get back at you.

NEVER REFER TO ME AS (long pause) your brother.

Conflict score - Extreme (5).

Interpretation; at core, angry, dissociated, rotten, searching.

M., Female, 42, Phase IV

Imagine three different boxes. One is large, one is medium, and one is small. (Pause.) Now imagine seeing something in each box. (Long pause.) Now tell me what you see in the boxes.

LARGE BOX-IMAGE: Table for two, couple of T-bone steaks, set for dinner. Candlelight and two steak dinners.

SPEAKING AS IF YOU ARE THE IMAGE, FINISH THE SENTENCE: I FEEL hungry.

THE ADJECTIVE THAT BEST DESCRIBES ME IS congenial.

I WISH life was that simple.

I MUST work on relationships.

I SECRETLY hate reality.

I NEED warmth.

I WILL grow.

NEVER REFER TO ME AS mean.

Conflict Score - Low (2).

Interpretation: Wants to be seen as wanting relationship, willing to work, aware of the problem.

MEDIUM BOX-IMAGE: A baby is in one of the boxes.

SPEAKING AS IF YOU ARE THE IMAGE, FINISH THE SENTENCE: I FEEL hungry.

THE ADJECTIVE THAT BEST DESCRIBES ME IS helpless.

I WISH my mom would come.

I MUST cry until she comes.

I SECRETLY (laughs) am afraid.

I NEED love.

I WILL grow.

NEVER REFER TO ME AS unwanted.

Conflict score - Medium (3).

Interpretation; copes by some dependency, but dealing with issues as best she can.

SMALL BOX-IMAGE: The first thing that comes to mind is a book.

SPEAKING AS IF YOU ARE THE IMAGE, FINISH THE SENTENCE: I FEEL I know all the answers.

THE ADJECTIVE THAT BEST DESCRIBES ME IS KNOWLEDGEABLE.

I WISH I was the solution.

I MUST add pages.

I SECRETLY don't know my purposes.

I NEED concentration.

I WILL become valuable with age.

NEVER REFER TO ME AS pointless.

Conflict score - Medium (3).

Interpretation; at core, feels competent, if a little uncertain, working on self.

As these representative protocols suggest, there is more conflict evident in the imagery of phase two residents who are perhaps more in touch with their internal process. By phase four, the level of internal conflict has, in this very small sample, been reduced.

The therapist can use these views of the inner world of the client to see the world as the client does, meet the client in that world without giving up his/her own reality, confirm the client's otherness without giving up his/her own, and help facilitate the healing journey that is the purpose of their being together.

DISCUSSION

This project was undertaken to learn something about the degree of conflict present in members of a therapeutic community as they progressed through the phases of the program. It was found that rather than a continuous reduction in conflict, there was a trend toward a peak in phase two, perhaps as a result of these residents being in better touch with their internal conflict than phase one residents, and then a trend toward a reduction in conflict in phase four residents as they had resolved some of their internal difficulty. As the residents progress through the program, the degree of conflict becomes even more apparent, and then decreases as they become more at ease with themselves and more able to function without psychosis in the world. This project was also undertaken to discover if The Three Boxes could be used to facilitate access to the inner world of these initially very disturbed individuals so that their therapists could meet them there and still maintain their own ground in reality. We found that even quite dysfunctional residents, who are unable to maintain focused attention for more than a few minutes, could effectively respond to the imagery and give results that could be usefully scored and interpreted.

REFERENCES

Fitzpatrick, M. P. (1985). Evolving communities. Lemon Grove, CA: International Association of Therapeutic Communities.

Friedman, M. (1985). The healing dialogue in psychotherapy. New York: Jason Aronson.

Shorr, J. E. (1983). Psychotherapy through imagery, 2nd ed. New York: Thieme-Stratton.

Shorr, J. E. and Tansey, D. A. (1976). Manual for the Shorr Imagery Test. Los Angeles: Institute for Psycho-Imagination Therapy.

EVOLVING TO THE STUDY OF IMAGERY AND AROMAS

Milton Wolpin

Department of Psychology
University of Southern California

Imagery has fascinated me for many years. The first paper I ever wrote, after my dissertation, was with Roy Hamlin, who was my chair; that was in 1958. He was a man who, in spite of the behavioral zeitgeist of the times, was open to the study of non-readily observable events, e.g., images that occur during the falling asleep and waking up states--hypnogogic and hypnopompic phenomena and during hypnosis, what we might today call "altered states of consciousness." We co-authored a paper at that time entitled "Loosening of thought controls and the creative process." Essentially what we were concerned about were the thoughts and images that come to us when we are in a state other than our wide awake one. It seemed to us, and we supported our thesis by referring to the literature, that the thoughts and images in these other states might be both unusual and of such a nature that they could be utilized to enhance one's creativity. I guess an instance that intrigued us, and that has been widely reported, was Kekule's experience, as he was awakening from sleep one day, of seeing the benzene ring projected on the wall in front of him. The solution to a very difficult problem had suddenly come to him in the form of an image and without conscious effort, at that moment, in that direction.

The literature, indeed, contains many examples of a similar nature. And so occasionally over the years, I have touched on the question of how imagery changes, e.g., as muscle states vary, as we repeat imaging something over and over, and as a function of role playing. At present something else I have been into recently has captured my attention a bit more forcefully. Actually it is in many ways consistent with my general interest in imagery and the ways in which it changes, but it also touches more directly on the utility for behavioral and emotional change that images have. What I would like to do now is to share with you some of my thoughts about aromas and to indicate to you that what may be developing is the rapidly increasing use of aromas, for a variety of purposes, including therapeutic.

I expect that some of the recent developments may seen to us of no great import, but then again, who knows? At any rate, it is interesting to observe that the use of aromas for entertainment, after some earlier false starts, may be beginning to take hold.

The L.A. Times of June 15, 1982 reported that "This fall Charles of the Ritz will introduce the Aromance Aroma Disc System which features miniature "records" injected with fragrance oil. Insert the discs in an electronic

Aroma Disc Player which resembles a tape deck and the scent fills the room. "It's an entirely new technology, says Barbara Carver, Ritz vice president of new products. Aroma Disc isn't a conventional room deodorizer or air freshener. It's home entertainment." Carver and her staff developed more than 40 different kinds of scents with such names as Fireplace, Babbling Brook, etc. "We wanted scents that would evoke pleasant memories," she says. We wanted scents that would help people fantasize. The June 20, 1982 issue of Time magazine has the same basic story. There was also an interesting story in Mainliner magazine of November 1980, one of those take-with publications that help one to while away the time on airplanes.

Hardly what one would call scientific but it does arouse one's curiosity and is indeed consistent with the suggestions in the scientific literature which I shall try to point out.

What I would like to do now is touch briefly on some of the history of the interest in odors for therapeutic purposes. Rovesti and Columbo (1963), in a paper presented at a Congress of Pharmaceutical Aerosols, say that "Leading physicians of antiquity, such as Galen and Celsus, advocated the use of aromatic herbs as sovereign remedies against hysterical convulsions and report that sometimes they stopped attacks immediately." They also summarize a 1925 report by Gatli and Cojola who they say have "clearly shown," among other things, that patients in an anxious state improved rapidly with gradual attentuation of the symptoms of angst, by spraying mixtures of essential oils such as geranium patchouli, vanilla and amber onto patches of cotton wool and then applying them with a face mask while also spraying the surroundings.

They suggest that odors can be used as either stimulants or sedatives and to relieve anxiety and depression. They even point to some specific odors to relieve depression, i.e.,the oils of citrus fruits, e.g., lemon, orange, verbena, rectified citronella and ylang ylang.

They also report on the use of aromas in industrial situations and summarize their sense of some of the possibilities of aromas stating, "It is clear that there is a sense of liberation, not only physical but also psychical since through the evocative action of memory the human being, subjected to the stress of work, is able to escape at both conscious and unconscious levels." (It does seem clear, from their description of these settings, that indeed escape is what one might hope for. Alternatively, of course, one might try to make some more serious change in the daily life of workers but that is probably a topic for another time.)

Their reference to "memory" is consistent with a great deal of anecdotal literature which suggests that odors have a reputation of being powerful, in contrast to other kinds of stimuli, e.g., visual and auditory, in evoking memories in the form of images accompanied by strong emotions. Some examples from the work of Laird, in the 1930's, is probably fairly representative. He studied "254 distinguished living persons" and obtained retrospective reports from them on their "odor associations and effects in their personal experience."

His statement, at the end of his paper, is interesting. He states that "closer observation of the patients' odor associations, preference and experiences than is customary in (psycho)analytic work would apparently not only speed up the process, but also give a more resonant abreaction and more satisfactory analysis." Kenneth (1927) reported one of the few experimental studies relating aromas, images and emotions. In this study, he exposed 63 subjects to a wide variety of odors and asked them to report their associations.

Two things stand out from this study, (a) that subjects agree substantially, but also vary considerably with regard to how pleasant or unpleasant the experience of each odor is, and (b) it is very common for subjects to have memories, in visual form, as well as other imagery experiences, accompanied by emotions. One of his suggestions, based on these results, is that olfactory stimuli could be used to bring back memories of specific occurrences in a person's life. He also states, in a very brief report in 1927 in Nature, unaccompanied by data, that "In the treatment of neuroses on analytic lines, the overcoming of a high resistance in certain patients by means of images recalled by olfactory stimuli has been found recently to be of considerable value."

Kenneth's impressions are similar to some others of the time, e.g., Daly and White (1922). In a paper on Psychic Reactions to Olfactory Stimuli, they suggest that "The employment of odours as an active aid to association in psychoanalytical therapy, particularly in the deeper stages, may in the future be found to be productive of invaluable results." They suggest that some of the outstanding analysts of the times, e.g., Ferenczi and Jones (1923) were interested in the emotional effects, such as enthusiasm, of aromas. They also quote a statement by Marlette (apparently another analyst) who says, "Nothing on earth makes the past so living as does odour."

Daly and White refer to the thinking of Havlock Ellis in attempting to acount for the power of odors; Ellis (1936) also writes of aromas being very capable of bringing up "ancient memories" and ties this in with the fact that the sense of smell is mediated by "the most ancient part of the brain," which would have "primitive emotional associations."

What I have tried to indicate is that as far back as antiquity, during the time of Galen and Celsus, and in more very recent times, i.e., the 1920's and 1930's, there is reason to believe that aromas were used for a variety of purposes, especially therapeutically, and that this, clearly during this century, seems to be connected with an understanding that odors are unusually capable of eliciting images and emotions.

At this time it might be worthwhile to take a brief look at brain structure for any light that might be shed on our subject. What we find is interesting. That part of the sensory apparatus called the olfactory bulb, which is indeed the most ancient neurological structure, and which mediates the sense of smell is apparently intimately tied up with the limbic system. In addition to sending fibers to the temporal lobe, it also sends some directly to the limbic system. Important in this regard is that no other sensory fibers go directly to the limbic system. The major structures of the limbic system, i.e., the mammalary body, septum, hippocampus, amygdala and cingulate cortex are involved in mediating sex, emotion and memory. Thus, it appears that olfactory stimuli are intimately involved indeed, neurologically (in what we see by way of behavior and self reports when we expose people to olfactory stimuli) in, e.g., sex, emotion and memory. Neurologically, it would appear that the many reports of the unique properties of olfactory stimuli may be well grounded.

I would like to now go on to some research that I have been involved in, tie it in with the work mentioned, and then suggest some paths to which all of this may lead us.

Several years ago, and I'm not sure how, I became impressed with anecdotal material much like that reported here, i.e., that there is a close connection between aromas and early memory. It seemed worth checking out, in the light of assumptions of various therapies, that it is important and/or helpful, depending on the therapy, to clients, to retrieve early memories. With this in mind, several graduate students, i.e., Charles Weinstein, William Faunce, and Patricia Gross and myself have completed two projects. We actually did the "early memory" one second, as some pilot data for the early memory project suggested something else intriguing that we had not considered. So in the first project with Charles Weinstein, what we did was have subjects imagine themselves in various situations. After about 15 seconds of the imagining, and with their eyes closed, and while still imagining the scene, we would have them smell something. What they would smell would be either congruent or incongruent with what they were imagining. For example, in one of the scenes, a subject images him/herself eating a peanut butter sandwich. In one condition they then smell peanut butter, in the other they smell soap. What happens is what one might predict, when they smell peanut butter they are much more in the scene, it is more ral to them and much less likely they are looking at themselves from a distance; they are, as it were, much more "in the moment." In the other condition one of two things happens, i.e., either the new stimulus is woven into the scene, e.g., a stimulus of coffee might lead them to imagine eating a peanut butter sandwich and drinking coffee, or else the image is driven away completely. Nothing especially startling about these results but not something we had thought or guessed about before this.

In the second study with William Faunce and Patricia Gross, our "early memory" study, we exposed subjects to various aromas with the prior instructions that when they smell something, they are likely to have a response in the form of a bodily sensation, a feeling, a thought or an image. We gave them these instructions as the pilot data indicated that without such instruction, they were much less likely to come up with any kind of response. Our major finding was that the modal response was an image; many of the images were of early memories. Nothing especially startling here either; we simply have some systematically collected data that is consistent with the anecdotal literature and with the work of Kenneth.

IMPLICATIONS

What are some of the implications of the previous remarks? It would appear to me that further research is likely to support the position that olfactory stimuli play an unusually strong role in eliciting images and emotions. I base this not only on the review of the literature and the work that Charles Weinstein, William Faunce, Patricia Gross and I have done, which I have briefly summarized for you here. I take this position because it appears consistent also with the way in which the brain is constructed. What we have, it seems, is that the structures that mediate processes we are deeply concerned about, e.g., sex, emotion and memory, are intimately involved with the olfactory system. If this is indeed the situation, then it would appear that, with stimuli that have been relatively long neglected by most therapists, and that may appear in some regards rather trivial, i.e., aromas, we may be able to have a rather significant effect on functioning in important areas. This, I think, is the major inference that I would like to make and that I feel it would be worth our while to set about testing.

To the extent that early memories are important, perhaps as we work with various clients, we might try to find out, for each of them, what aromas are best at accomplishing this. It seems likely that for each person at least several different aromas are likely to be of value.

It seems like it might take a bit of doing to find aromas that would make images more real--to help a person really get into something--peanut butter while imagining eating a peanut butter sandwich seems easy. However, perhaps it's not impossible and conceivably worthwhile. If one knew what aromas were associated with an important person in one's life, e.g., one's mother, those might be used--perfumes or maybe smells of certain foods--of flowers--or who knows. Maybe hospital aroma for traumatic situations--the smell of antiseptics.

The "opposite" of this seems fairly easy. It would be interesting to see if obsessive thoughts could be gotten rid of, at least temporarily, by smelling things incongruent with the thought--that should be easy. Another intriguing possibility is that of helping to develop emotional responses for people who block off feelings, again obsessive compulsive types come to mind. There clearly is one response that aromas elicit that it is likely to be difficult to arrange as compared with the other stimuli and that is disgust. But what about fear, or rage, or elation. Besides using stimuli to which these emotions may be a conditioned response, are there aromas to which we might automatically respond in such a way? Clearly the limbic system mediates such responses. There seems little doubt that if aromas could elicit these, that therapists could readily figure ways to use them productively.

What if one were to associate what was already experienced as a very positive aroma with a very positive experience--e.g., if you will allow an intrusion, orgasm. Could that significantly increase the likelihood of the odor eliciting a positive response--and would it be more intense than previously?

Creativity also seems relevant. There is some data that artists, as opposed to others, are more into imagery. Could one use aromas to increase the range of images available, as well as the accompanying emotions?

Is learning enhanced when aromas are present? Why is it that in various rituals, especially mediation, one often finds something like incense. Is it simply for the pleasant and possibly relaxing quality? Or is there more?

Aromas and imagery have not been studied much of late. Kenneth was a pioneer. but in recent times there has not been much follow through on his ideas; perhaps the time has come.

REFERENCES

Daly, C. D., and White, R. S. (1922). Psychic reactions to olfactory stimuli. British J. of Med. Psychol., 10, 70-87.
Ellis, H. (1936). Studies in the psychology of sex, Vol. 2, Part 3, Chapter 2, pp. 44-112. New York: The Modern Library.
Ferenczi, S. (1923). Sex psychoanalysis (Jones, E. tr.). Boston: R. G. Badger.
Kenneth, J. H. (1927). Odours and visual imagery. Nature, 119, 818-
Kenneth, J. H. (1927). An experimental study of affects and associations due to certain odors. Psychological Monographs, 171, 32-91.
Los Angeles Times, June 15, 1982.
Mainliner Magazine, November, 1980.
Rovesti, P., and Colombo, E. (1962). Aromatherapy and aerosols. Paper presented at the Congress on Pharmaceutical Aerosols, Milan, Italy.
Times Magazine, June 20, 1982.

[illegible] could be [illegible] which are automatically respond in such ways? [illegible] [illegible] [illegible] [illegible] [illegible] productive?

[illegible]

EMOTIVE IMAGERY AND PAIN TOLERANCE

Linda Diane Smith* and Milton Wolpin

Department of Psychology
University of Southern California

IMAGERY AND PAIN

This research considers the relationship between the individual's imagination, i.e., his or her particular imagetic milieu, and the cognitive evaluation of pain as suffering. Specifically, emotive imagery was manipulated to see if there is a relationship between the imagery being experienced, pain tolerance, and subjective ratings of pain intensity.

Investigations concerned with a behavioral technology for coping with pain have examined a variety of cognitive strategies for pain control (Chaves and Barber, 1974; Johnson, 1973; Kanfer and Seidner, 1973; Neufeld and Davidson, 1971), and sophisticated behavioral management programs (Sternbach, 1974). Some specific cognitive strategies used in pain relief have included imaginative inattention (Chaves and Barber, 1974); imaginative transformation of pain (Barber and Hahn, 1962), and imaginative transformation of context (Blitz and Dinnerstein, 1968). Non-imagery strategies have included somatization (i.e, focusing on the existence of bodily processes or sensations, to the exclusion of pain) and relaxation and controlled breathing (Elton and Stanley, 1976).

Reviews of the pain literature indicate the confounding effects of anxiety (Craig and Weiss, 1972; Sternbach, 1974). Wolpe (1961) contends that several types of responses may "reciprocally inhibit" anxiety, and his use of relaxation for that purpose has received wide attention. Although there is some disagreement regarding Wolpe's theoretical explanation (Evans, 1973), relaxation has been experimentally demonstrated to block anxiety (Himle, 1973; Persely and Leventhal, 1972). In addition, Lazarus and Abramovitz (1962) state that positive emotions, such as those engendered by self-assertion, also compete with anxiety, and can be used to assist recovery in phobic children. They described a method of producing such feelings as pride through positive images described by a therapist. This the authors termed "emotive imagery." Such a procedure is also used to foster feelings of relaxation and anger (Turk, 1978). Another response which may compete with anxiety is anger. Simonov (1962) reports some evidence in Soviet research for the existence of separate and reciprocally inhibitory centers for anxiety and anger in the area of the midbrain. Whatever the physiological case, anger induction has been used clinically

*Now at Casa Colina Rehabilitation Hospital

to inhibit anxiety responses (Goldstein, Serber and Piaget, 1970; Holmes and Horan, 1976). In general, sad or anguished imagery has been found to be correlated with feelings of boredom, despair and hopelessness associated with depression (Schultz, 1977). Thus, sad imagery may not inhibit anxiety but may in fact induce anxious feelings.

The activity of focusing on covert events or images incompatible with anxiety during actual overt uncomfortable situations has been called "in vivo" emotive imagery (Horan and Dellinger, 1974). The tension producing stimuli occur in real life rather than in imagination and simultaneously, rather than intermittently, with the positive fantasy. As a cognitive behavior therapy technique "in vivo" emotive imagery has been used in experimental and clinical investigations involving pain tolerance (Horan and Dellinger, 1974; Farr, 1974; Horan, Layng and Pursell, 1975). Images involving affect were more effective than neutral imagery or no imagery in increasing tolerance of painful stimulation (Horan and Dellinger, 1974; Westcott and Horan, 1977). Many of the behavioral-cognitive strategies developed for pain control thus far reviewed are concerned with the motivational-affective component of the pain experience. In particular, the reciprocal inhibition of anxiety has been the focus of a developing technology. Westcott and Horan (1977) examined the effects of "in vivo" emotive imagery on pain tolerance by random assignment of 80 subjects to either a no-treatment control, neutral imagery, angry imagery or relaxation imagery conditions. Subjects were asked to immerse their hands in ice water for as long as possible. Statistical comparisons showed that angry "in vivo" emotive imagery was significantly more effective for female subjects than no treatment control procedures, but relaxation was not. No significant differences were noted in the male sample. The purpose of the study was to explore the relative merits of anger and relaxation in enhancing tolerance of noxious stimulation.

Although the model for research, which Westcott and Horan developed, is an interesting one, there are several difficulties with the design which suggest the need for revision before attempting to replicate the findings. Because the study is concerned with reduction of anxiety and therefore a reduction of subjectively experienced pain, dependent measures should include some measure of the subject's perceived pain. The authors measure pain tolerance which would reflect the analgesic effects, if any, of emotive imagery, but the subjective perception of the pain is not isolated.

The authors made no pre-test of trait or state anxiety with the subjects participating in the study. Certainly the level of prior anxiety within the individual is a potential confounding variable when considering the alleviation of pain-related anxiety through in-vivo imagery. A pre-test measure for state-trait anxiety would assist the researcher in teasing out the effect this issue might have on any group within the design.

In using standardized imagery situations, the researchers may have attenuated their emotional effect. Kanfer (1974) reports that images chosen by the client as anger producing were more effective than standardized images in enhancing pain tolerance. In this study several forms of "in vivo" emotive imagery using the subjects' personal memories to evoke emotion, were utilized to enhance or decrease pain tolerance.

The additional difficulty is one of theoretical importance. Westcott and Horan are not unique in assuming that the anxiety which they are trying to alleviate is somewhat naturally attendant on the induction of experimental pain. Therefore, they, as well as other researchers in this area, do not induce anxiety experimentally in addition to pain induction. Although researchers may be correct in this assumption, theoretical literature which has been reviewed earlier would suggest that anxiety and sensory pain may behave as independent components of the pain experience. In this study, anxiety is conceptualized as an aspect of the motivational-affective component of pain. What an individual reciprocally inhibits by visualizing relaxing or angering imagery is the visualization of imagery of an anxiety-producing nature, not the perception of sensory pain or "anxiety" related to it. In clinical situations, sad thoughts concerning the meaning of pain, i.e., life threatening or severely life altering consequences, produce greater fear and less tolerance of pain (Beecher, 1969). It might be expected that the visualization of sad events might form a mental set for the experimental pain which would induce anxiety and greater subjectively experienced pain.

It was hypothesized (a) that the type of in-vivo emotive imagery utilized by the subject effects his or her cognitive appraisal of the painful stimuli as measured by subjective ratings of discomfort, (b) that the type of in-vivo emotive imagery utilized by the subject relates to his or her ability to enhance or decrease pain tolerance, and (c) that pleasant or angry imagery is expected to produce greater pain tolerance through reciprocal inhibition of anxiety-producing imagery, whereas sadness imagery is conceptualized as increasing anxiety, thus lowering pain tolerance.

Method

Subjects. All subjects completed the State-Trait Anxiety Scale (Spielberger, 1968) and the Creative Imagination Scale (Barber, 1980) to measure their anxiety and imagery ability.

Volunteers (50 male and 50 female) from psychology courses at a community college were randomly assigned to one of four imagery treatment conditions (Neutral, Anger, Pleasant, Sad), or to a no-strategy control condition.

Each subject was asked if any physical condition would affect the placing of his or her dominant hand in ice water. Those with cardiovascular or skin conditions were ruled out as were individuals with extensive meditative practice or athletic training, either of which might involve prior training in the use of imagery for physiological control.

Procedure

Individual appointments consisted of pre-recorded instructions for each of the various conditions. The experimenter was blind to the taped experimental condition the subject received. Subjects reporting for this appointment were randomly assigned to one of five groups. In the emotive imagery conditions, subjects were asked to imagine as vividly as possible a scene from their own experience in which they felt one of three emotions (anger, pleasure or sadness). In the neutral imagery condition subjects were instructed to count repetitively from 1 to 10 while visualizing the numbers. Subjects in the no-strategy control condition received no instruction regarding mental activity.

After an initial imagination task was completed to familiarize the subject with the task, the subject's dominant hand was exposed to circulating ice water kept at a constant temperature of 2 Centigrade. Each subject included in an imagery condition was asked to continue to imagine as vividly as possible his or her particular task while placing a hand in ice water for as long as possible. Subjects in the no-strategy control condition were asked to place their hand in the ice water for as long as they were able with no instructions regarding mental activity. The maximum amount of time a subject in any condition was allowed to maintain his hand in the water was five minutes. At this point numbness occurred with no possibility of tissue damage.

Prior to the painful stimuli all subjects were asked to rate the kind and strength of any emotions generated, and imagery vividness achieved during the initial task. After the cold pressor test was concluded and pain tolerance times recorded, subjects were asked to indicate again the strength of emotions, level of pain intensity, and imagery vividness during the painful stimuli. Subjects in neutral and no-strategy control groups received questionnaires appropriate to their conditions. All subjects were asked specifically by the experimenter's assistant about image, feelings and strategies used to determine if they had actually completed the task as suggested by the tape.

Verbal Taped Instructions

General lead for all conditions. "Thank you for volunteering to participate in this inquiry into human behavior. As in any psychological study you may withdraw from participation at any point you wish. This study is concerned with the relationship between specific mental activities and the individual's ability to tolerate discomfort. (Paulse.) to begin the first exercise, make yourself comfortable and close your eyes. Although we all have many thoughts which concern us each day, this is an opportunity to relax both your mind and your body."

Continuation for emotive imagery conditions. "With your eyes closed remember how the outside of your home looks as you approach from the street. As you stand in front of your house or apartment, notice the colors and objects around you; perhaps there are plants . . . a walkway . . . an automobile. Try to recollect these kinds of details as you imagine yourself approaching your front door, putting the key in the lock, and entering your home. Now let this memory go. As I name several objects, try to call each one to mind . . .

An orange . . . as you recall what an orange looks like, can you also remember its smell . . . its taste?

The ocean . . . try to imagine how it looks . . . sounds . . . smells . . . tastes.

Let the image go.

Without allowing any other distracting thought or feeling to enter your consciousness, recall an experience from your past which created (angry, sad, or pleasant) feelings for you. (Pause.) With your eyes still closed, imagine the scene as vividly as possible. What is the location? Are others present or are you alone? Try to use all your senses, vision . . . hearing . . . smell . . . taste . . . and touch to recollect vividly what occurred. As you recall the incident more and more completely, you can re-experience the feeling of (anger, sadness, or pleasure) as you did before. (Pause.)

When you are satisfied that you have recreated the incident and the feeling to the best of your ability, please complete the first form given to you (Imagery Vividness and Intensity of Emotion Rating Scales). (Pause.) Continue to imagine the previous scene as vividly as possible as you place your hand in the ice water and allow it to remain submerged for as long as possible."

The experimenter times the immersion.

Continuation for the neutral imagery condition. Without allowing any other distracting thoughts or feelings to enter your consciousness, count slowly from 1 to 10, trying to see each number as you hear yourself mentally repeating it. When you reach 10, repeat the process starting with 1 again. When you are satisfied that you have accomplished this task to the best of your ability, continue to count and imagine the numbers as you place your hand in the ice water and allow it to remain submerged for as long as possible.

Continuation for the control condition. Place your hand in the ice water and allow it to remain submerged as long as possible.

When each subject in an imagery condition had withdrawn his/her hand, the experimenter verbally instructs each subject to remove the headset and again complete the Imagery Vividness and Intensity of Emotion rating scales.

Results

Reported in Table 2 is the time in ice water for each group. A two-way analysis of variance was used with data having been logarithmically transformed due to within-group variance of the SADNESS group being significantly greater than that of the others. This created the variable TIMELN. Table 2 shows the arithmetic difference between the mean of the variable TIMELN at each level of the two independent variables and the overall or grand mean.

Table 1

Time in Ice Water (in seconds)

Variable	Mean	Standard Deviation
All Groups	81.52	69.31
Anger Group	108.25	81.24
Male	146.1	96.88
Female	70.4	36.94
Pleasure Group	95.85	72.1
Male	116.8	84.09
Female	74.9	54.14
Sadness Group	35.5	16.98
Male	43	19.6
Female	28	9.99
Neutral Group	89.05	67.1
Male	113.3	75.88
Female	64.8	49.59
Control Group	78.95	71.88
Male	94	85.05
Female	63	56.3

Table 2

TIMELN: Log Transformation of the Pain Tolerance Variable

Grant Mean - 4.092889

Variable and Category	N of Cases	Deviations Unadjusted
GROUP		
1 Anger	20	.30
2 Pleasure	20	.19
3 Sadness	20	-.63
4 Neutral	20	.19
5 Control	20	-.06
SEX		
1 Male	50	.25
2 Female	50	-.25

From the table it can be seen that the ANGER group displayed the greatest pain tolerance, followed by the PLEASURE and NEUTRAL groups respectively. All three of these groups had group means higher than the overall mean. The mean for the CONTROL group was just a little lower than the overall mean, while the SADNESS group was quite a bit below the overall mean, showing the greatest deviation of all the groups. It can also be seen from this table that males had a greater pain tolerance than females.

An analysis of variance by GROUP and SEX was performed on the dependent TIMELN. The results are summarized in Table 3.

Table 3

Results of Analysis of Variance of TIMELN
by Experiment Group and Gender

Source of Variation	Sum of Squares	DF	Mean Square	F
Main Effects	17.47	5	3.49	7.27*
GROUP	11.19	4	2.80	5.82*
SEX	6.28	1	6.28	13.08*
2-Way Interactions	.096	4	.03	.05
GROUP SEX	.096	4	.03	.05
Explained	17.57	9	1.95	4.06
Residual	43.24	90	.48	
Total	60.81	99	.61	

*Significant of .001 or better

As can be seen, both of the main effects are significant at the .001 level or better while the interaction of the main effects was not at all significant. This means that while there were significant differences across both GROUP and SEX, these effects are independent, i.e., the effect of each independent variable is the same within each level of the other independent variable. Their effects are essentially additive with no complications caused by interacion.

A Tukey test was performed in order to test the significance of the observed differences in the group means. This procedure has been developed in order to control the overall error when several statistical comparisons are made on the same set of data.

The results of a Tukey test at the .05 level showed that the ANGER, PLEASURE, and NEUTRAL groups were all significantly different from the SADNESS group, but that none of the former three groups were significantly different from each other and none of the experimental conditions were significantly different from the control group. A significant difference was found between the mean pain tolerance of the MALE and FEMALE groups. A summary of the results of the test for the experimental conditions is given in Table 4.

The Tukey test revealed then that the difference between experimental groups that the analysis of variance picked up were due to the difference between the ANGER, PLEASURE, and NEUTRAL group when compared to the SADNESS group. As can be seen from both Tables 2 and 4, the SADNESS group had a significantly lower pain tolerance than any of the experimental groups. When the Tukey B test is performed on the data, as indicated by the (#) symbol, a significant difference is also found between the CONTROL and SADNESS groups.

A two-way ANOVA was run on the self-reported pain variable (PAIN) by GROUP and SEX, the results of which are shown in Table 6.

Table 4

Tukey and Tukey B Tests for Experimental Groups
Using TIMELN Variable

	Mean	Sadness	Control	Neutral	Pleasure	Anger
Sadness	3.47	---	.56#	.81*#	.81*#	.93*#
Control	4.03	---	---	.25	.25	.37
Neutral	4.28	---	---	---	.00	.12
Pleasure	4.28	---	---	---	---	.12
Anger	4.40	---	---	---	---	---

Critical Value for Tukey - .63
Critical Value for Tukey B
W5 - 64
W4 - 62
W3 - 59
W2 - 55
*Significant for Tukey Test as .05 level
#Significant for Tukey B Test at .05 level

Table 5

Means for Subjective Pain Ratings

Overall	Anger	Pleasure	Sadness	Neutral	Control
12.40	12.75	11.50	14.10	11.25	12.40

As can be seen, there was no significant effect of the GROUP variable on the subjective PAIN variable, although the SEX factor was significant, with FEMALES reporting more pain than MALES.

Another possible explanation for the difference between the SADNESS group and the other groups is that there were basic differences between the subjects in the SADNESS group and those in the other groups. This was examined using a series of T-tests on the two anxiety variables (STATE, TRAIT) and the pre- and post-pain vividness of image and intensity of emotion variables. In no case were significant differences found between the SADNESS group and the combined other groups. Thus, the subjects in the SADNESS group were no more anxious than the other subjects and were not particularly better or worse than the other subjects in performing the experimental tasks of imaging or generating emotion.

<u>Relations Between Variables</u>

Table 7 shows the Pearson Correlation Coefficients for IMAGERY VIVIDNESS, EMOTIONAL INTENSITY, and the PAIN and TIME variables. Both the overall relationships and those within each group and sex are demonstrated.

Table 6

Analysis of Variance

Pain by GROUP
SEX

Source of Variation	Sum of Squares	DF	Mean Square	F	Significance of F
Main Effects	271.90	5	54.38	2.30	.05
GROUP	102.90	4	25.72	1.09	.37
SEX	169.00	1	169.00	7.16	.009
2-Way Interactions	121.10	4	30.28	1.28	.28
GROUP SEX	121.10	4	30.28	1.28	.28
Explained	393.00	9	43.67	1.85	.07
Residual	2125.00	90	23.61		
Total	2518.00	99	25.43		

There seems to be a tendency in all groups for the vividness and intensity of initial images and emotions to be positively correlated with the reported pain, although this is only strong enough to be significant in the SADNESS group, FEMALES, and overall. There also seems to be a trend in all groups except the SADNESS group of a negative relation between the vividness of images and intensity of emotions during the pain experience and the amount of reported pain, although this is only strong enough to be significant in the PLEASURE and NEUTRAL group. These trends are essentially reversed when the correlations with TIMELN (Pain Tolerance) are examined, as would be expected. There are strong overall positive correlations between the second vividness of images and emotions variables and TIMELN, which are especially strong in the PLEASURE and NEUTRAL group, as well as among MALES.

Table 7

Pearson R Values for Imagery Intensity and Emotion Vividness with TIME and PAIN

Vividness of Emotion or Intensity of Mental Imagery	Overall	Anger Group	Pleasure Group	Sadness Group	Neutral Group	Control Group	Male	Female
	Pain	Pain	Pain	Pain	Pain	Pain	Pain	Pain
Intensity of Emotion I	.26*	.27	.11	.40***	---	---	.14	.36*
Vividness of Mental Image I	.23*	.15*	.09	.48*	-.02	---	.26	.18*
Intensity of Emotion II	.04	.07	-.47*	.35	---	---	-.04	.09
Vividness of Mental Image II	-.18	-.16	-.60**	.25	-.45*	---	-.19	-.14
	Time	Time	Time	Time	Time	Time	Time	Time
Intensity of Emotion I	-.09	.01	-.25	-.01	---	---	-.07	-.06
Vividness of Mental Image I	-.02	-.10	-.07	-.06	.16	---	.03	-.09
Intensity of Emotion II	+.34**	.27	.55**	.19	---	---	.49**	.29
Vividness of Mental Image II	+.40**	.29	.57**	.13	.57**	---	.52**	.27

*p < .05

**p < .01 with two tailed test

***p < .05 with one tailed test

Finally, matched-pair T-tests were used to examine whether any differences existed between imagery vividness prior to pain and after the painful experience, as well as intensity of emotion prior to pain and after the painful experience.

Table 8

Means for Vividness of Imagery and Intensity of Emotion

Vividness of Imagery				
Pre-Pain				
Anger	Pleasure	Sadness	Neutral	Control
15.7	14.60	15.55	14.60	---
Post-Pain				
14.45	10.25	10.00	9.60	---
Intensity of Emotion				
Pre-Pain				
Anger	Pleasure	Sadness	Neutral	Control
12.60	13.40	13.30	---	---
Post-pain				
13.80	7.05	9.40		

Table 9

Means and T test for Vividness of Imagery and Intensity of Emotion Combined

Variable	No. of Cases	Mean	Standard Deviation	T Value	Degrees of Freedom	2-Tail Prob.
Vividness of Mental Image I	80	15.11	3.99	6.35*	79	.001
Vividness of Mental Image II	80	11.08	6.05			
Intensity of Emotion I	60	13.10	4.70	3.12*	59	.003
Intensity of Emotion II	60	10.08	6.53			

The mean of VIVIDNESS OF MENTAL IMAGE II was found to be 3.5 less than the mean of VIVIDNESS OF MENTAL IMAGE I, which is significant at the .001 level while the mean of INTENSITY OF EMOTION II was found to be 2.6 less than the mean of INTENSITY OF EMOTION II, significant at the .05 level. Although not always significant, the direction of the differences between the means was found to hold across all groups and sexes with the exception of the ANGER group where the mean for INTENSITY OF EMOTION II was found to be 1.2 units higher than the mean for INTENSITY OF EMOTION I. Generally then, both imagery and emotion were significantly less vivid after the painful experience. The exception was the emotion of anger which was more vivid after the painful experience.

DISCUSSION

A two-way analysis of variance evaluated the dependent variable pain tolerance (TIMELN), by experimental group and gender, resulting in the significance of both group and gender, with no significant interaction between them. A second ANOVA was completed comparing the effects of group and gender on the subjective ratings of pain (PAIN). This analysis demonstrated the significant effect of gender on reports of pain intensity, but no effect of group on perception of pain intensity. thus, the mental coping strategy used had no effect on perceived pain intensity, although it did on pain tolerance. Before discussing possible conceptualizations for this result, a discussion of related results is necessary.

In the initial ANOVA, a significant effect involving gender was noted with males showing greater pain tolerance than females. This result is corroborated by prior researchers (Westcott and Horan, 1977). The second analysis demonstrated that males generally reported lesser levels of perceived pain than did females. Thus, for males and females there is an inverse relationship between pain tolerance and subjective ratings of pain, with the males demonstrating greater pain tolerance and report of lesser perceived pain, and females demonstrating lesser pain tolerance and report of greater subjective pain. Whether this is due to physiological or complicated sociocultural factors, or both, is not a question that can be answered within the context of this research. These results follow the general trend established in research in this area. More interestingly, they do serve to demonstrate clearly that the <u>group effect</u> on pain tolerance reflected in the initial ANOVA test did result from actual changes in that dimension, rather than changes in the amount of pain perceived by either gender.

<u>Sadness</u>

A further examination of the significant effect of group on pain tolerance was performed using both the Tukey and Tukey B tests for differences between experimental groups. From both tests it can be seen that the sadness group alone was responsible for the significance of the main effect of group in the original ANOVA. All other conditions were not significantly different from one another.

To understand the singular effect of sadness on pain tolerance, it was necessary to ascertain whether or not the members of the sadness group were different than members of the other groups in their ability to image or their level of anxiety. T`tests to examine these differences were performed with no significant differences found between members of the sadness group and all other groups on these dimensions. Subjects in the sadness group were no more anxious than the other subjects in performing the experimental task of imaging.

The sadness group is unique, however, when Pearson Correlation Coefficients are performed on the Vividness of Mental Imagery and Intensity of Emotion variables in conjunction with subjective pain ratings. In the sadness group prior to the painful experience there is a significant positive correlation between the vividness of mental image, intensity of emotion and subsequent subjective report of pain. In addition, the sadness group shows a trend toward a positive relationship between vividness of images and intensity of emotions during the pain experience and the amount of reported pain. The general trend of all other groups was to show a negative relationship between vividness of images and intensity of emotions during the pain experience and the amount of reported pain. This relationship was significant for both pleasure and neutral groups.

In summary, the vividness of imagery and intensity of emotion for members of the sadness group both prior to and during the painful experience correlated with higher ratings of subjective pain. The vividness and intensity of image and emotion became statistically significant variables effecting heightened subjective perception of pain, only when sad thoughts were considered. In matched pair T tests it was demonstrated that the vividness of image and intensity of emotion prior to and during the painful experience declined over all groups. Despite this the sadness condition produced higher subjective pain ratings. Reflecting on the two components of pain in Melzack's theory, sensory-discriminative and motivational-affective, vividness of imagery and intensity of emotion would seem to be effecting the motivational/affective component resulting in subjective report of greater pain. However, this is true only in the context of sad imagery. The cognitive control exercised when sad images are vividly held and sad emotions strongly experienced works against the individual in pain. The finding suggests that imagery vividness, emotional intensity, sad context, and pain induction interrelate to produce greater subjectively felt pain.

The effect of sadness on pain tolerance was highly significant without relationship to vividness and intensity variables. It would seem then that the individual thinking sad thoughts while enduring experimentally induced pain rapidly removes himself from the painful stimuli without regard to the intensity of the emotion or vividness of image. The type of emotion, i.e., sadness, is sufficient to lower pain tolerance. Using Melzack's gate theory, the higher cognitive centers, by focusing on sadness, would be providing a "meaning" for the sensory stimuli which would make pain tolerance more difficult. The more vivid that mental image the more subjective "pain" is experienced.

Pleasure and Neutral groups

When the pain tolerance and subjective pain ratings of subjects in both Pleasure and Neutral groups were compared with the vividness of imagery and intensity of emotion variables, a significant correlation between them was demonstrated. Vividness of imagery was inversely related to subjective perception of pain for both groups. Vividness of imagery was positively correlated with pain tolerance for both groups. The intensity of the pleasant emotive condition was similarly related to pain perception and tolerance. Therefore the variables of intensity of emotion and vividness of imagery in the case of pleasant imagery allows the subject to heighten pain tolerance and lower subjective perception of pain by increasing vividness of image and/or intensity of emotion. However, this vividness of image alone allowed subjects in the neutral imagery group who had no emotive quality to their images to increase pain tolerance and decrease subjective pain. Thus vividness of imagery would seem the more important variable for pain control, as long as the content of sadness is avoided.

Anger

Although the anger group did not differ from the other conditions when ANOVAs were done relating the various group means to pain tolerance and subjective pain ratings, the means for pain tolerance were the highest of any of the groups. When means for intensity of emotion prior to and during the painful experience were analyzed, anger proved to be the only group in which the intensity of emotion increased during the painful experience. Although neither of these findings were statistically significant, they may indicate a logical relationship between increased anger and heightened pain tolerance. Earlier studies have indicated this relationship at levels of significance (Goldstein, Serber and Piaget, 1970; Holmes and Horan, 1976; Westcott and Horan, 1977). In conjunction with the data concerning the effect of sadness and pain tolerance, i.e., the flight experience and lowered pain tolerance, anger may indicate mobilization of the body for the "fight" response which may also increase pain tolerance.

Theoretical Implications

Lazarus's theory is that the content and intensity of emotion depend on a cognitive appraisal of the effect of a present event on a person's well being. Emotions then are psychologically construed as value responses. They follow from an appraisal of what we perceive as beneficial or harmful to some aspect of ourselves. Lazarus and Mason both suggest that the essential mediator of the flight or fight syndrome is the cognitive recognition by the individual of his or her plight. This study suggests that emotive imagery, particularly sadness, relates to the interpretation of pain as a threat, resulting in lowered pain tolerance as well as the interpretation of pain as suffering, i.e., subjective ratings of pain. The vividness and intensity of the emotive-imagetic milieu contributed to the meaning of the pain and thus to the individual's reaction to it.

Sadness was associated with the experimental pain by means of imagery which was totally unrelated to the event of pain induction. This may simulate the experience of the individual whose pain signals threatening dis- or injury. In extrapolating to clinical work with chronic pain patients, the cognitive strategies used for pain control in this study: anger, pleasure, neutral or no-strategy conditions, did not produce significantly greater pain tolerance. Perhaps this indicates that any coping strategy may improve the individual's chances of pain control simply because any imaging strategy or even no strategy is better than imaging sadness.

This study did replicate Westcott and Horan (1977) data regarding the gender effect in regard to pain tolerance. Males did demonstrate greater pain tolerance, females lesser pain tolerance. In addition, the current data demonstrated a gender effect for subjectively rated pain which was the inverse of the pain tolerance effect. These results seem intuitively correct. The explanation for the effect probably lies outside any independently manipulated variable in either study. Sociological or physiological differences may account for this stable effect.

Although Westcott and Horan did report an interaction between angry imagery in females and heightened pain tolerance, no similar interaction effect was found in the present study. It should be noted that in the Westcott/Horan study, anger in females only distinguished itself from the No-Treatment Control condition. It was indistinguishable from the neutral or relaxation imagery groups. The results of the present study found all of the above groups indistinguishable from one another with only sadness significantly different. There was no gender interaction with this group.

In combination, the results of the two studies would seem to indicate that clinical interventions which emphasize some form of imagery strategy for the pain patient might choose any of the above strategies with about the same effectiveness with the exception of sadness. The research cannot predict one strategy as more effective than the other in increasing pain tolerance, and only one, i.e., suffering, is remarkably more effective in lowering pain tolerance. The results seem to indicate what the patient needs to avoid doing, while suggesting that several techniques are equally effective at accomplishing this.

It may be then that what an individual reciprocally inhibits by visualizing relaxing or angering or neutral imagery is the visualization of imagery of an anxiety-producing nature. In addition, the vividness of the imagery and intensity of emotion significantly correlate in the case of sad imagery with heightened subjective report of pain sensitivitity. With pleasure and neutral imagery vividness of imagery and intensity of emotion negatively correlate with subjective pain sensitivity. This data indicates that psychologists might do well to train pain patients to increase the vividness of their imagery while directing this imagery toward pleasing, positive events. The more fully the client can perceive his or her imagery, the better chance he or she has for decreasing subjective report of pain.

REFERENCES

Barber, R., and Hahn, K. (1962). Physiological and subjective responses to pain producing stimulation under hypnoticallay suggested and waking-imagined "analgesia." Journal of Abnormal and Social Psychology, 65, 411-418.

Blitz, B., and Dinnerstein, A. (1968). Effects of different types of instructions on pain parameters. Journal of Abnormal Psychology, 73, 276-280.

Chaves, J., and Barber, T. (1974). Cognitive strategies, experimenter modeling, and expectation in the attentuation of pain. Journal of Abnormal Psychology, 83, 356-363.

Craig, K. D., and Weiss, S. M. (1972). Verbal reports of pain without noxious stimulation. Perceptual and Motor Skills, 34, 943-948.

Elton, D., and Stanley, G. V. (1976). Relaxation as a method of pain control. Australian Journal of Physiotherapy, 22, 121-123.

Evans, I. M. (1973). The logical requirements for explanation of systematic desensitization. Behavior Therapy, 4, 506-514.

Farr, J. H. (1974). The effect of "in vivo" emotive imagery on the tolerance of two types of noxious stimulation. Unpublished doctoral dissertation, Pennsylvania State University.

Goldstein, A., Serber, M., and Piaget, G. (1970). Induced anger as a reciprocal inhibitor of fear. Journal of Behavior Therapy and Experimental Psychiatry, 1, 67-70.

Hilgard, E. R., and Hilgard, R.J.R. (1975). Hypnosis in the relief of pain. Los Altos: William Kaufmann, Inc.

Himle, D. P. (1973). Effects of instruction upon an automatic response: An analogue of systematic desensitization. Psychological Reports, 32, 767-773.

Holmes, D. P., and Horan, J. J. (1976). Anger induction in assertion training. Journal of Counseling Psychology, 23(2), 108-111.

Horan, J. J., and Dellinger, J. K. (1974). In vivo emotive imagery: An experimental test. Perceptual and Motor Skills, 39, 359-362.

Horan, J. J., Layng, F. C., and Pursell, C. H. (1976). Preliminary study of effects in "in vivo" emotive imagery on dental discomfort. Perceptual and Motor Skills, 42, 105-106.

Johnson, J. (1973). Effects of accurate expectations about sensations on the sensory and distress components of pain. Journal of Personality and Social Psychology, 27, 261-275.

Kanfer, F., and Seidner, M. (1973). Self-control factors enhancing tolerance of noxious stimulation. Journal of Personality and Social Psychology, 25, 381-389.

Lazarus, A. A., and Abramovitz, A. (1962). The use of emotive imagery in the treatment of childrens' phobias. Journal of Mental Science, 108, 191-195.

Neufeld, R., and Davidson, P. (1971). The effects of vicarious and cognitive rehearsal on pain tolerance. Journal of Psychosomatic Research, 15, 329-335.

Persely, G., and Leventhal, D. (1972). The effects of therapeutically oriented instruction and of the pairing of anxiety imagery and relaxation in systematic desensitization. Behavior Therapy, 3, 417-424.

Schultz, K. D. (1976). Fantasy stimulation in depression: Direct intervention and correlational studies. Yale University.

Simonov, P. (November, 1987). Studies of emotional behavior of humans and animals by Soviet physiologists Paper presented at the Conference on Experimental Approaches to the Study of Emotional Behavior. New York Academy of Sciences.

Sternbach, R. A. (1974). Pain patients: Traits and treatment. New York: Academic Press.

Terrh, D. C. (1978). Cognitive-behavioral techs. in management of pain. In J. P. Foregt and D. P. Rathjen (Eds.), Cognitive-behavior therapy: Research and application. New York: Plenum.

Westcott, T. B., and Horan, J. (1977). The effects of anger and relaxation forms in in vivo emotive imagery on pain tolerance. Canadian Journal of Behavioral Science, 3, 9.

Wolpe, J. (1961). The systematic desensitization treatment of neuroses. Journal of Nervous and Mental Disease, 132, 189-203.

SEXUAL JEALOUSY: EVALUATION AND ASSESSMENT USING THE PRINCIPLES OF PSYCHO-IMAGINATION THERAPY

Pennee Robin and Jack Connella

Institute for Psycho-Imagination Therapy
Los Angeles, CA

The imaginal components of jealousy are almost identical to those of love. The images of love can include idealized images of the loved one, remembered moments of bliss, and images of future happiness. Although the love images focus primarily on the benign and blissful, there can also be painful and tormenting images of misunderstandings and fearful images of unthinkable separation. The latter images usually arise because of feared or actual situations which invoke jealousy.

All of the love images are distorted by the emotions of jealousy. With jealousy the idealized image of the loved one is seen all too often from a position of low self-esteem, unworthiness, and fear of loss. For a jealous person the moments of love involve a rival rather than the self and are no longer blissful. The hopes for future happiness are replaced by visions of the loved one forever out of reach and in the arms of another.

Sometimes there is a legitimate cause for such images. The loved one has truly gone off with someone else. The expectation of a relationship has been replaced by the reality of loss. Grief for the loss of love mirrors the grief of loss through death. In such a case the bereft one must deal with the anguish and come to terms with reality. While it is no easy task to live through such a loss, most bear up under the pain and move forward at some point.

If jealousy is not based on fact but is the result of neurotic fears, unsubstantiated suspicions, and imagined scenarios, there is no healing until in some fashion the jealous party faces the distortions, overcomes the neurotic perspective, and begins to deal with the pain in a healthy and therapeutic fashion.

Whether the jealousy is engendered by neurotic fear or a real event, the ensuing images are just as powerful. The lover who images torrid love scenes between the loved one and a rival often has the same visceral reactions and behaves much as the lover who has indeed uncovered such a situation in reality.

Irene was in a relationship for seven years with a man who was uncontrollably jealous. She was victimized by his unfounded images of her infidelity. "Everything would be going great and we would go out and all of a sudden . . . it's like this monster came out of him. He'd say, 'I know who you were thinking about when you watched that movie. You turned your back on me.' He'd keep saying I turned away from him and go on ranting and raving until I got hysterical aqnd started crying and screaming." His behavior was based on his own vivid images rather than on her actual behavior, but the results were the same. The relationship was destroyed eventually by his inability to deal with his neurotic jealousy.

On the other hand, Eric, whose case is the main focus of this article, was faced with an actual situation which activated his jealousy. He and his wife, Jody, were married when they were very young; he was 19, she was 16. Both were raised in what he describes as a puritanical, midwest background. He states, "We have been married for 27 years. We had always been very monogamous. We hadn't had any affairs. I hadn't even had a woman before my wife and as far as I know it was the same way with her. We were very single-minded when it came to sex.

"Jody is the type of woman who normally has seven, eight, or ten orgasms, and she will do that maybe three of four times a week. All through our marriage we were very sexually compatible, but in the past five years I was going downhill and Jody was going uphill in sexual needs."

Eric told us that two years prior to coming to the Shorr Clinic to participate in a jealousy research project, both he and Jody had each attempted, and was discovered in, an unsuccessful extra-marital affair. They were both extremely jealous and there were numerous scenes. Somehow they managed to maintain an uneasy truce for a while.

Gradually their situation deteriorated. They both had job problems and the domestic scene worsened. His impotence increased to the point where he consulted a doctor, who indicated the problem was not physical. After what Eric referred to as "a particularly bad weekend where I was not able to perform satisfactorily," he and Jody arranged to swap mates the following weekend with another couple they had been friendly with for a while.

Eric stated, "With the full cooperation of everybody involved, and probably with the instigation of me more than anybody else, we decided we would swing . . . I thought I was an adult and intelligent enough to accept that sort of thing. We were all in the same room, which was probably a mistake. It became very obvious that Jody and Felipe were very compatible. Unfortunately I was not able to do very much, in fact, almost nothing.

"Jody and Felipe did try to separate from us two or three times, but I kind of insisted we stay together. They acted like two elephants in the rainforest bellering (sic) and carrying on like you never heard in your life. It kept going on and on. So to make a long story short--and this is the heart of the thing that I could not understand--despite my instigation and all of our agreements, my frustration grew, and it became very obvious that I was mad. I seemed to be the only one of the four that was mad. And I was very mad--holding it in as best I could--but obviously mad."

When the other couple left after the swinging fiasco, "another thing happened that triggered more anger," Eric told us. "Jody was really in favor of all that had been going on. In fact, she had even said to me, 'Goodbye, Eric, go on home with Elise.' She wanted to stay with Felipe. That infuriated me.

"After they had finally gone she was lying on the bed and I just blindly struck out and hit her with my hand on her rear end--very, very hard --and called her a nasty four-letter name. She has interpreted that since as being beat up. At that point in time, as soon as I struck her I realized that I had no understanding of why I did it. It was a totally visceral reaction as I later tried to explain. The point is, I did it. And from that time there seems to have been a very traumatic difference in the way she has related to me. It was almost as if I had turned on her and caused this whole thing to happen. A total exaggeration, because, as I said, I did not beat her up with my fists, but she got a good slap on the ass."

Surprise though it may have been to him, Eric's violence did not end at that time. His suppressed anger surfaced again several months later when Jody accompanied him to an out-of-town seminar. He refers to the events as "The Night of Disaster." They went into the hotel bar in the evening and Jody apparently was flirting with some of the men there. Eric said, "We had both been drinking too much, and I got very mad about her behavior. So I jerked her back to the room. She said in a rage that she was going back to the bar alone. I said she wasn't, and we did a very physical thing. I did not strike her, but I grasped her very strongly and she fell on the side of the water bed and bruised herself quite extensively to the point where she went to the hospital later on to be sure she was not really hurt badly, that the bruises were not really critical. She indicated, of course, that I had just beaten the shit out of her, which I had not done. I had rassled with her."

Eric's narrative reveals much of the complexity and range of emotions and behavior often evident in cases of jealousy. Fear, anger, shock, resentment, confusion, and powerlessness are often felt and manifested by jealous persons. The accompanying behaviors may range from withdrawal into a silent suppressed or repressed rage to a violent acting out as we see in Eric's case. The sense of "I don't know why this happened" or "Why did I do this?" is a common feeling in jealous persons.

Obviously, the long term history of these individuals and their relationship prior to the 'jealous experience' is of primary importance in understanding and unraveling the underlying dynamics, conflicts and motivations in such a complex case. However, this article is specifically focusing on understanding Eric and his jealousy episode.

A complex case of sexual jealousy is often a challenge for the most competent clinician in the initial attempts at assessment, evaluation, and treatment planning. Quite often the persons involved may be "non-psychological" in their understanding of their experiences. They may often be severely repressed individuals with little understanding or self-awareness. These persons may be fixed at a level of shock, confusion and naivete. In order to engage this type of patient in a therapeutic alliance, we believe it is of the utmost importance that this initial resistance by bypassed with speed and accuracy.

These authors have found the systematic use of waking visual imagery to be an invaluable tool in evaluating and assessing such difficult cases. Imagery, unlike other modes of communication, usually has not been punished in the past, and is, therefore, less susceptible to personal censorship in the present. Joseph E. Shorr (1981) emphasizes subjective meaning by recognizing that the patient's images are uniquely his, coming from his own storehouse of knowledge and experience. In the process of describing his image, the patient begins to relate it to something of meaning in his life. S. K. Escalona (1973) suggests that mental imagery offers an opportunity to study the integration of perception, motivation, subjective meaning and realistic abstract thought. Thus, imagery provides a powerful projective technique resulting in a rapid, highly accurate profile of the individual's personality dynamics, defenses, dominant drives, conflicts and emotions. The interpersonal and intrapersonal interactions, as well as the individual's strategies within the self-other relationship, are often best revealed through imagery.

These authors have found the most systematic and researched use of waking visual imagery that also has a strong theoretical basis is found in Psycho-Imagination Therapy (Shorr, 1967, 1981, 1983a), and the Shorr Imagery Test (1974). Psycho-Imagination Therapy is a phenomenological and dialogical process with major emphasis on subjective meaning through the use of waking imagination and imagery. Psycho-Imagination Therapy puts the individual, through his own imagery, into a particular situation which can evoke a set of interactions that are useful in revealing major problems in the significant areas of his life, and which also permit him to relive experiences.

Shorr (1978) has systematically categorized over two thousand Imaginary Situations (IS) which have proved in the clinical setting to reveal specific information about the patient's personality, world view, self definition, areas of conflict, and style of defenses. Other categories are specifically for focusing on change and for facilitating the process. Furthermore, responses to the categorized imagery usually elicit hidden or repressed material more efficiently than direct questioning by the therapist. When Imaginary Situations are used diagnostically, Shorr incorporates the use of the Finish-The-Sentence (FTS) technique as a method of focusing on the particular image for further meaning.

Shorr states that the theoretical purpose of using Imaginary Situations is based not only on seeing how the patient views his world, but also in being able to open up the "closed system of internal reality" (Fairbairn in Guntrip, 1964). Shorr contends that the better able the patient and the therapist are to see this "tight inner world," the easier it will be to deal with the whole of the patient in his world.

The clinician is cautioned that when using imagery for either or both diagnosis and treatment, it is necessary to have a body of images to analyze and compare. No single image is sufficient to reveal basic internal conflicts or personality structure, no matter how apparent the meaning may seem to be. A psychotherapist trained in the uses of imagery can use a body of imagery in conjunction with dialogue and other techniques to find patterns of behavior and congruities in values and attitudes which will enable both patient and therapist to develop a viable approach to treatment and a possible resolution of conflict.

After taking a brief history, we administered the Shorr Imagery Test (SIT) to Eric along with the Finish-The-Sentence (FTS) technique. The SIT is an individually administered projective test of adult personality. The SIT consists of 15 items in which the testee is asked to imagine a particular Imaginary Situation (IS) and then to expand in a directed way upon the image evoked. The test yields both a quantitative conflict score and a qualitative personality analysis. When taking the test the subject is instructed to sit back, relax, close his eyes and trust the images he sees in his head. The subject is then presented with an Imaginary Situation. (The reader is encouraged to do the same as each image is presented in the text. It is helpful to write down your images and your sentence completions. If you are familiar with the use of mental imagery, the subjective meaning of your answers may be readily apparent to you, yet present some surprises. The use of Shorr's books (1983a, 1983b), and the Shorr Imagery Test Manual (1974) will further enhance your understanding of these images.)

One of the most powerful and revealing Imaginary Situations on the Shorr Imagery Test is "The Three Boxes":

(IS) You are to imagine three different boxes.

One is large, one is medium, and one is small.

Now imagine seeing something in each box.

Now tell me what you see in each box.

After reporting all three images, the testee is then instructed:

Imagine that you <u>are</u> the image that you see in the large box. Now, speaking as that image, finish the following sentences:

I feel____

The best adjective to describe me is__________________

I wish____

I must____

I secretly____________________________________

I need____

I will____

Never refer to me as__________________________

The testee is then instructed to do the same sentence completions with the image in the medium box, and then with the image in the small box.

The following is the verbatim report of Eric's responses to "The Three Boxes":

LARGE BOX-- IMAGE: an elephant

I feel: crowded in here

The best adjective to describe me is: overheated

I wish: I could get out

I must: not do this anymore

I secretly: wish I were in the jungle

I need: some hay

Never refer to me as: a big lug

MEDIUM BOX--IMAGE: A dog

I feel: warm and comfortable

The best adjective to describe me is: cozy

I wish: I could sleep here all the time

I must: bring my bone with me next time

I secretly: wish I had a little girl dog with me

I need: some loving

I will: go out tomorrow

Never refer to me as: a dumb dog

SMALL BOX--IMAGE: A flea

I feel: uptight

The best adjective to describe me is: itchy

I wish: I could hop out

J must: leave as soon as possible

I secretly: would like to get on the dog

I need: a good warm home

I will: get one as soon as possible

Never refer to me as: an insect

Extensive clinical experience has demonstrated that "The Three Boxes" image is a reliable indicator of three levels of personality. The large box represents the outer social manifestations of behavior and interaction --the style with which the subject relates to the world. This is the image presented to others--the outer self--and the conflicts about this outer self. The middle box seems to relate to the person's defenses or style of coping with the barriers and conflicts inside him. The small box seems to indicate how the person feels about his inner self or core--the inner aspect of himself. By subjecting the image in each box to the seven sentence completions, one obtains much amplification of the feelings and many other aspects of the personality. The seven FTS for each image found in the boxes serve to round out the structure, and their interrelatedness can help the therapist make sounder judgments as to their total value.

The following evaluation is based on Eric's answers to the entire Three Boxes imagery. These interpretations are not intended to be a thorough analysis of the imagery, but are a starting point from which the experienced clinician can bring to bear his own knowledge for further interpretation. He is encouraged to look at the three box images not only separately, but also as an entirety, and to look for the interrelationships of all three images, keeping in mind that this imagery purportedly reveals the three levels of personality.

LARGE BOX: (elephant)

This imagery shows that Eric probably often feels a sense of discomfort in relation to others, to the point of wanting to leave. However, he probably adapts in some manner, possibly by focusing on his own needs and satisfaction to the exclusion of others. Others probably view him and refer to him as insensitive or unaware. He shows some negative concern about his size.

MEDIUM BOX: (dog)

Eric's coping style is to avoid conflict and retreat to basic dependency needs. He feels inadequate to compete in the world. His insecurity is probably manifested in his inability to be alone too long without compulsively seeking personal encounters or sexual gratification. He may be sexually aroused all of the time.

SMALL BOX: (flea)

Eric struggles with a severely despised self image. He feels insignificant and powerless. He feels as uncomfortable inside himself as he feels in the outer world. He has strong dependency needs and seems to need to touch others constantly. He appears to have a singular ability to adapt to anything to get these needs satisfied. Again he is very concerned about his size.

An overall view of the Three Boxes image shows that Eric has a rotten, despised self image with feelings of great inadequacy. He probably has strong sexual drives with a constant concern about sexual needs. He has little ability to be independently on his own, however, he constantly wants to "leave." He has developed chameleon-like personality characteristics as a coping style.

The following is another of Eric's imagery productions taken directly from the SIT:

> (IS) Imagine you are in a room. Go to the middle of the room. You will see a hole in the floor. Now imagine looking through the hole and tell me what you see. Then I want you to imagine going down into the hole and tell me what you see, feel and do.

Eric's response was: "I see a light bulb on--an empty cellar. When I go down it's cold and damp--cobwebs. I just look around."

He was then asked to finish the seven sentences speaking as the person down in the hole. These are his responses:

I feel: inquisitive

The adjective that best describes me is: cold and damp.

I wish: I could find something precious.

I must: get out before I catch cold.

I secretly: would like a wine cellar like this at home.

I need: a sweater on.

I will: get one and come back.

According to Shorr (1983a), 98% of respondents to this image are revealing some aspects of sexuality and/or relationships. The remaining 2% generally relate to death when going down into the hole. Additionally, when a person is asked to imagine going down into the hole and then asked how he feels, what he does, and what he sees, a great deal of additional sexual material can be elicited. These authors using this image in treatment sessions have found it to be productive in uncovering the most sensitive and guarded information about the patient's sexuality. This image has an uncanny ability to help the patient explore what is often the most shame-ridden areas of his personality.

Eric's imagery suggests that there is a great void in his sexual/intimate life, with an inability to find the "something precious" he is looking for--namely, the warmth and intimacy. He most likely struggles with this emptiness by adaptation rather than resolution. Others probably complain of his lack of warmth. He appears to be persistent and compulsive in his sexual drives and shows strong concern about his sexual attractiveness and is fearful of sexual rejection.

According to Karen Horney (1945), inner conflicts are caused by the opposition of two strong and incompatible forces, neither of which can be satisfied without exacting pain, fear, guilt, or some other emotional penalty. If a patient is deadlocked between two equally compelling forces, we must ask the question: Between what divisive aspects of himself is the patient caught, or between what polarized aspects of himself and others? In short, what are the patient's internal conflicts that are struggling within such a deadlocked position?

Shorr's use of Dual Imagery (1967; 1983a, 276-7) helps both the therapist and the patient observe these complementary opposites within experience. He states:

> A rather remarkable phenomenon appears to occur when a person is asked to imagine two different forces, dolls, trees, animals, impulses, etc., and then to contrast each of them in line with the projected imagery. In the great majority of the reported imagery (but not all) there appears to be some form of polarization between them.

The opposing or contrasting forces can be enhanced by focusing through further dialogue within the imagery or with further imagery. The degree of polarization usually correlates with the degree of conflict.

In his initial interview Eric did appear to be in great conflict, yet he was almost totally unaware of the forces involved in the conflict. He did, however, show signs of a great discrepancy between how he "felt" versus what he "thought." The following Dual Image from the SIT is intended to reveal the forces within the conflict and the degree of conflict.

> (IS) Imagine an animal coming out of your head and an animal coming out of your guts. (Pause) Now imagine them walking down a road together. What happens?

The following is the verbatim dialogue between Eric and one of the authors:

E: You mean any kind of animal?

A: Yes, just imagine an animal coming out of your head.

E: I suppose a fox. He would be a very wise animal and he would be trying to follow the normal way of existence. Trying to exist and trying to be intellectual about it at the same time.

A: What kind of animal would come out of your guts?

E: Suppressed tiger. A tiger that would want to go about doing things the way he wants to do it. He'd want to go screw the world. Find as many women as he could and take them all on.

A: What would happen? Just close your eyes and imagine the two of them walking down a road together, the fox and the tiger. See if you can just get a picture of the two of them walking down the road together.

E: It's got to be an awful fight. A terrible one. One of them would probably die. No doubt about it. Mostly the fox. Undoubtedly. (Laughs ruefully)

A: That's about where you are in your life, isn't it?

E: I guess you're right. It's the thought beneath your conscious and the subconscious. The subconscious has come out in me in the last year. That's what it's all about--over and above my objections and my religious hang-ups.

Eric's imagery does reveal extreme polarized conflict between his affective and cognitive functions. On one hand he appears to be trying to maintain control through his intellect by being "wise" and "normal." Yet the price he pays in the "suppression" of his feelings is enormous. On the other hand, when the suppressed feelings surface they take over to the point of destroying any rational ability. He jumps from one polarity of the conflict to the other in a neurotic attempt at solution, only to find that the real conflict remains unresolved. The potential of such extreme polarity of conflict could be manifested in an impulsive and severe acting out with a high probability of loss of control.

Eric's responses also reveal his intense concerns about his sexuality and the underlying suppressed feelings which seem to drive him in a sexually compulsive manner. While Eric demands of himself that he behave in a "moral" and "normal" manner, he is probably sexually aroused all the time while exhibiting little real warmth or caring for others.

As one can readily see, there is a wealth of information that is revealed in Dual Imagery. The possibilities for further therapeutic investigation along many different paths are infinite.

Eric initially presented himself as a man who had little interpersonal or intrapersonal conflict in his life, except for his "recent sexual impotence and my wife's increased sexual needs." He saw his only problem as his wife's distancing herself from him after he had become so unexplainably angry that he lost control and struck out at her violently.

In reviewing only three of Eric's imagery productions, along with a brief history taking, we quickly begin to see a clear picture emerging of his personality, conflicts, motivations, attitudes, values, coping styles and accompanying behavior. We see a man struggling with a severely despised self image with feelings of great inadequacy and impotence in most areas of his life. He constantly enmeshes himself more deeply in his despised image by avoiding direct confrontation of his problems. Instead he indulges in self-destructive behavior to escape the anxiety engendered by his powerlessness. For example, rather than try to improve his relationship with his wife, he acts out his compulsive need for sexual gratification by arranging a mate-swap which guarantees the sexual rejection he is trying to avoid. Eric states, "I thought I was intelligent enough to accept swinging," but the "suppressed tiger" (his emotion) breaks loose and overcomes his moral stance. Not only has he accomplished exactly what he wanted to avoid, but he has increased his feelings of inadequacy by failing to resolve his neurotic conflict.

Sexual jealousy is not a single emotion, but rather a combination of emotional reactions. Insecurity, inadequacy, anxiety, anger, and fear of loss are only part of the emotional flux. The jealous person often feels out of control, depressed, and suspicious. Jealous people may have difficulty in feeling empathy for others and may exhibit paranoia. Their discomfort is often exacerbated by the guilt and shame that they experience for feeling or expressing their jealousy.

Characteristically, the sexually jealous person attributes his misery to external forces and seldom looks within himself for the roots of the problem. He blames the loved one for being too provocative or the rival for being too seductive. In an ineffectual attempt to improve the situation, he addresses only the immediate circumstances and overlooks the underlying causes of his feelings and behavior.

Eric is almost a classic example of the jealous person. He deals only with the symptoms. He attributes his sexual inadequacy, his anger, and his acting out to his wife's behavior, and he attempts to maintain control of his life and his sexuality by changing the circumstances rather than exploring his own inner conflicts.

We have attempted to show that the use of waking imagery can lead to a rapid and accurate uncovering of extremely sensitive and guarded thoughts, motives, feelings and conflicts. We have used the principles and techniques of Psycho-Imagination Therapy specifically because of its strong theoretical base in interpersonal interactions. The wealth of information elicited through the examination of but three Imaginary Situations and the complementary dialogue and sentence completions attest to the value of this approach for speedy and accurate evaluation of a specific individual. The work of developing a treatment plan is always a challenge, but it can be enhanced and facilitated through the use of imagery.

REFERENCES

Connella, J. (1983). The uses of self-image imagery in psycho-therapy. In J. E. Shorr, G. Sobel-Whittington, P. Robin, J. Connella (Eds.), Imagery: Theoretical and clinical applications. New York: Plenum Press.

Escalona, S. K.(January, 1973). Book review of mental imagery in children by J. Piaget and B. Imhelder (New York, 1969). In Journal of nervous and mental disease, 156, 70-71.

Guntrip, H. (1961). Personality structure and human interaction. New York: International Universities Press.

Horney, K. (1945). Our inner conflicts. New York: W. W. Norton.

Laing, R. D. (1971). The self and others. New York: Pelican Books.

Robin, P. (1980). Theory and Application of Psycho-Imagination Therapy. In J. E. Shorr, G. E. Sobel, P. Robin, and J. A. Connella (Eds.), Imagery: Its many dimensions and applications. New York: Plenum Press.

Robin, P. (1983). The integration of Sullivanian theory and the use of imagery in couples therapy. In J. E. Shorr, G. Sobel-Whittington, P. Robin, and J. A. Connella (Eds.), Imagery: Theoretical and clinical application, Vol. 3. New York: Plenum Press.

Robin, P. (1986). The clinical use of psycho-imagination therapy in the treatment of sexual jealousy. In M. Wolpin, J. E. Shorr, and L. Krueger (Eds.), Imagery: Recent practice and theory, Vol. 4. New York: Plenum Press.

Shorr, J. E. (1967). The existential question and the imaginary situation as therapy. In Existential psychiatry, 6, 24, Winter, 443-462.

Shorr, J. E. (1974). Shorr imagery test. Los Angeles: Institute for psycho-imagination therapy.

Shorr, J. E. (1976). Dual imagery. In Psychotherapy: Theory, research, and practice, 13, (2).

Shorr, J. E. (1978). Clinical use of categories of therapeutic imagery. In J. L. Singer and K. Pope (Eds.), The power of human imagination. New York: Plenum Press.

Shorr, J. E. (1981). An overview of psycho-imagination therapy. In R. Corsini (Ed.). Innovative psychotherapies. New York: Wylie Interscience.

Shorr, J. E. (1983a). Psychotherapy through imagery. New York: Thieme Stratton.

Shorr, J. E. (1983b). Go see the movie in your head. Santa Barbara: Ross-Erikson.

MEASURING MANIFEST DREAM CONTENT*

William E. Snell, Jr., Scott Gum, Roger L. Shuck, and Jo A. Mosley

Southeast Missouri State University
Cape Girardeau

ABSTRACT

Manifest dream content refers to the descriptive nature of people's dreams. The present investigation was concerned with the relationship between manifest dream content and gender, personality, and stress. For this purpose, an assessment instrument was developed to measure a variety of different types of manifest dream content, the Manifest Dream Scale (MDS). Factor analysis indicated that the items on the Manifest Dream Scale clustered into five separate groups: (a) positive social activity, (b) undesirable negative experience, (c) death, injury, and natural events, (d) entertainment and recreation, and (e) mundane activities. Gender was found to be related to some but not all of the manifest dream categories. A more consistent pattern of relationships was found between manifest dream content and (a) instrumental and expressive personality attributes, and (b) gender role tendencies. In addition, a final set of results indicated that a recent history of stressful life experiences produced an impact on the manifest content of women's and men's dreams.

Dreams have fascinated psychologists for a number of decades. Dreaming itself refers to the psychological processes that correspond to the neurophysiological activity of the sleeping nervous system (Cohen, 1976). Prior to the advent of contemporary sleep research, the most common explanation of dreaming was Freud's (1965). According to Freud, dreams serve as a type of safety valve through which people find psychological release for unacceptable wishes and impulses. In addition, Freud argued that dream content is often forgotten because the content is so frightening and unacceptable that people actively repress their memory.

---

*Portions of these data were presented at the annual meeting of the American Association for the Study of Mental Imagery, New Haven, CT, June 1988. Gratitude is extended to David Cohen for his helpful comments on an earlier version of this manuscript. Request for reprints and copies of the MDS should be sent to William E. Snell, Jr., Department of Psychology, Southeast Missouri State University, Cape Girardeau, MO 63701

An alternative perspective has begun to emerge in recent years (Cohen, 1969, 1970, 1972, 1973a, 1973b, 1974a, 1975b). According to this approach, dream content reflects the influence of presleep events in a direct and continuous manner. As such, this theory contends that there should be a considerable degree of correspondence between dream content and aspects of people's personality and their individual life style. The results of several studies are consistent with Cohen's (1976) continuity theory of dreams. In two of these investigations, presleep mood was found to correlate significantly with the affective quality of dreams (Cohen, 1974b; Cohen and Cox, 1975). Another study dealing with "sex-role orientation" and dream content was also interpreted as supportive of Cohen's continuity theory of dreaming (Cohen, 1973b). In this study, people who described themselves in terms of gender-related personality attributes reported similar themes in their manifest dream content.

The purpose of the present investigation was to further examine the notion that dreams directly reflect the nature of people's personality and their current lifestyle concerns. To accomplish this goal, dreams were content analyzed to identify the range and variety of manifest dream themes characterizing them. Content categories were then identified through the use of factor analyses, and subscales were constructed on the basis of the factor loadings. Next, the resulting dream categories were correlated with (a) a measure of stressful life experiences, the Angry Life Experiences Scale (ALES; Snell, Belk, Gum, Shuck, and Mosley, 1988), (b) a measure of instrumental and expressive personality attributes, the Personal Attributes Questionnaire (PAQ; Spence, Helmreich, and Holohan, 1979; Spence, Helmreich and Stapp, 1975), and (c) a measure of global masculinity and global femininity, the Personal Attributes Questionnaire (PAQ; Spence and Helmreich, 1978). It was anticipated that these stress and personality tendencies would be directly reflected in the manifest dream content of women and men (cf. Hall, 1966, 1984).

METHOD

Subjects

A sample (N = 405) of college women and men were asked to participate in a research study on dreams. In return for their participation, the subjects received extra credit counting toward their course grades. The number of subjects reported in the following analyses occasionally varies since not all the subjects completed each and every item.

Procedure

When the subjects arrived at the testing room, they were asked to read and complete an informed consent form. All subjects volunteered to participate and were then asked to complete several assessment instruments (described below). Two-hour sessions were scheduled for the experiment; however, most subjects completed the experimental material in about one hour. The average number of subjects attending each session was about 45.

Instruments

Manifest Dream Scale (MDS). The Manifest Dream Content Scale (MDS) was designed to measure how often certain types of themes characterize the manifest content of people's dreams. The instructions asked the subjects to indicate how often they had dreamed each of 50 types of dream content during the past three nights of sleep (cf. Urbina, 1981). To indicate their responses, the subjects used a 5-point Likert scale (numerical codes are enclosed in parentheses): (0) I don't remember dreaming about this [content] during the last three nights; (0) I definitely did not dream about this [content] during the last three nights; (1) I dreamed about this [content] one time during the last three nights; (2) I dreamed about this [content] two times during the last three nights; and (3) I dreamed about this [content] three times during the last three nights. Thus, higher scores corresponded to more frequent dreaming of the 50 thematic content categories measured by the Manifest Dream Scale (MDS).

Angry Life Experiences Scale (ALES). The Angry Life Experiences Scale (ALES; Snell, Belk, Gum, Shuck, and Mosley, 1988) was designed to measure 48 different types of anger-eliciting events and experiences. For each item, the subjects were asked to indicate how often they had experienced each of the events during the last month of their lives (e.g., five times in the last month). In addition to providing this frequency information for each item, the subjects were asked to rate how angry the events had made them feel. A 6-point Likert scale was used to assess their responses; not at all angry (0), not very angry (1), somewhat angry (1), moderately angry (3), very angry (4), and extremely angry (5). This procedure thus resulted in frequency and affective intensity ratings for each of the 48 anger-eliciting experiences, with higher scores corresponding to (a) more frequent occurrence of angry life experiences, and (b) greater angry affect associated with the impact of the angry life experiences, respectively.

Personal Attributes Questionnaire (PAQ). The PAQ is a measure of socially desirable instrumental and expressive personality attributes (Spence et al., 1979). Each of these two subscales consisted of eight items (e.g., can make decisions easily). Each item was scored on a 5-point Likert scale (0-4), and then the eight items constituting each subscale were summed to create subscale scores, higher scoring corresponding to greater instrumentality and expressiveness. Two other items were also included on the PAQ, a global masculinity item (not very feminine-very feminine). These two items were scored on a 5-point Likert scale, high scores reflecting more "global masculinity" and "global femininity."

RESULTS

The results are reported in three separate sections. Section one presents the psychometric analyses for the Manifest Dream Scale (MDS), including factor analysis and reliability analyses. The second section reports the correlational results associated with the Manifest Dream Scale (MDS) and the measure of stressful life experiences, the Angry Life Experiences Scale (ALES; Snell et al., 1988). The third section examines the relationship between gender and the dream categories, and the fourth and final section presents the results associated with the gender-related measures of instrumental and expressive personality attributes and the two measures of global masculinity and global femininity.

Manifest Dream Scale (MDS)

The subjects' responses to the 50 dream themes on the Manifest Dream Scale were subjected to principle axis factor analysis with varimax rotation. A five factor solution was identified (see Table 1).

The first factor was labeled pleasant social activity, since the highest loading dream themes involved people (.71), themselves (.70), and friends (.70). The dream themes on the second factor (e.g., negative affect-emotion, humiliation, verbal aggression) dealt with issues related to undesirable negative experiences. Factor 3 was characterized by dream themes dealing with death, injury and natural events (e.g., water, active natural forces, outdoors, and death). The fourth factor solution dealt

Table 1

Varimax Rotated Factor Structure Loadings
for the Manifest Dream Scale (MDS)

MDS Factors	Factor Labels	Eigenvalues (% of (Variance)	Factor Loadings	MDS Item Descriptions
I	Positive Social Activity	11.19 (22.4)	.71	(7.) People
			.70	(9.) Self
			.70	(32.) Friends
			.63	(38.) Positive Affect
			.61	(28.) Pleasure
			.55	(18.) Interpersonal Relationships
			.55	(21.) Motion
			.55	(31.) Family
			.54	(34.) Adults
			.52	(1.) Sensory Vividness
			.51	(14.) Indoors
			.49	(12.) Time
			.48	(48.) Dating-Courting
			.47	(16.) Familiar Settings
II	Undesirable Negative Experiences	3.03 (6.1)	.64	(42.) Negative Affect-Emotion
			.60	(29.) Humiliation
			.56	(4.) Achievement-Mastery
			.53	(5.) Achievement-Competition
			.52	(11.) Verbal Aggression
			.49	(23.) Aloneness
			.49	(3.) Achievement-Work
			.49	(45.) Mental State-Condition
			.41	(6.) Achievement-Fear of Success
			.40	(35.) Moral Authority
			.38	(25.) Power
			.36	(41.) Body Image
			.30	(2.) Human Body
III	Death, Injury, and Natural Events	1.97 (3.9)	.61	(36.) Injury
			.59	(47.) Water
			.55	(10.) Physical Aggression
			.51	(37.) Active Natural Forces
			.50	(15.) Outdoors
			.48	(19.) Death or Dying
			.48	(43.) The Sky
			.41	(22.) Illness and Sickness
			.40	(20.) Drinking
			.39	(40.) Vehicles
			.34	(8.) Animals
IV	Entertain-ment and Recreation	1.41 (2.8)	.49	(46.) Music
			.45	(17.) Past-time Entertainment
			.43	(26.) Physical Sports
			.42	(13.) Sex
			.36	(49.) Sleep
V	Mundane Activities	1.14 (2.3)	.46	(30.) School
			.43	(33.) Children
			.42	(44.) Academic Classes
			.41	(39.) Food or Eating
			.35	(27.) Boredom

Note: N=379. A principal axis factor analysis with varimax rotation was conducted. Scale numbers refer to item sequencing on the MDS. Items with loadings greater than .30 were used to describe each factor. Items with multiple loadings greater than .30 were assigned to the higher loading factor. Higher scores for each item correspond to more frequent dreaming of the manifest dream content.

with entertainment and recreation (e.g., music, past-time entertainment). Mundane everyday activities was the identifying characteristic of Factor V (e.g., school, classes, eating).

Five subscales on the MDS were constructed by summing the subjects' responses to the items on these factors. Loadings greater than .30 were used to assign items to the appropriate factor, and items with multiple loadings greater than .30 were assigned to the highest loading factor. Internal reliability analyses were then conducted by computing Cronbach alpha's. These reliability coefficients are presented in Table 2. The alpha's ranged from a low of .60 to a high of .90 (average alpha = .76). All of these measures of internal consistency were sufficiently high to warrant using the five dream subscales in the analyses reported below.

Next the five subscales on the Manifest Dream Scale were intercorrelated to determine how related the various subscales were. These results are also presented in Table 2. An inspection of Table 2 indicates that the five dream categories on the Manifest Dream Scale (MDS) were moderately correlated with each other (range = .30 to .61; average = .46).

Stress and Dreams

It was anticipated that a recent history of stressful life experiences would influence the types of manifest content reported in the subjects' dreams. To examine this prediction, the Manifest Dream Scale (MDS) was correlated with a measure of stressful life experiences, the Angry Life Experiences Scale (ALES; Snell et al., 1988). For each subscale on the

Table 2

Internal Reliabilities and Intercorrelations for the Manifest Dream Scale (MDS)

Manifest Dream Subscales	Standardized Cronbach Alpha's	Gender	MDS Subscales (1.)	(2.)	(3.)	(4.)	(5.)
1. Positive Social Activity	.90	Both	.--				
		Males	.--				
		Females	.--				
2. Undesirable Negative Experiences	.85	Both	.57	.--			
		Males	.64	.--			
		Females	.57	.--			
3. Death, Injury, and Natural Forces	.80	Both	.47	.55	.--		
		Males	.58	.60	.--		
		Females	.47	.53	.--		
4. Entertainment and Recreation	.66	Both	.56	.43	.43	.--	
		Males	.57	.40	.47	.--	
		Females	.61	.45	.42	.--	
5. Mundane Everyday Activities	.60	Both	.45	.30	.4d	.40	.--
		Males	.45	.31	.48	.50	.--
		Females	.46	.43	.46	.37	.--

Note: N for all subjects = 386-390; n for males = 97.99; and n for females = 287-291. Higher scores correspond to more frequent dreaming of the manifest content. All correlation coefficients are statisticalaly significant, $p < .001$.

Angry Life Experiences Scale, the subjects indicated how often they had experienced the relevant events in the past month (frequency ratings) and how angry the experiencing of these events made them feel (intensity ratings). Each of these two sets of anger ratings were correlated with the five subscales on the Manifest Dream Scale. The results are displayed in Table 3.

Table 3

Correlations Between the Manifest Dream Scale and the Angry Life Experiences Scale

Angry Life Experiences Subscales (ALES)	Positive Social Activity	Undesirable Negative Experiences	Death Injury, and Natural Forces	Entertainment and Recreation	Mundane Everyday Activities
Frequency Ratings					
1. Narrow-Minded Selfishness	.08	$.22^{d}$	$.11^{a}$	.05	.04
2. Personal Inadequacies and Failures	.03	$.12^{b}$	.02	-.01	-.01
3. Impersonal Frustrations	$.11^{a}$	$.20^{d}$	.09	.01	.08
4. Bigotry and Prejudice	.05	$.14^{c}$	.05	.07	.06
5. Social Friction	.00	.08	.02	.01	-.03
6. Violation of Social Rules	-.04	$.09^{a}$	$.14^{c}$	.03	.01
7. Loss of Control	.06	$.13^{b}$	$.16^{d}$	$.09^{a}$	.05
Intensity Ratings					
1. Narrow-Minded Selfishness	$.13^{c}$	$.21^{d}$	$.13^{b}$	$.16^{d}$	.05
2. Personal Inadequacies and Failures	$.11^{a}$	$.27^{d}$	$.09^{a}$	$.15^{d}$	$.09^{a}$
3. Interpersonal Frustrations	$.10^{a}$	$.23^{d}$	$.13^{c}$	$.15^{c}$	$.09^{a}$
4. Bigotry and Prejudice	.08	$.19^{d}$	$.13^{c}$	$.16^{d}$	$.11^{a}$
5. Social Friction	.07	$.16^{d}$	.07	$.16^{d}$	.06
6. Violation of Social Rules	$.12^{b}$	$.19^{d}$	.08	$.17^{d}$	.06
7. Loss of Control	.02	$.12^{b}$	$.10^{a}$	$.14^{c}$	-.01

Note: N for intensity rating = 382 - 386; n for frequency ratings = 355 - 378. Higher scores on the MDS subscales correspond to more frequent dreaming of the manifest dream content assessed by the MDS subscales.

$^{a}p < .05$ $^{b}p < .01$ $^{c}p < .005$ $^{d}p < .001$

Anger Frequency Rating. An inspection of Table 3 indicates that those individuals whose dreams were characterized by undesirable negative experiences reported that they had recently experienced a large number of anger-producing events associated with narrow-minded selfishness, personal inadequacies and failures, interpersonal frustrations, bigotry and prejudice, social friction, violation of social rules, and loss of control. Similarly, those who dreamed about death, injury and natural forces reported a large number of angry life experiences concerned with narrow-minded selfishness, violation of social rules, and loss of control. Additionally, it was found that people who dreamed about the positive social activities reported the occurrence of angry life experiences related to interpersonal frustrations. A final pattern of results indicated that dreams characterized by entertainment and recreation were associated with anger-related experiences stemming from loss of control.

Anger Intensity Ratings. An inspection of Table 3 also reveals several significant relationships between the thematic content of people's dreams and how intensely angry they felt (i.e., their affective ratings) in response to the stressful life events measured by the Angry Life Experiences Scale. Those whose dreams were characterized by undesirable negative experiences reported that they had recently experienced a considerable amount of anger stemming from events associated with narrow-minded selfishness, personal inadequacies and failures, interpersonal frustrations, bigotry and prejudice, social friction, violation of social rules, and loss of control. In addition, it was found that intense feelings of anger due to these same seven types of experiences were associated with dreams of entertainment and recreation. The results also indicated that dreams characterized by positive social activity were associated with angry feelings arising from narrow-minded selfishness, personal inadequacies and failures, and interpersonal frustrations; and that dreams characterized by death, injury and natural forces were associated with angry feelings stemming from narrow-minded selfishness, personal inadequacy and failure, interpersonal frustrations, bigotry and prejudice, and loss of control. Finally, the results indicated that mundane dream content was related to angry feelings generated by personal inadequacies and failures, interpersonal frustrations, and bigotry and prejudice.

Gender and Dreams

A number of psychologists have argued that men and women dream about different types of phenomena (e.g., Brenneis, 1970; Cohen, 1973b; Hall and Domhoff, 1963; Hall and Van de Castle, 1965, 1966). To examine the similarities and differences between men's and women's dreams, a MANOVA was conducted, with gender as the independent variable and the eight dream subscales as the dependent variables. The results are presented in Table 4.

The multivariate effect for gender was highly significant, $F(5,372) = 9.51$, $p < .001$. An inspection of the univariate results shown in Table 5 indicates that on three of the subscales on the Manifest Dream Scale (MDS), men and women were quite similar. However, women relative to men did report more dream content concerned with positive social activity; and men reported more dream content associated with entertainment and recreation than did women.

Dreams and Gender-related Tendencies

One of the goals of the present study was to examine the relationship between manifest dream content and several gender-related tendencies (cf. Cohen, 1973b). To accomplish this, the subjects were asked to complete the Personal Attributes Questionnaire (PAQ; Spence et al., 1979), a measure of instrumental and expressive personality attributes as well as

Table 4

Means and Standard Deviations on the Manifest Dream Scale for Women and Men

Scale Labels	Women	Men	Both	F	p
1. Positive Social Activity	18.57 (10.20)	14.69 (9.06)	17.61 (10.06)	10.77	.001
2. Undesirable Negative Experiences	8.09 (7.06)	7.76 (7.22)	8.01 (7.09)	<1	n.s.
3. Death, Injury, and Natural Forces	4.79 (4.77)	5.43 (5.79)	4.94 (5.04)	1.14	n.s.
4. Entertainment and Recreation	2.38 (2.60)	3.22 (3.03)	2.59 (2.73)	6.89	.009
5. Mundane Everyday Activities	1.80 (2.11)	1.71 (2.16)	1.78 (2.12)	<1	n.s.

Note: N for Women = 284; n for men = 94. Standard deviations are shown in parentheses. Higher scores on the MDS subscales correspond to more frequent dreaming of the manifest dream content assessed by the MDS subscales. MANOVA $F(5,372) = 9.51$, $p < .001$.

global masculinity and femininity. The correlations between the Manifest Dream Scale and the gender-related tendencies on the PAQ are shown in Table 5.

Several significant findings were found for the subscales on the PAQ. Higher levels of instrumentality among the female subjects were associated with dreams about positive social activity; death, injury and natural forces; and entertainment and recreation. By contrast, lower levels of expressive personality attributes among female subjects were associated with dreams characterized by death and injury. Similarly, males with lower levels of expressiveness reported dreaming about death and dying, as well as mundane everyday activities. Two other sets of findings dealing with global masculine and feminine self-descriptions were also found. Females who described themselves as "not very feminine" reported dreaming about undesirable negative experiences, death, injury and natural forces, and entertainment and recreation. Among males, by contrast, those who described themselves as "masculine" reported a greater frequency of dreams characterized by death, injury, and natural forces.

DISCUSSION

The purpose of the present investigation was to examine whether women's and men's dreams would reflect the influence of their personality characteristics and their gender-related tendencies, as well as a recent history of angry life experiences. To examine these ideas, the Manifest Dream Scale (MDS) was constructed to assess the types of content that people dream. Psychometric analyses of the Manifest Dream Scale indicated that it contained five clusters of dream themes: (a) positive social activity, (b) undesirable negative experiences, (c) death, injury and natural forces, (d) entertainment and recreation, and (e) mundane everyday activities.

Table 5

Correlations Between the Manifest Dream Scale (MDS) and Gender-Related Measures

Personal Attributes Questionnaire	Manifest Dream Subscales				
	Positive Social Activity	Undesirable Negative Experiences	Death Injury, and Natural Forces	Entertainment and Recreation	Mundane Everyday Activities
1. PAQ Instrumentality					
All Subjects	.10[a]	.08	.15[c]	.16[d]	.06
Males	.01	.13	.14	.11	-.01
Females	.16[c]	.07	.15[b]	.16[c]	.09
2. PAQ Expressivity					
All Subjects	.10[a]	-.01	.00	-.04	-.02
Males	-.00	-.10	-.22[a]	-.13	-.29[c]
Females	.09	.02	-.14[a]	.06	.09
3. PAQ Global Masculinity					
All Subjects	-.06	.03	-.12[a]	.11[a]	-.05
Males	-.03	.16	.22[a]	.02	-.11
Females	.07	.00	.05	.05	-.04
4. PAQ Global Femininity					
All Subjects	.09[a]	-.04	-.09[a]	-.14[c]	.05
Males	-.05	-.12	-.13	.01	.06
Females	-.04	-.11[a]	-.11[a]	-.13[a]	.04

Note: N for all subjects = 368-378; n for males = 93-98; and n for females = 272-279. Higher scores correspond to more frequent dreaming of the manifest content; and greater instrumentality, expressiveness, global masculinity, and global femininity.

[a] $p < .05$ [b] $p < .01$ [c] $p < .005$ [d] $p < .001$

The results confirmed the expectation that manifest dream content tended to reflect in a direct and continuous manner the influence of personality, gender-role tendencies, and current life experiences (e.g., Breger, Hunter, and Lane, 1971). For example, people who reported dreaming about <u>undesirable negative experiences</u> reported a high incidence of angry life experiences concerned with narrow-minded selfishness, personal inadequacies and failures, interpersonal frustrations, bigotry and prejudice, social friction, violation of social rules, and loss of control--as measured by the Angry Life Experiences Scale (ALES; Snell et al., 1988). Also consistent with several gender stereotypes (cf. Belk and Snell, 1986), it was found that women reported more dream themes dealing with <u>positive social activity</u> and that men reported more dream themes characterized by <u>entertainment and recreation</u> related activities.

Additional results revealed that the gender-related personality attributes measured by the Personal Attributes Questionnaire (PAQ; Spence et al., 1979) were also predictive of men's and women's manifest dream content. Those females who described themselves as having socially desirable instrumental attributes reported having dreams characterized by positive social activity, death and injury, and entertainment and recreation. Also, highly expressive women were found to report fewer dreams characterized by death and injury types of themes. Among males, less expressivity was also associated with a greater frequency of dreams containaing the themes of death and injury as well as mundane everyday activities. Thus, both instrumental and expressive personality characteristics were associated with positive types of dreams. Additionally, it was found that males who described themselves as "masculine" reported dreaming about death, injury and natural forces. By contrast, those females describing themselves as "not very feminine" reported dreaming about death, injury and natural forces, entertainment and recreation, and undesirable negative experiences.

All of these findings combine together to provide additional support for the continuity theory of dreams (Cohen, 1974c, 1976; Cohen and MacNeilage, 1974). According to Cohen, dream content reflects presleep experiences and personal tendencies in a direct and continuous manner. And in fact the present evidence showed that angry life experiences were associated with the dream themes of undesirable negative experiences, that women dreamed more often than men about positive social activities and that men dreamed more often than women about entertainment and recreation, and that gender-related attributes and global-descriptions were associated with conceptually consistent dream themes. In light of these findings, psychologists may want to consider the possibility of another theory complimenting Freud's (1965) notion that dreaming functions as a safety valve for the psychological expression of unacceptable impulses and desires. Clearly, a large amount of research evidence offers support for the additional view that dreams directly reflect the content of people's everyday life experiences and their personality.

REFERENCES

Belk, S. S., and Snell, W. E., Jr. (1986). Beliefs about women: Components and correlates. Personality and Social Psychology Bulletin, 12, 403-413.

Breger, L., Hunter, I., and Lane, R. W. (1971). The effect of stress on dreams. Psychological Issues, 7(27).

Brenneis, B. (1970). Male and female modalities in manifest dream content. Journal of Abnormal Psychology, 76, 434-442.

Cohen, D. B. (1969). Frequency of dream recall estimated by three methods and related to defense preference and anxiety. Journal of Consulting and Clinical Psychology, 33, 661-667.

Cohen, D. B. (1970. Current research on the frequency of dream recall. Psychological Bulletin, 73, 433-440.

Cohen, D. B. (1972). Presleep experiences and home dream reporting: An exploratory study. Journal of Consulting and Clinical Psychology, 38, 122-128.

Cohen, D. B. (1973a). A comparison of genetic and social contributions to dream recall frequency. Journal of Abnormal Psychology, 82, 368-371.

Cohen, D. B. (1973b). Sex role orientation and dream recall. Journal of Abnormal Psychology, 82, 246-252.

Cohen, D. B. (1974a). Effect of personality and presleep mood on dream recall. Journal of Abnormal Psychology, 83, 151-156.

Cohen, D. B. (1974b). Presleep mood and dream recall. Journal of Abnormal Psychology, 83, 45-51.

Cohen, D. B. (1974c). Toward a theory of dream recall. Psychological Bulletin, 81, 138-154.

Cohen, D. B. (1976). Dreaming: Experimental investigation of representational and adaptive properties. In G. E. Schwartz and D. Shapiro (Eds.), Consciousness and self regulation: Advances in research, Vol. I.

Cohen, D. B., and Cox, D. (1975). Neuroticism in the sleep laboratory: Implications for representational and adaptive properties of dreaming. Journal of Abnormal Psychology, 84, 91-108.

Cohen, D. B., and MacNeilage, P. F. (1974). A test of the salience hypothesis of dream recall. Journal of Consulting and Clinical Psychology, 42, 699-703.

Freud, S. (1965). The interpretation of dreams. New York: Random House.

Hall, C. S. (1966). The meaning of dreams. New York: McGraw-Hill.

Hall, C. S. (1984). "A ubiquitous sex difference in dreams" revisited. Journal of Personality and Social Psychology, 46, 1109-1117.

Hall, C. S., and Domhoff, B. (1963). A ubiquitous sex difference in dreams. Journal of Abnormal and Social Psychology, 66, 278-280.

Hall, C. S., and Van de Castle, R. L. (1965). An empirical investigation of the castration complex in dreams. Journal of Personality, 33, 20-29.

Hall, C. S., and Van de Castle, R. L. (1966). The content analysis of dreams. New York: Appleton-Century-Crofts.

Snell, W. E., Jr., Belk, S. S., Gum, S., Shuck, R. A., and Mosley, J. A. (1988, April). Assessing the impact of angry feelings and angry life experiences. Paper presented at the annual meeting of the Southwestern Psychological Association, Tulsa, Oklahoma.

Spence, J. T., and Helmreich, R. L. (1978). Masculinity and femininity: Their psychological dimensions, correlates, and antecedents. Austin: University of Texas Press.

Spence, J. T., Helmreich, R. L., and Holohan, C. K. (1979). Negative and positive components of psychological masculinity and femininity and their relationships to self-report of neurotic and acting-out behaviors. Journal of Personality and Social Psychology, 37, 1673-1682.

Spence, J. T., Helmreich, R. L., and Stapp, J. (1975). The Personal Attributes Questionnaire: A measure of sex-role stereotypes and masculinity-femininity. JSAS Catalog of Selected Documents in Psychology, 4, 43. (Ms. No. 617)

Urbina, S. P. (1981). Methodological issues in the quantitative analysis of dream content. Journal of Personality Assessment, 45, 71-78.

CONTRIBUTORS

1. Robert Kunzendorf; Diane Hoyle
Dept. of Psychology
University of Lowell
Lowell, MA 01854

2. James Honeycutt
Louisiana State University
Dept. of Speech Communication
Baton Rouge, LA 70803-3923

3. Leonard Giambra; Alicia Grodsky
4940 Eastern Ave.
Baltimore, MD 21212

4. John Caughey
University of Maryland
College Park, MD 20742

5. Nicholas Brink
202 S. Second St.
Lewisburg, PA 17837

6. Helaine Rosenburg; William Trusheim
Pequannock Township Schools
Fine and Performing Arts
Pompton Plains, NJ 07444

7. Isabella Colalillo-Kates
The Rainbow Light & Co.
431 Whitmore Ave.
Toronto, Ontario, Canada
M6E 2N7

8. Imants Baruss; Robert Moore
Kings College
266 Epworth Ave.
London, Ontario, Canada
N6A2M

9. Don D. Rosenburg
6318 No. Monticello
Chicago, IL 60659

10. Mary S. Cerney
Menninger Clinic, Box 829
Topeka, KS 66601

11. Joseph E. Shorr
170 S. Barrington Place
Los Angeles, CA 90049

12. Mark Ettin
375 Snowden Lane
Princeton, NJ 08540

13. David Tansey
7670 Opportunity Road #165
San Diego, CA 92111

14. Milton Wolpin; Linda Smith
Psychology Department
University of Southern California, SGM 502
Los Angeles, CA 90089-1061

15. Jack A. Connella; Pennee Robin
111 No. La Cienega Blvd.
Beverly Hills, CA 90211

16. William Snell Jr.; Scott Gum; Roger L. Shuck; Jo A. Mosley
Southeast Missouri State University
Cape Girardeu, MO 63701

INDEX

MIX
Papier aus verantwortungsvollen Quellen
Paper from responsible sources
FSC® C105338

If you have any concerns about our products,
you can contact us on
ProductSafety@springernature.com

In case Publisher is established outside the EU,
the EU authorized representative is:
Springer Nature Customer Service Center GmbH
Europaplatz 3, 69115 Heidelberg, Germany

Printed by Libri Plureos GmbH
in Hamburg, Germany